Criminology: A Reader's Guide

Criminology:
A Reader's Guide

EDITED BY:

JANE GLADSTONE

RICHARD V. ERICSON

CLIFFORD D. SHEARING

PUBLISHED BY THE
CENTRE OF CRIMINOLOGY
UNIVERSITY OF TORONTO

ISBN 0-919584-67-5

Canadian Cataloguing in Publication Data

Main entry under title:

Criminology

Includes bibliographical references.
ISBN 0-919584-67-5

1. Criminology. I. Gladstone, Jane. II. Ericson,
Richard V., 1948– . III. Shearing, Clifford D.,
1942– . IV. University of Toronto. Centre of
Criminology.

HV6028.C75 1991   364   C91-093115-1

Contents

Preface

Criminology: A Reader's Guide is a collection of essays and reading lists on various aspects of criminology, written by members of the faculty of the Centre of Criminology, University of Toronto. The book is intended for the general, nonspecialist reader as well as for the student of criminology, and those who work in criminology or related fields.

The *Guide* is not a textbook, nor does it provide an exhaustive survey of the entire field. Chapters are grouped by category: Crime, Policing and Punishment; Law Reform and Policy; and Social Hierarchies, Crime and Justice. The reading lists provided with each chapter are a special feature of the volume. Most of the reading lists are annotated, that is, they include notes on a book's scope and contents, or a brief assessment for the reader.

While the names of the editors appear on the cover of the book, several other people were also involved in turning the manuscript into a book. A great deal of credit is due to Audrey Sinco for her dedication and hard work at the word processor, and for her careful reading of the text. Rita Donelan's knowledge of administration and handling of a myriad of details to do with the manuscript has been invaluable. Gwen Peroni's skill and speed in the crucial work of preparing the book for the printer are greatly appreciated. John Beattie, Director of the Centre, has offered encouragement and support throughout the project, and in guiding our separate or collaborative efforts. Many thanks to Catherine Matthews, Renana Almagor and Tom Finlay at the Centre Library. All associated with the project appreciate the excellent library resources and have benefitted from the congenial working environment at the Centre.

We are grateful to the Ministry of the Solicitor General of Canada for their contribution to the Centre of Criminology which helped to facilitate the production of this book.

Jane Gladstone

CRIMINOLOGY: A READER'S GUIDE

Introduction: An Institutional Approach to Criminology

Richard V. Ericson and Clifford D. Shearing

In this volume members of the Centre of Criminology at the University of Toronto conduct idiosyncratic guided tours of the criminological literature. The volume celebrates the Centre's diversity and its deeply entrenched view, instilled by its founding Director, John Ll.J. Edwards, that Criminology is a field that can and should be tilled with the conceptual and methodological implements of a variety of disciplines. John Edwards believed that bringing scholars from different disciplines together under one roof would facilitate a subtle interpenetration of ideas and perspectives, eventually leading to new shared understandings and points of fundamental agreement that would inform and shape the work of each of its members. The essays reveal the fruits of this conception. They lay bare the features of our collective foundation, features that we believe coalesce in what we have termed an 'institutional approach to criminology.' In introducing each of the essays we use the views of our contributors to identify this institutional approach, and to show how it informs, and is developed by, each authors' perspective on Criminology.

The outline of this approach to Criminology was first articulated by Richard Ericson in a report on 'Law as a Social Phenomenon' prepared for the Council of Canadian Law Deans. The opportunity to prepare this report allowed him to reflect on the conception of Criminology that has emerged at the Toronto Centre. In preparing this report he benefitted from the comments of scholars elsewhere in Canada who share aspects of the institutional approach, including Bruce Archibald, Neil Boyd, Gus Brannigan, John McMullan, Robert Menzies, Vince Sacco, Laureen Snider and Toni Williams. Important contributions were also made by Clifford Shearing and Rosemary Coombe of the Centre of Criminology. We are grateful to Rosemary Coombe for allowing us to draw on her paper 'Contesting the Self,' which has since appeared in *Studies in Law, Politics and Society*; we use this work in our discussion of the way law operates to constitute subjectivities.

Criminology seeks an understanding of crime, criminality, law and justice. The Centre of Criminology at the University of Toronto has specialized in particular topics and approaches to this broad area of study. While the Centre's researchers have not eschewed other major fields of inquiry, they have given relatively little attention to, for example, the aetiology of criminal behaviour, or to narrow questions concerning the effectiveness of particular measures for controlling crime. The Centre's focus has been on the institutional dimensions of criminal justice, studied in empirical detail. Research has pursued an understanding of how crime, criminality, law and justice are constituted within major institutions, especially law, the polity, the economy, science and culture.

A starting point for criminological inquiry is the legal institution itself. A great deal of research at the Centre has examined the operation of criminal law and justice as seen through the discretionary activities of police, prosecutors, lawyers, judges, prison operatives, and parole officials. There has also been considerable work on understanding the relation between criminal law and other types of law, for example, comparing the deterrence mode of criminal law enforcement with the compliance mode of administrative law enforcement.

The political institution is a fundamental part of crime and criminal justice. All crimes, and all reactions to crime, are defined politically. Research has centred on processes in law reform, including efforts to subject certain activities to the criminal law or more intensive criminal sanctions (criminalization), as well as efforts to reduce criminal sanctions or to subject certain activities to forms of regulation other than criminal law (decriminalization). Research has included consideration of key people and organizations involved in reform processes, whether they represent the state or outside interest groups pressuring the state, and has led to efforts to theorize the role of the state. A related concern is the policy process, and in particular the place of scientific expertise and evidence in law reform and policy. Connected to the research on discretion by law enforcement officials is work on the practical effects of changes in legislation. For example, the fact that a great deal of legislation remains unenforced, and is sometimes largely unenforceable, casts light on the ways in which law reform is sometimes an end in itself, seen as the fitting ending to a political narrative that has its locus in public political culture rather than the everyday realities of the administration of justice.

Crime and criminal justice are also infused with the economy. Research has been undertaken on the ways in which fiscal considerations shape criminal justice policy, for example, the turn to community correctional alternatives that are less expensive than prisons. Researchers at the Centre have also examined the place of the private corporate sector in the political economy in terms of the powers available to that sector to shape law and law enforcement in accordance with its particular interest in capital gains. The institution of private property, and the legal entitlements traditionally available to private property owners in Western political economies, allow private corporations relative autonomy in insulating themselves from state legal regulation while at the same time establishing their own forms of private policing. Research in this area also raises fundamental questions regarding traditional political and legal distinctions, such as those separating the public and private spheres, and the state from civil society.

Crime, criminality, law and justice are also constructed through cultural institutions and practices. For example, the mass media are the predominant everyday means through which people experience crime, criminality, law and justice. Mass media serve as an important *part of* the justice system, used by law enforcers to mobilize public assistance as well as to promote their organizational and professional ideologies; mass media are also used by the people as a mechanism of alternative justice and as a resource in seeking law reform.

Science is another important cultural institution with respect to crime, criminality, law and justice. Both policy officials and law enforcers increasingly turn to scientific expertise, including technologies developed by scientists, to inform and justify their decisions. This 'scientification' of the working environment of law enforcers arguably has a much greater impact on their everyday tasks and decisions than does the law.

The cultural sphere is linked to aspects of the political economy. Research focuses on how particular problems – e.g. abortion, pornography, child abuse – become defined as important public issues in need of law reform and particular forms of regulation. Attention is given to the 'symbolic politics' involving various organizations and professions who vie for 'ownership' of problems and their preferred forms of legal regulation. At the core of such inquiries is the relationship between the symbolic dimensions mediated by the cultural institutions, and the instrumental dimensions of how changing ideologies and sensibilities translate into the hard realities of control practices in the form of new laws, law enforcement practices, security devices, and so on. For instance, how has the Canadian Charter of Rights and Freedoms, *the* exemplar of law in symbolic politics, provided a symbolic canopy for new forms of law enforcement practice?

Underlying the approach of the Centre of Criminology is a concern to understand how the particular mechanisms of criminal justice decision-making, organization, institutional arrangements, and inter-institutional relations contribute to social order and disorder.

Social order includes three fundamental components: morality, procedure and hierarchy. Morality addresses whether something is in or out of order, good or bad. A basic question concerns how criminal law and justice help delineate moral sensibilities and moral boundaries and thereby help to constitute moral order. For example, historical research on changing sensibilities about the limits to criminal punishment has been especially fruitful in understanding constitutive elements of moral order. Research on law reform is also especially revealing of the dialectic between law and moral order. There are areas in which criminal law reform is accomplished routinely because it is already rooted in moral consensus (e.g. child abuse); areas in which the moral consensus has to be constructed through legal change (e.g impaired driving; narcotics); areas in which any effort at law reform perpetuates moral conflict (e.g. abortion); and areas which are not even on the reform agenda because there is moral ambiguity or moral concerns are silenced (e.g. some areas of administrative law and forms of private policing).

Order is also constituted procedurally, in terms of acting in accordance with established rules and in established sequences. Research focuses on the reciprocal influence between criminal procedure and the procedures adopted by other forms of law, social institutions, organizations and groups. Researchers are also interested in how procedures, combined with moral considerations, provide a general sense of procedural propriety that functions to sustain the legitimacy of organizations and institutions. For example, researchers examine how the social discourse, specific provisions, and case decisions of the Canadian Charter of Rights and Freedoms influence the procedural conceptions and norms of various institutions, organizations and groups. Research addresses the extent to which the procedural conceptions and norms of criminal law and justice permeate the orders of various institutions (e.g. medical, welfare, corporate, educational) and thereby affect their autonomy, result in a merging of practices, and influence the interchangeability of both their professional staffs and their clienteles. Another topic of inquiry is how the conceptions and norms of procedure fostered by law relate to accountability and legitimacy in various institutions, and thus to the constitution of institutional authority.

Order is also a matter of hierarchy, of class, status, distinctions as to quality, exclusion, and inequality. Research addresses how criminal law and justice reproduce economic, political, cultural and social hierarchies.

Researchers have examined how criminal law reproduces economic inequality. For example, there are studies of the differential treatment of economic crimes, showing the leniency granted in cases of tax fraud compared to welfare fraud. More generally researchers have shown that the criminal law mainly addresses relatively petty property crimes committed by the most marginal members of society while corporate wrongdoing is mainly dealt with, if at all, through less severe regulatory and compliance mechanisms under administrative law.

Criminal law and justice also contribute to political hierarchies. Research demonstrates how specific law reforms and policy options respond to and enhance particular political interests to the exclusion of others. Research on private policing mechanisms compared to the state's criminal justice mechanisms reveals the considerable political purchase available to private property owners in both offsetting the state's regulatory incursions and using the state as a convenience.

In the cultural sphere criminologists have considered a number of ways in which knowledge as cultural capital is differentially distributed through criminal law and justice mechanisms. A basic question concerns the mechanisms through which the criminal justice institution regulates knowledge possession and use, resulting in the accretion of knowledge/power advantages to some over others. For example, the criminal justice system polices its own institutional boundaries with respect to the types of expertise it allows and disallows as evidence in dispute settlement. Thus legal rules of evidence and legal judgements protect the authority of legal reasoning and discourse over the claims of forensic psychiatrists and their peculiar reasoning and discourse. The institutional hegemony of law is maintained by protecting its own ways of producing meaning, its own knowledge system, in the wider environment of other professional and institutional discourses with claims to authority.

Criminologists have also researched how criminal justice agencies, especially the police, are members of the deviance defining elite with preferred access to the mass media. Most immediately, this access allows them to frame how particular events, issues and problems are to be thought about, and therefore what outcomes and solutions are deemed viable. More generally, preferred access allows them to create the contemporary myths of crime, law and justice, to turn stories of what is into stories of what ought to be with important implications for our everyday understanding of moral life, procedural propriety, and hierarchical orders.

The criminal law also participates in the construction of cultural identities. As Coombe notes, it authoritatively determines the identities people can claim, and the ways in which personhood and experiences of self can be legitimately represented. These determinations, as Coombe makes clear, silence particular alternative representations of identity, which in turn reproduce social relations of power. They also feed back into the criminal law institution where issues of intent, malice and other indicia of consciousness are central. On the other hand these determinations are not deterministic: the self can resist them and thereby negate, lessen or alter hegemonic aspects of criminal law and thus participate in the reconstruction of legal and other institutional structures.

Criminological research also examines the role of criminal law and justice in the reproduction of social hierarchies in terms of, for example, age, gender, and ethnicity. Taking the example of gender, research focuses on how criminal law is framed in terms of traditional cultural conceptions and social relations of patriarchy, so that patriarchy is enforced and reproduced in the administration of criminal justice. This bears implications not only for social ordering practices, but also for the very ways in which we see those practices and the identities of people involved in them.

The challenge for criminologists is to not only empirically establish hierarchy and inequality in the above terms, but also to specify the mechanisms through which hierarchy and inequality are constituted and perpetuated. In particular there is a need to understand how the mechanisms of criminal justice system and legal institution intersect with those of other social institutions in the reproduction of legal order and legal inequality.

An issue that cuts across each of the dimensions addressed to this point is the growth in criminal law, and in law more generally. Thus another significant area of research is mapping the growth in legislation, in policing capacity (the size and characteristics of bureaucracies involved in legal regulation), in levels of enforcement (the populations subject to control, potentially and actually), and in law talk in political culture and popular culture (influencing how we think and imagine the real). Criminologists seek to explain growth in law in various ways. Law is seen as replacing other institutional discourses as a cultural tool for imagining order and for accomplishing order. The growth of law is seen as being associated with an increasingly complex division of labour, and the attendant features of social distance and social inequality. The growth in law is analyzed in terms of its association with the growth and complexity of knowledge, especially scientific knowledge, and of technology. Another important consideration is the extent to which there are legal add-ons because of structural features of our political culture. The contemporary political sensibility sees legislation as the preferred, even 'natural' ending to the political narrative. That is, legislation is seen as the happy ending to reform processes, and thus as an end in itself regardless of whether it is otherwise reasonable, enforceable or practical as an ordering device. The above considerations in turn allow criminologists to understand how law affects processes of democratic decision-making, reform and social change.

In summary, an institutional approach to criminology entails a conception of criminal law and justice as an ordering system that functions to allocate resources (e.g. by guaranteeing and protecting relationships; by intervening to enforce policies and programmes); to regulate and resolve conflict (e.g. by providing principles and procedures for doing so); and to keep the peace (e.g. by establishing rules of behaviour and enforcing violations with sanctions). The mechanisms of criminal law and justice coordinate institutional activities, and help to constitute society's authority system. As such they are not only a set of rules and bureaucratic roles and practices, but also a distinctive way of construing the reality of social order, telling people what to be as well as what to do. In this formulation the mechanisms of criminal law and justice are seen in terms of a dialectic between agency (ordering) and structure (order). Going beyond simple binary oppositions – for example, between repression and liberation, enabling and constraining features, due process and crime control – criminologists seek an understanding of the mechanisms of criminal law and justice in their wider institutional contexts: as, for example, sites of political conflict and struggle; vehicles for perpetuating political, economic, cultural and social dominance; and, tools for construing culture and expressing dominant cultural values. The struggle over social order, the activity ('legal' or otherwise) that seeks to guarantee social order, and the activity ('legal' or otherwise) that resists the realization of this guarantee, is what unites the field of criminology.

The individual contributions to this volume of course reflect each author's particular, specialized understanding of the field. However, they each include elements of the institutional approach to criminology that has guided research programmes at the Centre of Criminology. In the remaining sections of our introduction we indicate how each essay exemplifies the institutional approach to criminology we have outlined.

Crime, Policing and Punishment

Some of the most significant recent advances in criminology have been provided by social historians. In the past two decades social historians have initiated a great deal of research into crime, policing and punishment because the topic accords with their scholarly interest in the constitution of authority and social order through everyday institutional practices; and, because the present-day public concern over crime and social control urges an understanding of the way it was in order to better appreciate and deal with the way it is.

John Beattie examines the early modern age in English history – from the end of the Middle Ages to the onset of the modern industrial world in the nineteenth century – a period in relation to which research has been especially active and fruitful. A major thrust of this work has been to place crime, policing and punishment in institutional contexts. Crime, policing and punishment are understood in relation to social, economic, political and cultural (ideological) structures. In seeking this understanding historians have increasingly gone beyond sources internal to the criminal justice system (e.g. court records), for example, relying on literary sources, parliamentary debates, and the popular press. Crime, policing and punishment are researched by historians with sensitivity to local institutional contexts and local knowledge, i.e. in terms of the particulars of time and place. As John Beattie emphasizes, this research has enhanced understanding of the variable nature and social function of criminal law and justice, and in particular its function as an ideological system. It has also enhanced understanding of how criminal law was engaged by ordinary people, for example, how riotous activities were not simply unthinking reactions of 'the mob' to adversity, or orchestrated by paid subversives on behalf of self-interested factions of political elites, but disciplined forms of political engagement rooted in peoples' views about their rights under law. This research has also enhanced understanding of how 'crime' and 'criminals' were a product of institutional decision-making processes – in particular, the decision to prosecute – which varied across jurisdictions according to local institutional arrangements, resources and contexts.

In relation to these emphases, researchers have produced fine-grained detail on decision processes as these reveal the institutional roles and relationships of officials, e.g. justices of the peace, parish constable, night watchman, and later, the New Police, lawyers, and prison administrators. Changes in the administration of criminal justice are increasingly well documented, but with a sensitivity to local variations, resistances, and unevenness in acceptance by time and place. There is greater understanding, for example, of the shift from private to public prosecutions; changes in the trial process resulting from police involvement in prosecution and the involvement of lawyers in defending the accused; and, changes in punishment, with a gradual reduction in the use of capital punishment and transportation and a gradual increase in the use of imprisonment.

John Beattie's own research, as well as the work of some scholars he cites, indicates that in the late eighteenth century there was not a sharp break of old regime institutions under the impact of the Industrial Revolution and the rationalism of the Enlightenment. Rather, changes in crime, policing and punishment were long-term, continuous, and piecemeal. The lesson here reflects the Centre of Criminology's research tradition. When one seeks fine-grained empirical detail about structures and processes, not only within the criminal justice institution but in its relations with other institutions, the task of explanation is complicated even while the explanatory possibilities and level of sophistication are enhanced.

Jim Phillips examines the evolution of Canadian criminal justice between 1750 and 1920. In keeping with the institutional approach to criminology, he emphasizes that criminal justice history addresses not only the obvious areas of substantive criminal law, policing, courts and prisons, but also social, economic, political, and cultural history, including, for example, histories of social reform, labour unrest, popular culture and political disaffection. He shows that within Canada there has been considerable variation by time and place in how and why the criminal justice system developed as it did, and in its social, economic, political and cultural functions.

Examining the literature on the institutionalization of criminal justice in Canada, Jim Phillips cautions that there are many gaps in our knowledge, and that many of the sources available present incomplete analyses or are of poor quality. He reviews the transplantation of British criminal justice into Canada over the period 1750–1840. Of course it was not only the British laws and institutions that were transplanted, but also the ideological imprints they bore. For example, the penitentiary was imported in the early 1800s as a product of received ideologies about social order and reform. The penitentiary was not only an instrumental means of segregating troublesome people, but also a 'moral architecture' that symbolized dominant ideology. However, British legal ideology and practice met considerable resistance, especially in post-conquest Quebec, where it was associated with a kind of military overlordship in the eyes of the conquered.

The period 1840–1867 in the Maritimes and the Province of Canada was marked by rapid social change. Historians have shown how the criminal justice system was at the forefront of governmental efforts to deal with a range of social problems associated with urbanisation and modernisation. Moreover, the authorities' solutions to the crime problem were entwined with new health, education and welfare institutions that were evolving along with the legal institution and criminal justice system.

The inter-institutional nature of the response to crime, and the use of the criminal justice system at the vanguard of the reforming state, continued in the post-Confederation period, especially with respect to Western settlement. In particular the North West Mounted Police were used as the main policy tool of central Canadian continental expansionism. The North West Mounted Police provided a general colonial administrative service that included criminal law enforcement as only one of many tools for protecting European settlers and their claims to property and capital expansion. While in popular culture the Mounties symbolized the legal ideals of fairness and justice, their practices tended to reproduce the morality, procedure, and hierarchy of European interests.

Jim Phillips proceeds to review literature on how crime and reaction to it were constituted by particular social, political, economic and cultural features of Canadian society. In doing so he adds to our appreciation that crime and its control cannot be understood in isolation from an understanding of wider institutional structures and social processes. In particular he focuses on studies of how women, aboriginal peoples, and racial minorities have been dealt with in the criminal justice system. These studies reveal structured inequalities in Canadian society and how these inequalities have been reproduced in and through criminal law. Throughout Jim Phillips provides valuable pointers to further research. His essay exemplifies the institutional order approach to criminology and how it has been and can be used to enhance the history of Canadian criminal justice.

Philip Stenning and Clifford Shearing have developed a conception of policing that is central to an institutional order approach to criminology. Policing involves ordering, that is using particular methods or procedures, as demanded by a group with the power to sustain its own version of procedural propriety (method), sense of morality, and power (hierarchy). There are various forms of policing or ordering regarding various orders to be protected. For example, regular policing (the public police) is concerned with responding to threats to order guaranteed by government. Political policing is concerned with responding to threats to government as a guarantor of order. Private policing is concerned with responding to threats to private order as defined by each particular private property owner.

Philip Stenning and Clifford Shearing indicate that most research has examined regular policing and has been organized in terms of basic questions regarding police decision-making. The central focus has been on police officer discretion, defined as autonomy in decision-making. The relative influences of police officer culture, police management, courts, the law, and various publics have been researched, providing detailed evidence of relevance to debates about police accountability. This research has been especially fruitful in making evident the limits to regular policing. The most fundamental limitation is the institution of privacy, as underpinned by the institution of private property, which makes regular policing heavily dependent upon the reactive mobilization of others (individuals, organizations, institutions) for information and various forms of assistance. These restrictions on regular policing have led to experiments with different forms of public police organization, including various programs under the rubric of community policing.

Awareness of the limits to regular policing has led researchers to study alternatives. Philip Stenning and Clifford Shearing have pioneered research into private policing, revealing its distinctive purposes, forms of organization, and goals. Private policing is based in the private morality of particular private interests that are usually not consistent with the public interest. Private policing entails quite different procedures than those employed by the regular police. It is organized to protect profit and prevent loss, and not only with respect to crime. It is usually embedded in other roles and relationships within the private organization concerned, and within technologies of surveillance. Finally, private policing has a different conception of, and relation to, hierarchical order compared to regular policing. It involves multi-national corporations that cut across nation-state jurisdictions and therefore the boundaries, functions, and forms of accountability of regular policing. It thereby alters hierarchies, for example, going beyond traditional political hierarchies and their means of holding police accountable.

Richard Ericson addresses the contributions of the institutional ordering approach to penology, a sub-field of criminology concerned with the sentencing and punishment of criminal offenders. In keeping with the previously noted trends regarding historical research and research on policing, penology has traditionally examined rather narrow political and constitutional issues. It has been technocratic, pragmatic and administrative, for example, assessing the effectiveness of various penal sanctions in terms of their deterrent value for maintaining social order; examining the effectiveness of various forms of prison social organization in terms of the maintenance of order in prisons; and, researching the discretion of judges, prison officials and parole authorities in terms of how it might be regulated more effectively. However, in the past two decades penology has been enhanced considerably by the work of the new social historians, also discussed in John Beattie's essay, and by sociologists.

Historians and sociologists broadened inquiry by viewing the penal system from below, through the eyes of ordinary people including criminal offenders, and moving on to research how penal practices contribute to the construction of political authority and reproduction of social order. In particular a group of revisionist social historians has challenged the parameters of legal discourse and its base in liberal political theory. They place penal reform at the centre of inquiry, treating reform as being as much a part of the penal system as prisons and guards, and emphasizing how reform is always in need of reform. They emphasize the role of the human sciences, including penology itself, in penal structures and processes. They examine the relation between penal practices and macro social, economic, political and cultural forces.

Influenced by revisionist historians, sociologists have taken up the same questions with respect to contemporary penal reform movements and practices. For example, there is substantial sociological literature regarding the contemporary decarceration or community corrections movement. Sociologists have also examined how penal institutions are entwined within a broader inter-institutional network in society and shaped by political economy and cultural sensibilities. Research focuses on the professionalization and bureaucratization of punishment, the inter-changeability of dependent populations across health, welfare and penal institutions, and the ways in which penal control is embedded in various aspects of community organization.

The recent work by historians and sociologists has raised fundamental questions that link the study of penal sanctions to social and political theory. It has sparked theorizing about the relative autonomy of the state, the relation between public and private spheres, processes in bureaucratization and professionalization, and the constitution of order in terms of morality, procedure and hierarchy. The disciplines of history and sociology have been brought closer together, with fruitful exchanges regarding research questions, the methods to be used in answering them, and the interpretation of research results. These exchanges have also bridged over into political science, as discussed in the next section.

Law Reform and Policy

It is obvious that criminal law and justice are infused with politics. Nevertheless, in common law jurisdictions criminological research on political institutions has only developed significantly in the past two decades. Peter Solomon attributes the previous lacuna in part to the fact that jurists in common law countries have traditionally downplayed the political origins of laws; in contrast, the significance of 'criminal policy' has been long recognized by jurists in, for example, France and Russia. Peter Solomon observes that the study of politics and crime in common law countries has flourished in the past two decades as a result of four broad influences: the interest of the new social historians in criminal law and justice; the parallel sociological focus on crime and justice, especially the work of the new criminologists; the development of the critical legal studies movement among legal scholars, with their emphasis upon the political origins and impact of law; and, last but not least, the heightened interest of American political scientists in criminal law and justice in the context of the 1960s civil rights movement and the politics of law and order it fostered.

Peter Solomon addresses three areas in which an understanding of crime, criminal law and justice in the context of political institutions has been fruitful. The first area is political policing which, as mentioned above, concerns how government responds to threats to its role as a guarantor of order. There has been some research on the practices of political policing agencies, and substantial research on the manufacture of political deviance in times of crisis. The second area of research addresses criminal law policymaking. Research in this area assists in understanding the relative importance of social groups and political actors in government, for example, the influence of state operatives ('insider' reformers) compared to non-state interest groups ('outsider' reformers). It also helps understand the role of the criminal law in social change by researching, for example, criminalization (as opposed to other forms of law or no law) and the intensification of law (through law and order crackdowns involving increased enforcement and penal sanctions). Additionally, it is a means of understanding the role of science, technology and expertise in law and government. The third area of research addresses politics in the administration of justice. There is a great deal of research on the politics of controlling the discretion of criminal justice officials, showing, for example, how controlling discretion at one stage of the criminal process often serves to enhance discretion at another stage.

Chet Mitchell brings the above issues to life through a case study of narcotics law reform and policy. Narcotics laws have been created largely on the basis of anecdotal claims, not scientific evidence. Chet Mitchell makes the telling point that there is considerable public attention to sensational cases, such as that of Donald Marshall, regarding false evidence and wrongful conviction at trial, while at the criminal law system's most important stage – the creation of criminal offences – legislators routinely employ incomplete, discredited, or false evidence, or no evidence at all. Unlike the courts, Parliament is under no legal obligation to consider relevant evidence before passing a law. Hence accused persons can be tried carefully, but under ill-considered laws, and they are not allowed to challenge the validity of the laws they are charged with breaking. While Canada has been a leader in research on illicit narcotics – for example, through the Le Dain Commission of Inquiry, and the ongoing work of the Addiction Research Foundation of Ontario – scientific evidence continues to have minimal influence on law in face of 'the war on drugs' in political culture.

The greatest source of influence on narcotics legislation has been anecdotal claims from particular interest groups, especially 'insider' reformers such as the police. Legislators respond to lobbyists and bureaucrats – members of the deviance-defining elite – rather than to a general public that has little knowledge or interest. Hence narcotics laws exemplify the way in which law leads public opinion as opposed to being a response to it. The evil of 'drugs' is dramatized through very high criminal penalties that are set arbitrarily rather than in terms of known risks established scientifically.

Chet Mitchell completes the picture by examining the politics of narcotics law enforcement. Historical research reveals that the law as written and enforced has been discriminatory, targeting drugs that tend to be used disproportionately by marginal immigrants, ethnic minorities, particular labour groups, and dissidents. Narcotics law enforcement also exemplifies what Gary Marx has termed the 'ironies of social control,' escalating and compounding problems it was designed to minimize and regulate.

Kent Roach offers a case study of an especially significant law reform, the enactment of the Canadian Charter of Rights and Freedoms. Roach outlines three 'political' stories about the Charter and its impact. One story has it that the Charter expresses progressive continuity with previous law: it simply embodies, and makes more plain, where we were headed anyway. A second story accounts for the Charter as an agency of political conflict and change, especially at the level of symbolic politics in the public sphere. A third story characterizes the Charter as an agency of regressive continuity: far from providing for greater social equality, the Charter continues the more general repressive function of law, the constitution of 'legal' inequality.

Reported decisions on the Charter indicate that the primary use has been in matters pertaining to criminal law and justice, especially challenges to the conduct of law enforcement officials. Kent Roach indicates that judges have used the Charter to take a strong stand on the right to counsel, but have been weak with respect to constraining police investigations and the practices of penal officials. The Charter has been used unevenly, a fact that seems related to the enabling features of the Charter for judicial discretion. As such the Charter seems to reflect the Canadian penchant for what Doreen McBarnet calls 'loophole law,' and therefore has taken us only partway toward the American law. While the advent of the Charter has entailed increased reliance on American legal authority, Kent Roach argues there is little threat in practice of there being a straightforward importation of American ideas.

Another significant case study in law reform and policy is provided in Chris Webster's analysis of how mental disorder is dealt with in the criminal justice system. While the criminal law recognizes that it is unjust to commit to trial a person who is mentally unfit or who was insane at the time of the offence he or she is alleged to have committed, the criminal justice system has had great difficulty determining questions of fitness, insanity and dangerousness. The law itself is not precise in its definitions. Psychiatrists, psychologists and other health professions within the institution of medicine have been mobilized as experts, but their definitions are also imprecise. For example, the American Psychiatric Association lists 350 mental disorders, which are constantly undergoing revision. Clinicians disagree on classifications in general as well as in their diagnoses of particular cases.

Chris Webster shows how these definitional problems have an impact at every stage of the criminal justice process. The use of particular clinical diagnoses is often influenced more by institutional pressures than by scientific and clinical criteria: for example, clinicians often use a diagnosis that will achieve the court disposition they favour. Dispositions often depend on the availability of custodial and treatment facilities, and the claims they make about being able to help the offender. The definitional problems are exemplified in efforts to define and predict dangerousness. Due to institutional pressures, clinicians err on the side of caution by over-predicting dangerousness, leading to the unnecessary detention of some people. More generally, there are no valid psychiatric or psychological tests for the prediction of violence, and it is in any case difficult to predict behaviour which occurs at such a low rate.

These considerations urge reform of dangerous offender legislation and procedures, which are based on the assumption that medical professionals do have the ability to engage in reliable and accurate forecasting.

Chris Webster's contribution is especially significant in the details it provides regarding how criminal law is entwined with another major social institution. It points to the ways in which criminality, along with other forms of deviance, has become increasingly medicalized. It makes evident the ways in which medical operatives become *part of* the criminal justice system. It raises important questions about the ways in which scientific expertise and technologies are embedded in criminal justice. It addresses significant aspects of bureaucratic and professional power, as two major institutions, medicine and law, interface for the accomplishment of practical tasks. The complicated issues regarding mental disorder and the criminal justice system continue to induce important policy developments and significant reforms in both law and medicine.

Social Hierarchies, Crime, and Justice

As indicated previously, the study of crime, law and justice provides an excellent way to understand social order as hierarchy. Two fundamental aspects of social hierarchy are gender, which is addressed in Mariana Valverde's essay on feminist perspectives in criminology, and age, which is addressed in Gordon West's essay on juveniles.

Mariana Valverde specifies the significant contributions of feminist perspectives. Feminist perspectives have advanced understanding about some of the fundamental limitations of dominant paradigms in criminology. They have made evident the shortcomings of contract theory, the ground of classical criminology. Contract theory perpetuates the split between the public and private spheres both in legal discourse and in everyday life. It thereby masks gender domination, especially as it leaves the private sphere, the primary workplace of women, largely unregulated. Feminist perspectives have also challenged positivist criminology which, with its dichotomy between observer and observed, knowing subject and known object, constructs people as objects to be studied, but not as fully rational subjects in their own right. This framework continues to be applied more to women offenders than to men.

Mariana Valverde points out that scholars using feminist perspectives have not been in search of a grand theory to fit women offenders, but rather seek to challenge basic social categories and their implications for social organization and control: family, civil society, the state, criminal law and other law, deviance and normality. Scholars adopting feminist perspectives have focused in particular on the state, both to critique how it contributes to the constitution of unequal power arrangements and relationships, and to understand how it can be engaged for social change. This focus has sparked greater appreciation among criminologists that crime and criminal law cannot be analyzed adequately in isolation from analysis of the state, and that law is a central component in struggles for social change.

Mariana Valverde stresses that for scholars who take feminist perspectives, criminal law is analyzed in conjunction with other areas of law, and all legal analyses are linked to broader questions of social justice. In the lived experiences of women criminal law is entwined with family law and administrative law. While women suffer as victims of crime, there is more widespread suffering in the context of social structures that create a series of injustices, for example, inadequate child care facilities, welfare benefit inequalities, and pornographic representations that treat women as objects.

Seeing law, social control and justice in terms of the everyday mechanisms by which men subordinate women urges reflection on criminology itself. While there are publication outlets for scholars with feminist perspectives, these continue to be marginalized. Women tend to be included only in discussions about selected topics, such as sexual deviance. Gender is not a central analytical category in mainstream criminology, as exemplified in the other contributions to the present volume.

Our society also structures inequality in terms of age. The young and the old are subject to various types of social exclusion, for example, from employment, particular forms of housing, particular leisure activities, and some leisure habits. Gordon West focuses on the young, offering the poignant observation that 'In Canada, ironically it has become illegal for a person under eighteen to act as an adult.' There are many activities that are illegal only for children and youth, for example, truancy, sexual activeness, using tobacco products, and consuming alcoholic beverages. There are recurrent moral panics about children and youths, used to justify waves of legal intervention. These often target particular groups (e.g. ethnic minorities, lower classes, females) and therefore reproduce structured inequality, even though self-report and observational research evidence indicates that youth crime is widespread across all social classes and groups.

Gordon West traces how children and youth have been treated very differently than adults under criminal law. Between 1908 and 1984 in Canada, the *Juvenile Delinquents Act* enabled wide judicial and administrative discretion with respect to children and youth deemed to be in the condition of 'delinquency.' It linked the criminal process for juveniles into the health, education and welfare institutions. It thereby provided sanctions for errant young people who were merely offensive, as well as for those who were offenders, and penalized the deprived as well as the depraved. Gordon West argues that one of the main functions of the *Juvenile Delinquents Act* was to symbolically and ritually dramatize popular concerns about the 'bad child' and to construct the image of 'the good child.' That is, it was directed as much at constructing moral order as at preventing crime and guaranteeing public safety.

The *Young Offenders Act* was enacted in 1984. It aims to limit official discretion by confining delinquency to acts specified in the *Criminal Code* and by introducing various other elements of legalism, such as more due process protections for accused persons, including a right to legal representation, and a maximum penal sanction of three years incarceration. Gordon West observes that, as with all legal changes, many aspects of the situation under this new law are not dramatically different. Problems in the administration of juvenile justice continue, including unevenness across jurisdictions, and arbitrariness in decision-making. At the level of public culture, the politics of childhood and adulthood continue to be played out in moral panics about crime and vice among marginalized young people. The social hierarchies and practices which perpetuate age-grading are too solid to be shifted in the short-term by a particular law reform and specific legal challenges.

The essays and bibliographies in this volume explore the institutional focus of scholarship at the Centre of Criminology, and our links with criminological scholarship conducted elsewhere. Collectively, the following pieces illustrate the value of research on the institutional processes and structures that constitute crime, law and justice, and on how these articulate with the moralities, procedures and hierarchies of social order.

Crime, Policing, and Punishment

1

Crime, Policing, and Punishment in England 1550–1850

J.M. Beattie

Introduction

As crime, especially violent crime, has appeared to increase sharply in Western Europe and North America over the last thirty years or so, the history of crime and of policing and punishment has taken on a particular urgency. This wider public concern surely helps to explain why historians have become interested in studying crime and past societies' responses to it, and why there has been a recent explosion of writing on the criminal law and the administration of justice. But more narrowly, such matters have also been explored as a central aspect of what has been called 'the new social history,' a history that has taken on a set of questions largely neglected by an older historical tradition that had focused particularly on political and constitutional issues. Social historians have not in fact ignored questions of politics and power, or the history of institutions, but they have been preoccupied over the last two decades with the experience of those hitherto largely excluded from the historical record, and with issues central to the social life of ordinary men and women in the past – with the labouring population, the history of work, of women, children, marriage and the family, the life cycle, education and literacy, and such matters as poverty and the circumstances and conditions under which social order was established and maintained. In this context the study of crime and the changing nature of the criminal law and its administration has taken on a particular interest. Indeed, because these matters bear on the broader social context and on the changing economic circumstances of society, and because the records of the courts illuminate in such concrete ways the lives of people for whom historical evidence is not easy to come by, the study of crime and the way it was dealt with have proven to be particularly attractive areas of study. In the case of England, the most fruitful and active period of research has been that between the end of the Middle Ages and the onset of the modern industrial world in the nineteenth century, the period known in English history as the early modern age. It is that period I will largely concentrate on here, noting briefly contributions to the study of crime, as well as work on the forms of policing, the process of prosecution and trial, and the history of punishment.

Crime

Inevitably, in a developing field of this kind, much of the best work published so far has been in articles and case studies. But a number of monographs and other longer works have appeared in recent years, including two general and synthetic studies which provide very useful introductions to the periods 1550–1750 (Sharpe, 1984) and 1750–1900 (Emsley, 1987). These are both very informative, helpful on the sources available for the history of crime and the administration of the law and on the problems they pose, and provide valuable introductions to the most recent work on these subjects. Other surveys of recent work can be found in Bailey (1980), Hay (1980), Jones (1982), Sharpe (1982, 1988), and the especially valuable essay by Innes and Styles (1986). What these surveys reveal is that while the study of crime and the administration of justice in early modern England has been marked over the last two decades by a variety of interests and approaches, there has been a common concern to get beyond the anecdotal, piecemeal and 'literary' evidence that has served so often to characterize crime in the past. This has meant an effort to exploit the records of the English courts, records which survive in some jurisdictions from the mid-sixteenth century on. One main line of work has aimed to learn who was charged and with what offences, and the way in which such cases were dealt with by the courts – at least with regard to the most serious crimes against property and the person. The government kept no such statistics until the early nineteenth century and much of the early systematic study of crime has involved the creation of a form of criminal statistics built up principally from the documents that set out the formal charges against the accused and recorded the outcome of the cases. Historians have varied a good deal in the way they have gathered and interpreted such statistics, and their meaning and value has been the subject of a good deal of discussion. But the systematic exploitation of the records of the main criminal courts has informed much of the work done over the past twenty years.

Much of this work has inevitably concentrated on offences against property – burglary, robbery, theft – since they accounted for the vast majority of charges brought before the main criminal courts in England over this period. Such offences were prosecuted at a level that makes comparisons possible among jurisdictions and over time. How these data are to be interpreted, what they tell us about crime or the process of prosecution, has been a matter of some dispute, as we shall see. But the analysis of court records has made it possible for questions to be posed about patterns of prosecutions for property offences across several centuries (for the period before 1800, see Beattie, 1974, 1986; Cockburn, 1977; Hay, 1982; Herrup, 1987; Lawson, 1986; Samaha, 1974; Sharpe, 1983, 1984). Most of these studies have taken the county as the unit of analysis because the counties were the jurisdictions within which the main criminal courts – the assizes and quarter sessions – were organized. After 1810, the national government began to collect and publish criminal statistics, and historians have been able to use these, as well as county-level data, to construct regional and national patterns of prosecution in the nineteenth century, and to forge more explicit comparisons of different parts of the country (Gatrell and Haddon, 1972; Gurr, Grabosky and Hula, 1977; Jones, 1982; Philips, 1977). Gatrell (1980) is a particularly valuable essay from a methodological as well as substantive point of view. Tobias (1967) explicitly rejected published statistical evidence on the grounds of its inherent biases; for a critical evaluation of that argument, see Philips (1977).

Much of the early work on the data derived from court records has turned on the extent to which fluctuations in prosecutions can be related to changing social and economic circumstances – the price of food, for example, or the effect of warfare on the labour market and thus on employment levels and incomes. Whether the correlations that have been identified between prosecutions for property offences and such economic factors illuminate the nature of theft in the early modern world depends to a considerable extent on what historians make of the character of the court data – and particularly whether fluctuations in prosecutions are thought to reflect changes in the actual incidence of offences or merely the propensity of victims to report suspects and of the authorities to apprehend them and bring them to trial. Most historians take prosecutions to be the outcome of an interaction between offences and prosecution decisions, though there is a good deal of disagreement about the way the balance is likely to have been struck, and thus what kinds of questions are most appropriately posed of the court records (for discussion of these matters, see for example, Beattie, 1972, 1986; Cockburn, 1977; Gatrell, 1980; Hay, 1982; King, 1984, 1987; Lawson, 1986; Philips, 1977; and for a sceptical evaluation of the value of such analyses of serial data see Innes and Styles, 1986).

This debate has had the considerable value of encouraging increased attention to the nature of the court records (for which see also Cockburn, 1975, 1978). It has led more recently to an important emphasis being placed on the prosecution process, especially on the factors that affected the victims' decisions to prosecute, and the way constables and magistrates employed their considerable discretionary powers. Apart from attempts to uncover the social and economic contexts in which prosecutions for property crime occurred, historians have also begun to study the differing experiences of men and women as victims and offenders, differences in patterns of prosecution in urban and rural areas, the question of 'professionalism' among offenders and the extent and nature of criminal gangs over the early modern period, and the matter of juvenile crime (see the work cited in the previous paragraph, and also on these various subjects, Barlow, 1973; Beattie, 1975; Brannigan, 1987; Gillis, 1975; Howson, 1970; Margarey, 1978; May, 1973; McMullan, 1982, 1984; Pollock, 1950; Tobias, 1967; Wiener, 1975) .

The history of violent offences over the past five hundred years has not yet been studied in detail, but the changing experience of physically violent behaviour in society that the records of the courts can illuminate – if only dimly and at some remove – and the changing attitudes toward such behaviour that they reveal more sharply, promise to provide insights into the circumstances and social relationships of ordinary men, women and children whose lives are rarely documented. The level and character of interpersonal violence has not yet been studied sufficiently to permit firm conclusions to be reached about the reality of changing levels of violent conduct over time. And the implications of the evidence that has been uncovered have been disputed (Beattie, 1985, 1986; Davis, 1980; Gatrell, 1980; Gatrell and Hadden, 1972; Gurr, 1981; Macfarlane, 1981; Philips, 1977; Sharpe, 1985; Stone, 1983, 1985). But the broad picture seems almost certainly to be of a falling level of physical violence in English society over the past five hundred years, at least into the early decades of this century. That conclusion rests largely on prosecutions for murder – the only violent offence that is likely to have been reported and prosecuted with any consistency over this period (for homicide, in addition to work cited above, see also Cockburn, forthcoming; Green, 1972, 1976; Hartman, 1977; Havard, 1960; Sharpe, 1981). But it also seems to be supported by evidence of a heightened sensitivity to violence in the late eighteenth century, when the authorities and the courts seemed increasingly anxious to prosecute and punish forms of violent behaviour – assault for example – that had earlier been treated largely as matters of private concern. Such changing attitudes are also signalled by an increasing revulsion against the use of violence in the punishment of criminal offenders – at least when practised in public – and lie behind the attack on capital punishment and public whipping which were sharply constrained in the one case and entirely abolished in the other in the early decades of the nineteenth century (see further on this below).

Apart from studies of trends in prosecutions for homicide over time, there has also been some important work on a number of other forms of violence: infanticide (Hoffer and Hull, 1981; Malcolmson, 1977; Rose, 1986; Sauer, 1978; Wrightson, 1982); suicide (Anderson, 1978, 1987; Andrew, 1988; McDonald, 1986; Stevenson, 1987 'Rise,' 1987 'Contributions'; Zell, 1986); rape (Clark, 1987; Conley, 1986); and duelling (Andrew, 1980; Kiernan, 1988; Simpson, 1988).

A great deal of excellent and revealing work has also been done over the last two decades and more on a subject that is related to the uses or the threat of violence in past societies, to popular attitudes and the responses of the authorities: that is, the study of crowds, of protest, demonstration and riot. There is now a vast literature on this subject, stimulated in the English context by the pioneering work of George Rudé and an article of fundamental importance by Edward Thompson on food riots (Rudé, 1962, 1964, 1970; Thompson, 1971). They revealed the richness of the subject by demonstrating the falseness of the assumption that the riotous activities of crowds in London and the countryside, so common in England between the sixteenth and nineteenth centuries, could be dismissed as the reflexive, violent and unthinking response of the 'mob' to adversity, to dearth or changes in economic circumstances – understandable, but without historical meaning – or as the activities of rent-a-crowds, hired by and manipulated by factions of the elite for their own political purposes. The work of Rudé and Thompson and of many who followed them revealed that crowd actions were more complex than historians had imagined, that crowds were commonly very disciplined, and that they acted from a coherent set of views about the law and their rights under it. Such views opened up the subject of riot and violent protest in a variety of changing settings over several centuries, and that has led to a stream of work on crowd actions in urban and rural settings, and on the changing character of such actions over time, as political and economic circumstances changed. Some of the main work has been on the food riots that were stimulated by unfair prices and changes in marketing practices; on disturbances in the workplace; on protests against the invasion of common rights on the land; and on popular politics (for a sample of such work see Bohstedt, 1983, 1988; Dunbabin, 1974; Fletcher and Stevenson, 1985; Harris, 1986, 1987; Holmes, 1976; Holton, 1978; Malcolmson, 1980; Rogers, 1978, 1982; Rose, 1960; Sharp, 1980; Slack, 1984; Stevenson, 1979; Stevenson and Quinault, 1974; Underdown, 1985; Walter and Wrightson, 1976).

The hallmark of this work and of recent studies of crime has been the effort to place such behaviour in context – in the case of 'mainstream' crime, for example, to study property offences and violence in relation to social, economic, political and ideological structures. This has considerably enlarged the boundaries of the subject by bringing to bear more systematically than ever before the vast amount of contemporary comment on and response to crime in pamphlets, sermons, a popular literature of criminals' lives and confessions that proliferated from the sixteenth century on, and, increasingly in the eighteenth and nineteenth centuries, in newspapers and magazines and parliamentary sources. The meaning of so many offences brought to trial in the past – especially perhaps violent offences – is difficult to penetrate from the often sparse and formal record of the court itself. But a number of recent studies have shown how much can be learned about the context of offences, about changing definitions of what is criminal, and about attitudes toward offenders, from contemporary 'literary' evidence when that is used critically and with concern for its strengths and weaknesses and the questions it can and cannot answer (for such sources and work based in part on them see Davis, 1980, 1984; Faller, 1976, 1987; Harris, 1982; Linebaugh, 1977; McMullan, 1984; Sharpe, 1985 'Speeches').

The effort to place crime in context has been particularly fruitful with respect to the study of a range of offences that are sometimes called – misleadingly, or at least inadequately – 'social crimes' as a way of suggesting that their definition as crime was not universally shared, and indeed was actively disputed by some part of the public (Hobsbawm, 1972; Rule, 1979). Such offences as poaching, smuggling, the clipping or counterfeiting of the coinage and the embezzlement of materials from the workplace were all in varying degrees susceptible of rival characterizations and at certain times were enforced by the propertied on an unwilling or sceptical community. In this respect they were unlike robbery or theft or the more serious and straightforward forms of violence. Poaching, embezzlement and similar offences can only reveal their meaning when local circumstances and the particularities of time and place are studied in some detail. Several of the most interesting and influential pieces of work in the past two decades have been case studies of such offences in their local contexts which have revealed their contested character and which have opened up for discussion the nature and social function of the criminal law. Studies of poaching and the game laws, of coining and embezzlement have been especially revealing in these ways (Hay, 1975 'Poaching'; Jones, 1979; Munsche, 1977, 1981; Styles, 1980, 1983). And particularly important has been the work of Edward Thompson – in his study of the circumstances in which violent protests in forest communities near London led to the infamous Black Act in 1723 (Thompson 1975 *Whigs and Hunters*), and, along with several of his students, in the collection of essays entitled *Albion's Fatal Tree* (Hay, Linebaugh and Thompson, 1975). The essays in that volume deal with offences that gave rise to disputed definitions of the law – poaching, smuggling, wrecking, the sending of threatening letters – and aim to elucidate them by a study of the local circumstances in which they arose and were played out (Hay, 1975 'Poaching'; Linebaugh, 1975; Rule, 1975; Thompson, 1975 'Anonymity'; Winslow, 1975). But the collection is also important for the conclusions it drew about the nature of the criminal law more generally and the way it was made and administered. In both *Whigs and Hunters* and (in rather different terms and with different emphases) in Douglas Hay's introductory essay in *Albion's Fatal Tree*, the social function of the law as an ideological system is at the forefront of analysis. One of Thompson's concerns is the constraints under which the law was administered in the eighteenth century, and the way in which those constraints gave point and substance to the notion of the rule of law. Hay's brilliant and pathbreaking essay (Hay, 1975 'Property') sought to make sense of much that has been puzzling about the judicial system in the eighteenth century, particularly about the forms of trial and the function of pardon, and about the resistance of the gentry to the reform of the law in the face of growing objections to its harshness and its evident failure to prevent crime. In developing answers to these questions, Hay introduced an important argument about the way the unreformed law and judicial system worked to enhance the social and political authority of the propertied elite. The argument has been challenged on several grounds: for its narrow conception of eighteenth-century society, divided sharply between patricians and plebeians; for its assumptions about the ease with which the capital offences were passed through parliament; for its conception of the criminal law itself and the uses made of it by various groups in society (see Brewer and Styles, 1980; King, 1984; Langbein, 1983; and, in answer to this last piece, Linebaugh, 1985). But Hay's essay and Thompson's study of the Black Act raised some central issues and focused attention on questions that have continued to influence work on the social history of crime and the law not only in eighteenth century England but at other times and places.

Prosecution and Police

A particularly crucial question raised in recent work concerns the matter of who used the criminal law and for what purpose, a question that has also emerged from the statistical analysis of prosecutions. And this in turn has underlined the importance of the study of the process of prosecution itself – the machinery available for apprehending suspected offenders and bringing them to trial, as well as the work of magistrates, and the nature of policing.

Recent work on English magistrates has begun to alter the view of these men as a bunch of booby squires or illiterate and corrupt trading justices that has so often served to characterize them in past accounts of this period.

Justices of the peace exercised a wide range of powers and supervised virtually all local administration, including the poor law, the control of vagrancy, and the supervision of the gaols and houses of correction. They provided the principal arena for the settlement of local disputes by formal and informal means, and they wielded a great deal of authority to act summarily to enforce numerous laws and regulations either on their own or in pairs or at the regular meetings of local magistrates known as petty sessions that became common in this period. They held the court that was of fundamental importance to both the government of the counties and the administration of justice – the quarter sessions that met every three months to try a wide range of offences before grand and petty juries.

The magistrates also provided the link between the victims of serious offences and the assizes, the court that was held twice a year in most counties by the professional judges from Westminster to hear the major cases and clear the gaols. The magistrates' duty to ensure that complaints involving breaches of the criminal law – especially felonies – were brought to trial was clarified in two major statutes in the 1550s that established the conditions and circumstances under which the accused were to be examined before being sent for trial, and granted the magistrates' authority to ensure that the victim and his or her witnesses appeared in court to carry on the prosecution. How magistrates interpreted those powers has not yet been systematically investigated, but one important point is clear: that is, that over the early modern period the administrative process by which magistrates had been enjoined in the sixteenth century to send all accused felons to court was transformed into a preliminary hearing in which they were allowed to make judgments about the character of the evidence brought forward by the prosecution and to discharge the accused if that evidence was weak. By 1800 the essentials of a judicialized preliminary hearing were in place (Beattie, 1986; Langbein, 1974, 1983; Pue, 1983).

The administrative work of justices of the peace in this period was set out in a classic study of English local government in the early years of this century (Webb and Webb, 1906). As important as that has been as a foundation for later work, the Webbs' study was misleading in a number of ways: by concentrating on the justices in quarter sessions they missed the crucial development in the seventeenth and early eighteenth century of petty sessions and therefore failed to appreciate the range of work performed by justices in their own localities; and – partly as a result – they greatly exaggerated the ineffectiveness of local administration in the eighteenth century. Some very fine recent work has provided a fuller account of the work of eighteenth-century justices of the peace. It is now clear that the groundwork for the major developments in local administration in the early nineteenth century was laid very much earlier, a response in part to a rising expectation in the eighteenth century of the services that local government ought to provide (see especially Landau, 1984 and Munsche, 1981. For other work on JPs, see Cockburn, 1972; Crittall, 1982; Moir, 1969a, 1969b; Munsche, 1977; Philips, 1976; Silverthorne, 1978; Styles, 1982, 1983; Welby, 1974. And for work on the identity of the men who held office and how they were appointed, see Glassey, 1979; Gleason, 1969; Landau, 1984; Zangerl, 1971).

There has been a similar and parallel interest in recent years in the history of the parish constable and of the night-watchmen of the towns, men who have been subjected to caricature even more than the justices of the peace. Little is known about who the tens of thousands of constables and watchmen were over the early modern centuries and what they actually did or did not do. It has been all too easy for historians to take some vivid literary representations – Shakespeare's Dogberry and Verges – as accurate accounts, and assume the incompetence and ineffectiveness of such men in the face of crime and disorder. Recent research which has attempted to put the constables into context and to evaluate their work against appropriate standards, has begun to correct what has been a uniformly bleak picture (Kent, 1981, 1986; King, W.J., 1980; Wrightson, 1980). There has been as yet less work on the history of the watch, but that picture is also changing. Evidence is emerging that significant changes in the character of watch forces in the metropolis of London took place in the late seventeenth and early eighteenth centuries and that efforts were made then to ensure that both constables and watchmen were capable of carrying out their duties, that they had equipment and clearly defined tasks, and that they were supervised (Tobias, 1979).

The study of the police is one of several areas in which an emphasis on continuities and on the long-term, piecemeal development of ideas and practices is beginning to replace a picture that has long been dominant: that is, the view that the late eighteenth century saw a sudden and sharp reform of old regime institutions under the twin impact of the Industrial Revolution and the rationalism of the Enlightenment. It is not so much the importance and significance of change in a wide variety of institutions that has been brought into question, as the assumption of the totality and suddenness of change in this new world forming in the last third of the century. More careful investigation of the early eighteenth century has uncovered significant developments in a whole range of institutions in the century before 1760. And that in turn has encouraged some re-evaluation of the important and significant changes that undoubtedly did take place in the late eighteenth and early nineteenth centuries. Changes in policing have provided one focus for such work, and there has been a great deal of writing over the past two decades on the character of policing in the eighteenth century as well as on developments embodied in the establishment of the so-called New Police in the metropolis of London in 1829 and in the rest of the country – in the boroughs (1839) and the counties (1856) – over the next quarter century. The process by which salaried and uniformed police forces emerged, better trained and disciplined and more highly organized than was possible under the the old parish and ward structures, has thus been significantly extended back into the eighteenth century.

The literature on the police falls broadly into two categories: an older and until recently dominant tradition that concentrated on the police as an institution, largely internalist, and uncritical in tone; and a body of revisionist writing that over the past twenty years has questioned many of the assumptions and conclusions of these more 'conservative' writers – though these revisionist arguments are already in their turn being subjected to critical scrutiny. The older tradition tended to regard the emergence of police on modern lines as an inevitable development, given the economic and demographic changes after 1750. The main narrative line in the work of Reith and Critchley and Radzinowicz – volumes 2 and 3 of whose detailed and important work on English criminal law and its administration since 1750 are centrally concerned with the establishment of the New Police – concerns the way in which the opposition to reform was overcome, and the eventual triumph of the rational answer to the crime and social disorder of the urban and industrial world in the form of the new policing regimes. The tendency of such writers was to assume a consensus in society about the value of the police and thus to regard opposition to its establishment as essentially wrongheaded and unthinking.

It is against such assumptions that much of the recent work on the English police has been written. Perhaps the leading characteristic of the revisionists' vision – particularly exemplified in the work of Storch (1975, 1976) – has been their emphasis on the opposition aroused by proposals for the New Police, and the conflict that followed their successful disposition. Their emphasis is more on conflict than consensus, on the opposition of the gentry on constitutional grounds, and on the continuing opposition in the working population, as the New Police in the 1840s and 1850s were employed not merely with problems of serious crime, but also in attempts to eliminate forms of popular recreation that distressed the more respectable members of society. The policeman as 'a domestic missionary,' in Storch's phrase, aroused opposition and resistance in some parts of the country long after the institution of the police had been fully accepted as natural and necessary in much of the society. Recent writing has emphasized the variety of responses to the New Police and their unevenness over time and place (for recent writing on the police see: Davey, 1983; Emsley, 1982, 1983, 1985; Field, 1981; Foster, 1982; Jones, 1983; Lowe, 1983; Miller, 1975,

1977; Palmer, 1988; Philips, 1980; Reiner, 1985; Robinson, 1979; Silver, 1967; Smith, 1985; Steedman, 1984; Storch, 1975, 1976, 1977; Swift, 1988 'Urban Policing,' 1988 'Police Reform'; Weinberger, 1981).

The argument has been made recently that the revisionists have themselves accepted too uncritically the supposed newness of the New Police and have failed to take account of evidence of changes in policing arrangements over the previous hundred years and more – changes which require a more precise delineation of the character of the New Police and which broaden the context within which an explanation of their emergence will have to be sought (Styles, 1987). One further dimension of policing history has been pressed forward in recent work – that is the value of a comparative framework, in which the emergence of the New Police in England and Wales is set within the context of the creation of policing policies and practices and institutions in Ireland and the wider British colonial world (Brogden, 1987; Palmer, 1988).

The development of the new policing forces in England and Wales had important implications for several other elements in the administration of criminal justice, and for one in particular: the system of prosecution. In the early modern period the courts relied on private prosecution to put the criminal law into motion. That meant that if an accused was going to be charged and brought to court, the victim of the offence (or his relatives or agent) had to bring the matter to the attention of a magistrate, arrange for the appearance of the accused or get a magistrate's warrant directed to a constable to bring the accused in for questioning, and then appear in court to prosecute the case. The victim/prosecutor was also required to pay the official costs at various stages as the matter went forward, as well, of course, as the charges of his own witnesses.

Some of the most useful and interesting recent work on the early modern criminal justice system has dealt with this process of prosecution, and the discretionary powers it provided to the accused and to the authorities. The costs of prosecution have also been discussed and the matter of who the prosecutors were, and thus, what meaning can be assigned to the criminal law as a social institution (Beattie, 1986; Hay, 1983, 1984; Herrup, 1984, 1987; King, P., 1984; Knafla, 1983; Langbein, 1974; Lenman and Parker, 1980; Philips, 1977; Samaha, 1981; Sharpe, 1980). Attention has also been directed at the ways in which the state became increasingly involved in prosecution, either directly through some of its agencies like the Post Office or the Mint, or indirectly by paying for prosecutions. More typical of the way the state in the eighteenth century tried to encourage the effective administration of the criminal law was by supporting private prosecutors by paying their costs, and by offering rewards for the successful prosecution of certain classes of serious offenders. Recent work has also begun to uncover those schemes and some of their consequences in the eighteenth century – of the payment of rewards in particular – in the development of private thief-taking and in the encouragement they gave to malicious prosecution (Hay, 1983, 1984, 1989; Hay and Snyder, 1989 'Using'; Paley, 1989 'Thieftakers'). Work has also been directed at the attempts made to increase the effectiveness of private prosecution by the organization of local self-help groups – societies for the prosecution of felons – and by the increasing use of newspapers as ways of advertising information about the loss of goods (horses, for example) and the identity of suspects (King, P., 1987, 1989; Philips, 1989; Shubert, 1981; Styles, 1980, 1989). And finally, what is perhaps the major question surrounding this subject over the long-term has also been addressed in a useful though preliminary way: that is, the way in which the system of private prosecution was entirely undermined as the New Police gradually took over the prosecution of serious offences in the nineteenth century. The process by which the police came to assume decision-making power about who would be charged, and with what offence, was underway by the 1850s and was apparently well advanced by the 1880s. How and why it happened and what the ramifications were of such momentous alterations in the criminal justice system awaits detailed investigation (Hay and Snyder, 1989 'Using').

Trial

Finally, work in two other areas should be noted: studies of the process of trial; and of the changing character of punishment over time. The history of trial procedure in the ordinary criminal courts in the pre-modern period has only recently been uncovered, as historians have begun to exploit the printed accounts of London trials, the *Old Bailey Sessions Papers*. Two large themes have been at the centre of recent work. In the first place, the changing dynamics of the trial – a trial conducted until the eighteenth century without the involvement of lawyers, with the victim as prosecutor and with the accused defending himself as best he could, without having had any real opportunity to prepare for the moment in court when the evidence against him was laid out and he was required by the judge to answer it. For in the 'old' form of trial, which continued well into the eighteenth century, defendants were forbidden to engage counsel to help them in the courtroom, and prosecutors generally chose not to do so since the accused had to answer on their own behalf. In these circumstances, the judge emerged as a crucial force in the court. He acted as examiner and cross-examiner; he was free to comment on the evidence as it was given; and there was clearly immense scope for his influence over the jury. That 'old' form of trial has been studied in some detail, as have the consequences of the introduction of lawyers into the criminal courts in the course of the eighteenth century. A good deal remains to be learned about the transition to modern forms of trial in the eighteenth and nineteenth centuries, and about the bench and bar, despite some important contributions to those subjects. But a substantial foundation has been laid over the past fifteen years or so (Beattie, 1977, 1986; Cockburn, 1972, 1985; Duman, 1980, 1982, 1983; Landsman, 1990; Langbein, 1977, 1978, 1979, 1983; Prest, 1981, 1987; Pue, 1987).

Some good work has also been done in recent years on the composition and function of the jury. The criminal trial jury played a particularly crucial role in the administration of a criminal law that depended for many centuries on capital punishment as a deterrent to crime. The jury's ability to modify through its verdict the charge brought against the prisoner gave it the power to temper the harshness of the common law rule that made execution the only available punishment for felony. For the jury could not only acquit defendants; it could save others from the gallows by convicting them on a lesser charge. And that ability to mitigate the law was enlarged as the jury gained in independence from the bench in the seventeenth century. Its role in major state trials in the seventeenth and eighteenth centuries gave the English jury an almost mystical status as a guardian of liberty, a shield against illegality and oppression. At the level of the day-to-day criminal trial its capacity for independent judgment placed the jury between the government and the public, and gave it some ability to shape the application of the law according to the changing standards of the community.

How criminal trial juries chose to exercise those powers over the early modern period has been the subject of some excellent work. The jury's ability to nullify the law forms the central theme of an important history of the jury and of its place in constitutional and political thinking from its origins in the early thirteenth century to the dawn of the modern trial at the beginning of the nineteenth (Green, 1985). And the crucial matters of who sat on the jury and the patterns of jury verdicts has been investigated in a collection of essays covering the same period (Cockburn and Green, 1988). What these studies have revealed is that in the early modern period, criminal trial jurors were drawn from the middling ranks of property owners, and that they were, in addition, typically very experienced in all aspects of local administration as well as in jury service itself. There is some disagreement among the contributors to this volume about how this social analysis of jury composition should be interpreted: whether, on the one hand, the jurors' property ownership and their experience as local governors and as jurors increased their capacity for independent action; or, on the other, whether they were in reality part of the elite who made the law and who presided over the courts. That remains an important issue. But there is no doubt that this collection of essays has greatly advanced the study of one of the central institutions of criminal administration in England (see Beattie, 1988; Cockburn, 1988; Green, 1988; Hay, 1988; King, P., 1988; Lawson, 1988; Roberts, 1988. And for jurors in the seventeenth century, see also Herrup, 1987).

Punishment

When juries reached their verdicts, judges at the assizes and magistrates at the quarter sessions passed sentences upon those that had been convicted. The punishments were to a considerable extent fixed by law. In the Middle Ages and in the first part of the period we are dealing with, the range of possible punishments for serious offences – for felonies, including murder, arson, rape, and virtually all crimes against property – was very narrow indeed. In the case of lesser offences, the so-called misdemeanors, the judges had the latitude to choose among a number of penalties, including fines, imprisonment, whipping, branding and public exposure on the pillory. But felonies were punishable only by hanging. The study of punishment in this period and well into the eighteenth century is to a considerable extent a study of the way that common law rule was interpreted by the courts, and the way capital punishment was in fact administered. It is clear from recent work that the rigour of the law was blunted by a range of discretionary powers available to juries, the judges, and the king. A great deal has been learned about the way the harshness of the law was mitigated by jury verdicts, by the device known as benefit of clergy and by the monarch's power to pardon. The study of punishment in the early modern period thus turns in large part on the social function of capital punishment and the public ceremony around which it was organised (Beattie, 1986; Bellamy, 1973; Campbell, 1984; Hanawalt, 1979; Hay, 1975; Linebaugh, 1975; Radzinowicz, 1948; Samaha, 1978; Sharpe, 1983, 1984, 1985; Spierenberg, 1984. For the end of public execution in England in the 1860s, see Cooper, 1974).

The history of punishment over the last two hundred years has been dominated by accounts of the movement to reform the criminal law and of the rise of the prison and the sanction of imprisonment which became regularly available to the English courts as a punishment for convicted felons only toward the end of the eighteenth century. The first volume of Sir Leon Radzinowicz's massive and magisterial work on the administration of the criminal law in England since 1750 is centrally devoted to the campaign in the late eighteenth century and the early decades of the nineteenth against the excessive use of the death penalty for relatively trivial offences, a campaign that resulted in the substantial dismantling of the old 'bloody code' in the 1820s and 1830s. And the Webbs (1922) long ago outlined the story of the reform of the prisons, as an aspect of their history of local government. The assumption behind much of this work is of a close linkage between the loss of faith in capital punishment after 1760 and the emergence of the idea of imprisonment as a means of reformation and rehabilitation, an idea given expression in the new purpose-built penitentiaries that arose in England in the late eighteenth and early nineteenth centuries. The sense that there was a close connection between the reform of the law and the rise of the modern prison in the same period derives ultimately from the arguments and ideas of those who pressed for such changes, from the work, writings and speeches of such reformers as John Howard, Jeremy Bentham, William Eden, Elizabeth Fry, Samuel Romilly and others. The account derived from their testimony and their arguments inevitably emphasized the sharpness of the break with the past that these changes represented. Just as inevitably, that account also incorporated an explanation of the motives of the reformers that has stressed their humanitarian revulsion against deterrence by terror and the disgraceful condition of the local gaols, and their struggle to do something about both. The story of penal change at the end of the eighteenth century and in the first half of the nineteenth has thus been couched in heroic terms, and what has long been the orthodox account has fully accepted both the chronology of change and the forms of explanation that derived from the reformers themselves (Babington, 1971; Gruenhut, 1948; Howard, 1958; Phillipson, 1923; Radzinowicz, 1948; Whiting, 1975).

An alternative framework for the study of imprisonment was provided fifty years ago by Rusche and Kirchheimer (1939), whose account, European in scope, rested on a much longer period than English studies had typically dealt with, and sought explanations grounded in economic experience, particularly the fluctuating condition of the labour market. But the dominant version of the English experience remained in place until it came to be re-examined in the light of other work on aspects of the law and criminal administration over the last twenty years. The more recent alternative account – inevitably labelled 'revisionist' – has sought to place English penal developments in a broad social context, and to challenge explanations of the rise of the penitentiary and new forms of prison discipline as uncomplicated expressions of the progressive and humane ideas of the reformers. As a result, the social history of punishment has been one of the leading areas of interest in recent work.

This work was very much underway before Michel Foucault's account of the rise of the penitentiary as a central institution of surveillance and control in modern society appeared in 1975 (and in English translation in

1977), but that book clearly focused attention on the importance of the prison. The discussion was also fed by other wide-ranging work on European and North American penal history (Melossi and Pavarini, 1981; Rothman, 1971, 1980; Spierenburg, 1984). In England, some important contributions to a newer understanding of prisons had been made by 1978 (see Henriques, 1972, for example), but the leading revisionist account in the English case was published in that year by Michael Ignatieff. His study of the emergence of a new carceral regime in the nineteenth century also searches for broad explanations – an intention announced in its subtitle. Ignatieff does not ignore the ideas and intentions of the reformers – indeed he places them, particularly Howard's, in a new and powerful light. But his emphasis is on locating the development of forms of imprisonment that emphasized solitary confinement and labour in a broad context that also incorporates political and economic forces. Several other recent studies of the law reform movement in England have similarly sought for broader explanations (McGowen, 1983, 1986, 1987, 1987–8, 1988; Morgan, 1977). And a great deal of work has been recently published on penal policy-making in the nineteenth century, on the various forms of discipline and labour by which new ideas and intentions were expressed, on the administrative innovations they gave rise to, and, in an excellent and revealing study, on the architecture of the institutions that were built and reconstituted in this period (Bender, 1987; Cooper, 1976; Evans, 1982; Henriques, 1972; McConville, 1981; Priestley, 1986; Radzinowicz and Hood, 1986; Stack, 1979; Stockdale, 1977; Tomlinson, 1978, 1981).

Not all of this work has, however, confirmed the picture that first emerged from the revisionist argument. Criticism of some of the revisionists' assumptions has indeed been led by Ignatieff in a subtle and important auto-critique (1981). And as more is learned about the prisons of the nineteenth century it is clear that too much has been made of the history of one or two institutions that came to embody the reformist ideology in a particularly clear way. Not all institutions were equally touched by the new ideas. In the absence of strong central direction until the second half of the century, a crucial variable was the degree of local interest in and commitment to penal questions. The result is an emphasis not on a massive universal transformation of prisons in the nineteenth century, which a reading of Ignatieff (1978) might lead one to expect, but rather on the unintended consequences that so often followed an effort at reform, on the importance of local circumstances and the diversity of experience in prisons in the nineteenth century (for these themes, see in particular DeLacy, 1981, 1986).

The revisionist account – and even more the traditional story of reform it sought to modify – has been open to challenge from another direction too, that is on the grounds that it posited too sharp a change in ideas and practice suddenly taking place in the last quarter of the eighteenth century (Garland, 1986). The implicit model in the work of both Radzinowicz and Ignatieff is of a system of punishment largely unchanging until the dependence on the gallows was challenged and then undermined in the last decades of the eighteenth century and the first half of the nineteenth. Both accept a chronology that concentrates attention on a takeoff point in the last decades of the century. This inevitably suggests a broad connection between changes in penal ideas and the large-scale changes going on at the same time, the movement of ideas identified as the Enlightenment and the complex of changes in the economy and society of England summarized as the Industrial Revolution. Recent research has begun to throw doubt on several aspects of that set of ideas by uncovering evidence of a much longer effort to strengthen the courts in the face of a perceived rise of crime, efforts going back into the seventeenth century and clearly involving a search for effective non-capital punishments. A period of experimentation can be seen to have taken place in the last decades of the seventeenth century (and perhaps earlier), an effort that included a few years in which the courts sentenced convicted offenders to terms of imprisonment at hard labour in the houses of correction, and that concluded with a change of the greatest significance – the establishment in 1718 of transportation to the American colonies. This gave the English courts for the first time a usable non-capital sanction for the punishment of felons. The establishment of transportation had a transforming effect not only on the structures of punishment, but on the conduct of trial, the management of prisons, the exercise of the royal prerogative of pardon, and indeed on all aspects of the system of criminal justice (for houses of correction, penal experiments and the establishment of transportation see Beattie, 1986; Ekirch, 1985, 1987; Innes, 1987; Smith, 1947). The system criticized by Beccaria, Howard and Bentham had in fact been changing significantly for a hundred years or more by the 1760s. When the American Revolution closed the door to transportation in 1776 and the English gaols filled up with convicted prisoners, it was clear that there could be no going back to the situation in the seventeenth century when capital punishment was the only sanction available to the courts. It was in these circumstances that incarceration at hard labour returned strongly, and now with a much more powerful ideological thrust. Transportation was re-established in 1787, though on different foundations and for a much smaller proportion of convicted offenders, with the opening of the penal colony at Botany Bay in Australia (Cobley, 1970; Frost, 1980, 1985; Gillen, 1982; Hughes, 1987; Martin, 1978; Shaw, 1966; Smith, 1982; Sweeney, 1981; Wilson, 1986).

An account of the transformation of English penal practices that emphasizes the search for effective secondary punishment in the late seventeenth and early eighteenth centuries and the decisive importance of the establishment of transportation in 1718 is useful mainly because it raises questions about a dominant tradition of explanation – whether by Radzinowicz or Ignatieff or Foucault – that focuses particularly on the late eighteenth century and links penal developments to the political and ideological and economic transformations of the age of the Industrial Revolution. It does not deny or diminish the importance of the changes that undoubtedly did take place in penal ideas and practice in England after 1776. Nor does it deny the need to see the law as a social institution. It does, however, make the task of explanation more complicated, just as the diversity of experience in the gaols of the nineteenth century complicates the story of reform in that period and the forces behind it. As we learn more about what actually happened, as the story of the criminal law, the police, the courts, the prisons, and the system of punishment, is filled out and the variety of experience is uncovered in all its messiness, so general explanations will be challenged and assumptions put to the test. What will emerge will be the need for more focused and more specific analyses of the social and political contexts within which offences were defined and committed, and the machinery of judicial administration was elaborated. That process of discovery has just recently begun. Considering the work now in progress, and the theses that have been completed over the last few years – many of them by scholars whose work has been noted in this essay – there is every reason to think that the next few years will see the publication of a range of major books that will take us much further toward a fully social history of crime, law, trial and punishment in England.

Reading List

Abel-Smith, Brian and Stevens, Robert. *Lawyers and the Courts: A Sociological Study of the English Legal System 1750–1965*. London: Heinemann, 1967

Anderson, E.A. 'The Chivalrous Treatment of the Female Offender in the Arms of the Criminal Justice System: A Review of the Literature.' *Social Problems* 23 (3, 1976): 350–7

Anderson, J. Maxwell. *Discovering Suicide: Studies in the Organization of Sudden Death*. London: Macmillan, 1978

Anderson, Olive. *Suicide in Victorian and Edwardian England*. Oxford: Oxford University Press, 1987

Andrew, Donna T. 'The Code of Honour and its Critics: The Opposition to Duelling in England, 1700–1850.' *Social History* 5 (3, 1980): 409–34

— 'Comment on MacDonald's Secularization of Suicide.' *Past and Present* 119 (May, 1988)

Babington, Anthony. *The English Bastille: a History of Newgate Gaol and Prison Conditions in Britain 1688–1902.* London: MacDonald and Co., 1971

Bailey, Victor. 'Bibliographical Essay: Crime, Criminal Justice and Authority in England.' *Bulletin of the Society of Labour History* 40 (Spring, 1980): 36–46

— 'The Metropolitan Police, the Home Office and the Threat of Outcast London.' In *Policing and Punishment in Nineteenth-Century Britain*, pp. 94–125. Edited by Victor Bailey, 1981

—, ed. *Policing and Punishment in Nineteenth-Century Britain.* London: Croom Helm, 1981

Baker, J.H. 'Criminal Courts and Procedure at Common Law 1550–1800.' In *Crime in England, 1500–1800*, pp. 15–48. Edited by J.S. Cockburn, 1977

Barlow, Derek. *Dick Turpin and the Gregory Gang.* London: Phillimore, 1973

Bayley, David H. 'The Police and Political Development in Europe.' In *The Formation of National States in Western Europe*, pp. 328–79. Edited by Charles Tilly. Princeton: Princeton University Press, 1975

— 'Police Function, Structure and Control in Western Europe and North America: Comparative and Historical Studies.' *Crime and Justice. An Annual Review of Research* 1 (1979): 109–44

Beattie, J.M. 'Towards a Study of Crime in England: A Note on Indictments.' In *The Triumph of Culture*, pp. 299–314. Edited by Paul Fritz and David Williams. Toronto: A.M. Hakkert, 1972

— 'The Pattern of Crime in England, 1660–1800.' *Past and Present* 62 (1974): 47–95

— 'The Criminality of Women in Eighteenth-Century England.' *Journal of Social History* 8 (4, 1975): 80–116

— 'Crime and the Courts in Surrey, 1736–1753.' In *Crime in England 1550–1800*, pp. 155–86. Edited by J.S. Cockburn, 1977

— 'Violence and Society in Early Modern England.' In *Perspectives in Criminal Law: Essays in Honour of John LL.J. Edwards*, pp. 36–60. Edited by Anthony Doob and Edward Greenspan. Aurora: Canada Law Book, 1985

— *Crime and the Courts in England, 1660–1800*. Princeton: Princeton University Press, 1986

— 'London Juries in the 1600s.' In *Twelve Good Men and True: The Criminal Trial Jury in England, 1200–1800*, pp. 214–53. Edited by J.S. Cockburn and Thomas A. Green, 1988

Bellamy, John. *Crime and Public Order in England in the Later Middle Ages*. London: Routledge and Kegan Paul, 1973

— *Criminal Law and Society in Late Medieval and Tudor England*. New York: St. Martin's Press; Gloucester, A. Sutton, 1984

Bender, John. *Imagining the Penitentiary*. Chicago: University of Chicago Press, 1987

Bohstedt, John. *Riots and Community Politics in England and Wales, 1790–1810*. Cambridge, MA: Harvard University Press, 1983

— 'Women in English Riots 1790–1810.' *Past and Present* 120 (August, 1988): 88–122

Brannigan, Augustine. 'Moral Panics and Juvenile Delinquents in Britain and America.' *Criminal Justice History* 8 (1987): 181–92

Breathnach, Seamus. *The Irish Police: From the Earliest Times to the Present Day*. Dublin: Anvil Books, 1974

Brewer, John and Styles, John, eds. *An Ungovernable People. The English and their Law in the Seventeenth and Eighteenth Centuries*. London: Hutchinson, 1980

Broeker, Galen. *Rural Disorder and Police Reform in Ireland, 1812–1836*. London: Routledge and Kegan Paul, 1970

Brogden, Michael. ' "An Act to Colonize the Internal Lands of the Island": The Empire and the Origins of the Professional Police.' *International Journal of the Sociology of Law* 15 (2, 1987): 179–208

— 'The Emergence of the Police: The Colonial Dimension.' *British Journal of Criminology* 27 (1, 1987): 4–14

Brundage, Anthony. 'Ministers, Magistrates, and Reformers: The Genesis of the Rural Constabulary Act of 1839.' *Parliamentary History* 5 (1986): 71–87

Campbell, R. 'Sentence of Death by Burning for Women.' *Journal of Legal History* 5 (1, 1984): 44–59

Carson, Kit and Idzikowska, Hilary. 'The Social Production of Scottish Policing, 1795–1900.' In *Policing and Prosecution in Britain 1750–1850*. Edited by Douglas Hay and Francis Snyder, 1989

Carson, W.G. 'Policing the Periphery: The Development of Scottish

Policing, 1795–1900.' Parts I and II. *Australian and New Zealand Journal of Criminology* 17 (1984): 207–32; and 18 (1985): 3–16

Clark, Anna. *Women's Silence Men's Violence: Sexual Assault in England, 1770–1845*. London: Pandora, 1987

Cobley, J. *The Crimes of the First Fleet Convicts*. Sydney: Angus and Robertson, 1970

Cockburn, J.S. *A History of English Assizes, 1558–1714*. Cambridge: Cambridge University Press, 1972

— 'Early Modern Assize Records as Historical Evidence.' *Journal of the Society of Archivists* 5 (4, 1975): 215–231

—, ed. *Crime in England, 1550–1800*. London: Methuen, 1977

— 'The Nature and Incidence of Crime in England 1559–1625: a Preliminary Survey.' In *Crime in England, 1550–1800*, pp. 49–71. Edited by J.S. Cockburn, 1977

— 'Trial by the Book? Fact and Theory in the Criminal Process 1558–1625.' In *Legal Records and the Historian*, pp. 60–79. Edited by J.H. Baker. London: Royal Historical Society, 1978

— *Calendar of Assize Records. Home Circuit Indictments, Elizabeth I and James I: Introduction*. London: HMSO, 1985

— 'Twelve Silly Men? The Trial Jury at Assizes, 1560–1670.' In *Twelve Good Men and True: The Criminal Trial Jury in England, 1200–1800*, pp. 158–181. Edited by J.S. Cockburn and Thomas A. Green, 1988

— 'Patterns of Violence in English Society: Homicide in Kent 1560–1985.' *Past and Present* (forthcoming, 1991)

Cockburn, J.S. and Green, Thomas A., eds. *Twelve Good Men and True: The English Criminal Trial Jury, 1200–1800*. Princeton, NJ: Princeton University Press, 1988

Conley, C.A. 'Rape and Justice in Victorian England.' *Victorian Studies* 29 (4, 1986): 519–36

Cooper, David D. *The Lesson of the Scaffold*. London: A. Lane, 1974

Cooper, R.A. 'Ideas and their Execution: English Prison Reform.' *Eighteenth-Century Studies* 10 (1, 1976): 73–93

— 'Jeremy Bentham, Elizabeth Fry, and English Prison Reform.' *Journal of the History of Ideas* 42 (1981): 675–90

Critchley, T.A. *A History of the Police in England and Wales*. London: Constable, 1967, reprinted 1978

Crittall, Elizabeth, ed. *The Justicing Notebook of William Hunt, 1744–1749*. Wiltshire Record Society 37 (1982)

Davey, B.J. *Lawless and Immoral: Policing in a County Town, 1838–1857*. Leicester: Leicester University Press, 1983

Davis, Jennifer. 'The London Garotting Panic of 1862: a Moral Panic and the Creation of a Criminal Class in Mid-Victorian England.' In *Crime and the Law: The Social History of Crime in Western Europe Since 1500*, pp. 190–213. Edited by V.A.C Gatrell, B. Lenman and G. Parker, 1980

— 'A Poor Man's System of Justice: The London Police Courts in the Second Half of the Nineteenth Century.' *Historical Journal* 27 (1984): 309–35

Davis, Jennifer S. 'Prosecutions and Their Context: The Use of the Criminal Law in Later Nineteenth-Century London.' In *Policing and Prosecution in Britain 1750–1850*. Edited by Douglas Hay and Francis Snyder, 1989

Dawson, John P. *A History of Lay Judges*. Cambridge, Mass.: Harvard University Press, 1960

DeLacy, Margaret. 'Grinding Men Good? Lancashire's Prisons at Mid-Century.' In *Policing and Punishment in Nineteenth-Century Britain*, pp. 182–216. Edited by Victor Bailey, 1981

— *Prison Reform in Lancashire, 1700–1850. A Study in Local Administration*. Stanford: Stanford University Press, 1986

Dinwiddy, J.R. 'The Early Nineteenth-Century Campaign Against Flogging in the Army.' *English Historical Review* 97 (383, 1982): 308–31

Donajgrodzki, A. *Social Control in Nineteenth-Century Britain*. London: Croom Helm, 1977

Duman, Daniel. 'Pathway to Professionalism: The English Bar in the Eighteenth and Nineteenth Centuries.' *Journal of Social History* 13 (4, 1980)

— *The Judicial Bench in England 1727–1875: The Reshaping of a Professional Elite*. London: Royal Historical Society, 1982

— *The English and Colonial Bars in the Nineteenth Century*. London: Croom Helm, 1983

Dunbabin, J.P.D. *Rural Discontent in Nineteenth-Century Britain*. London: Faber, 1974

Edwards, J. Ll. J. *The Law Officers of the Crown*. London: Sweet and Maxwell, 1964

— *The Attorney-General: Politics and the Public Interest*. London: Sweet and Maxwell, 1984

Ekirch, Roger. 'The Transportation of Scottish Criminals to America During the Eighteenth Century.' *Journal of British Studies* 24 (3, 1985): 366–74

— *Bound for America: The Transportation of British Convicts to the Colonies, 1718–1775.* Oxford: Clarendon Press, 1987

Elliott, B. 'Sources for the Study of Juvenile Delinquency in the Nineteenth Century.' *Local Historian* 13 (2, 1978): 74–8

Emsley, Clive. 'The Bedfordshire Police 1840–1856: A Case Study in the Working of the Rural Constabulary Act.' *Midland History* 7 (1982): 73–92

— *Policing and its Context 1750–1870.* London: Macmillan, 1983

— ' "The Thump of Wood on a Swede Turnip": Police Violence in Nineteenth-Century England.' *Criminal Justice History* 6 (1985): 125–60

— *Crime and Society in England, 1750–1900.* London: Longman, 1987

England, R.W. 'Investigating Homicide in Northern England, 1800–1824.' *Criminal Justice History* 6 (1985): 105–24

Erikson, Kai. *Wayward Puritans.* New York: Wiley, 1966

Evans, Robin. *The Fabrication of Virtue: English Prison Architecture, 1750–1840.* Cambridge: Cambridge University Press, 1982

Faller, Lincoln B. 'In Contrast to Defoe: The Rev. Paul Lorraine, Historian of Crime.' *Huntingdon Library Quarterly* 40 (1, 1976): 59–78

— *Turned to Account: The Forms and Functions of Criminal Biography in Late Seventeenth and Early Eighteenth-Century England.* New York: Cambridge University Press, 1987

Field, John. 'Police, Power and Community in a Provincial English Town: Portsmouth, 1815–1875.' In *Policing and Punishment in Nineteenth-Century Britain*, pp. 42–64. Edited by Victor Bailey, 1981

Fifoot, C.H.S. *Lord Mansfield.* Oxford: Clarendon Press, 1936

Finnegan, F. *Poverty and Prostitution: A Study of Victorian Prostitutes in York.* London: Cambridge University Press, 1979

Fletcher, Anthony and Stevenson, John, eds. *Order and Disorder in Early Modern England.* Cambridge: Cambridge University Press, 1985

Forbes, Thomas Rogers. *Crowner's Quest* [i.e. Coroner's Inquest]. *Transactions of the American Philosophical Society* 68 (1, 1978)

Forsythe, W.J. *A System of Discipline: Exeter Borough Prison, 1819–1893.* Exeter: University of Exeter, 1983

Foster, D. *The Rural Constabulary Act 1839: National Legislation and the Problem of Enforcement.* London: Bedford Square Press, 1982

Foucault, Michel. *Discipline and Punish: the Birth of the Prison*. New York: Pantheon Books, 1978

Frost, Alan. *Convicts and Empire: A Naval Question 1776–1811*. Oxford: Oxford University Press, 1980

— 'Botany Bay: An Imperial Venture of the 1780s.' *English Historical Review* 100 (395, 1985): 309–30

Garland, David. *Punishment and Welfare. A History of Penal Strategies*. Brookfield: Gower, 1985

— 'Foucault's *Discipline and Punish*: An Exposition and Critique.' *American Bar Foundation Research Journal* (Fall, 1986): 847–80

— 'The Punitive Mentality: Its Sociohistorical Development and Decline.' *Contemporary Crises* 10 (3, 1987): 305–320

Garland, David and Young, P., eds. *The Power to Punish*. London: Heinemann Educational Books, 1983

Gatrell, V.A.C. 'The Decline of Theft and Violence in Victorian and Edwardian England.' In *Crime and the Law: The Social History of Crime in Western Europe Since 1500*, pp. 238–338. Edited by V.A.C. Gatrell, Bruce Lenman and Geoffrey Parker, 1980

— Lenman, Bruce and Parker, Geoffrey, eds. *Crime and the Law. The Social History of Crime in Western Europe Since 1500*. London: Europa Publications, 1980

Gatrell, V.A.C. and Hadden, T.B. 'Criminal Statistics and their Interpretation.' In *Nineteenth-Century Society: Essays in the Use of Quantitative Methods for the Study of Social Data*, pp. 339–396. Edited by E.A. Wrigley. Cambridge: Cambridge University Press, 1972

Genovese, Elizabeth Fox. 'The Many Faces of Moral Economy: A Contribution to a Debate.' *Past and Present* 58 (1973): 61–168

Gillen, Mollie. 'The Botany Bay Decision, 1786: Convicts, Not Empire.' *English Historical Review* 92 (385, 1982): 740–66

Gillis, John R. *Youth and History: Tradition and Change in European Age Relations, 1770–Present*. New York: Academic Press, 1974

— 'The Evolution of Juvenile Delinquency in England, 1890– 1914.' *Past and Present* 67 (1975): 96–126

Glassey, Lionel K.J. *Politics and the Appointment of Justices of the Peace 1675–1720*. New York: Oxford University Press, 1979

Gleason, J.H. *The Justices of the Peace in England, 1580–1640*. Oxford: Clarendon Press, 1969

Green, Thomas A. 'Societal Concepts of Criminal Liability for Homicide in Medieval England.' *Speculum* 47 (4, 1972): 669–94

— 'The Jury and the English Law of Homicide, 1200–1600.' *Michigan Law Review* 74 (2, 1976): 413–499

— *Verdict According to Conscience: Perpectives on the History of the English Criminal Trial Jury, 1200–1800*. Chicago: University of Chicago Press, 1985

— 'A Retrospective on the Criminal Trial Jury, 1200–1800.' In *Twelve Good Men and True: The Criminal Trial Jury in England, 1200–1800*, pp. 358–400. Edited by J.S. Cockburn and Thomas A. Green, 1988

Gruenhut, Max. *Penal Reform: A Comparative Study*. Oxford: Clarendon Press, 1948

Gurr, Ted Robert, Grabosky, Peter N. and Hula, Richard C. *The Politics of Crime and Conflict: A Comparative History of Four Cities*. Beverly Hills: Sage Publications, 1977

— 'Historical Trends in Violent Crime: A Critical Review of the Evidence.' *Crime and Justice: An Annual Review of Research* 3 (1981): 295–353

Hair, P.E.H. 'Deaths from Violence in Britain: A Tentative Secular Survey.' *Population Studies* 25 (1,1971): 5–24

Hall, J. *Theft, Law and Society*. Indianapolis: Bobbs-Merrill, 1952

Hall, Stuart et al. *Policing the Crisis: Mugging, the State, and Law and Order*. London: Macmillan, 1978

Hanawalt, Barbara. *Crime and Conflict in English Communities 1300–1348*. Cambridge, Mass.: Harvard University Press, 1979

Harding, Christopher, Hines, Bill, Ireland, Richard and Rawlings, Philip. *Imprisonment in England and Wales: A Concise History*. London: Croom Helm, 1986

Harris, Michael. 'Trials and Criminal Biographies: A Case Study in Distribution.' In *The Sale and Distribution of Books from 1700*, pp. 1–36. Edited by Michael Harris and Robin Myers. Oxford: Oxford Polytechnic Press, 1982

Harris, Tim. 'The Bawdy House Riots of 1668.' *Historical Journal* 29 (3, 1986): 537–66

— *London Crowds in the Reign of Charles II: Propaganda and Politics from the Restoration until the Exclusion Crisis*. Cambridge: Cambridge University Press, 1987

Harrison, Brian. 'The Sunday Trading Riots of 1855.' *Historical Journal* 8 (2, 1965): 219–45

Hart, Jennifer. 'The Reform of the Borough Police, 1835–56.' *English Historical Review* 70 (1955): 411–27

— 'The County and Borough Police Act, 1856.' *Public Administration* 34 (4, 1956): 465–71

— 'Police.' In *Crime and the Law in Nineteenth-Century Britain*, pp. 177–209. Edited by W. Cornish. Dublin: Irish University Press, 1978

Hartman, Mary S. 'Crime and the Respectable Woman: Toward a Pattern of Middle Class Female Criminality in Nineteenth-Century France and England.' *Feminist Studies* 2 (1, 1974): 38–56

— *Victorian Murderesses*. New York: Schocken, 1977

Havard, J.D.J. *The Detection of Secret Homicide. A Study of the Medico-Legal System of Investigation of Sudden and Unexplained Deaths.* London: Macmillan, 1960

Hay, Douglas. 'Poaching and the Game Laws on Cannock Chase.' In *Albion's Fatal Tree*, pp. 189–254. Edited by Douglas Hay, Peter Linebaugh and E.P. Thompson, 1975

— 'Property, Authority and the Criminal Law.' In *Albion's Fatal Tree*, pp. 17–63. Edited by Douglas Hay, Peter Linebaugh and E.P. Thompson, 1975

— 'Crime and Justice in Eighteenth and Nineteenth-Century England.' *Crime and Justice: An Annual Review of Research* 2 (1980): 45–84

— 'War, Dearth and Theft in the Eighteenth Century: The Record of the English Courts.' *Past and Present* 95 (1982): pp. 117–60

— 'Controlling the English Prosecutor.' *Osgoode Hall Law Journal* 21 (2, 1983): 165–86

— 'The Criminal Prosecution in England and its Historians.' *Modern Law Review* 47 (1, 1984): 1–29

— 'The Class Composition of the Palladium of Liberty: Trial Jurors in the Eighteenth Century.' In *Twelve Good Men and True: The Criminal Trial Jury in England, 1200–1800*, pp. 305–57. Edited by J.S. Cockburn and Thomas A. Green, 1988

— 'Prosecution and Power: Malicious Prosecution in the English Courts, 1750–1850.' In *Policing and Prosecution in Britain 1750–1850*. Edited by Douglas Hay and Francis Snyder, 1989

Hay, Douglas, Linebaugh, Peter, Thompson, E.P., eds. *Albion's Fatal Tree: Crime and Society in Eighteenth-Century England*. New York: Pantheon Books, 1975

Hay, Douglas and Snyder, Francis, eds. *Policing and Prosecution in Britain 1750–1850*. Oxford: Clarendon Press, 1989

— 'Using the Criminal Law, 1750–1850: Policing, Private Prosecution, and the State.' In *Policing and Prosecution in Britain 1750–1850*. Edited by Douglas Hay and Francis Snyder, 1989

Henriques, U.R.Q. 'The Rise and Decline of the Separate System of Prison Discipline.' *Past and Present* 54 (1972): 61–93

Herrup, Cynthia. 'New Shoes and Mutton Pies: Investigative Responses to Theft in Seventeenth-Century East Sussex.' *Historical Journal* 27 (4, 1984): 811–30

— 'Law and Morality in Seventeenth-Century England.' *Past and Present* 106 (1985): 102–22

— *The Common Peace. Participation and the Criminal Law in Seventeenth-Century England*. Cambridge: Cambridge University Press, 1987

Hinde, R.S.E. *The British Penal System, 1773–1850*. London: G. Duckworth, 1951

Hobsbawm, E.J. 'The Machine Breakers.' *Past and Present* 1 (1952): pp. 57–70

— *Primitive Rebels*. Manchester: Manchester University Press, 1959

— 'Distinctions between Sociopolitical and Other Forms of Crime: Social Criminology.' *Bulletin of the Society of Labour History* 4 (1972): 5–7

Hobsbawm, E.J. and Rudé, George. *Captain Swing*. London: Lawrence and Wishart, 1969

Hoffer, Peter C. and Hull, N.C. *Murdering Mothers: Infanticide in England and New England, 1558–1803*. New York: New York University Press, 1981

Holmes, Geoffrey. 'The Sacheverell Riots.' *Past and Present* 72 (1976): 55–85

Holton, R.J. 'The Crowd in History: Some Problems of Theory and Method.' *Social History* 3 (2, 1978): 219–33

Horle, Craig W. *The Quakers and the English Legal System 1660–1688*. Philadelphia: University of Pennsylvania Press, 1988

Howard, D.L. *John Howard: Prison Reformer*. London: C. Johnston, 1958

Howson, Gerald. *Thief Taker General: The Rise And Fall of Jonathan Wild*. London: Hutchinson, 1970

Hughes, Robert. *The Fatal Shore*. New York: Alfred A. Knopf, 1987

Ignatieff, Michael. *A Just Measure of Pain. The Penitentiary in the Industrial Revolution, 1750–1850*. New York: Pantheon Books, 1978

— 'State, Civil Society and Total Institutions: A Critique of Recent Social Histories of Punishment.' *Crime and Justice: An Annual Review of Research* 3 (1981): 153–93. Reprinted in *Social Control and the State*, pp. 75–105. Edited by Stanley Cohen and Andrew Scull. Oxford: Martin Robertson, 1983

Inciardi, J.A., Block, A.A., Hallowell, L.A. *Historical Approaches to Crime: Research Strategies and Issues.* Beverly Hills CA: Sage Publications, 1977

Ingram, M.J. 'Communities and Courts: Law and Disorder in Early Seventeenth-Century Wiltshire.' In *Crime in England 1550–1800*, pp. 110–34. Edited by J.S. Cockburn, 1977

— 'Ridings, Rough Music and the 'Reform of Popular Culture' in Early Modern England.' *Past and Present* 105 (1984): 79–113

Innes, Joanna. 'The King's Bench Prison in the Later Eighteenth-Century: Law, Authority and Order in a London Debtors' Prison.' In *An Ungovernable People. The English and their Law in the Seventeenth and Eighteenth Centuries*, pp. 250–98. Edited by John Brewer and John Styles, 1980

— 'Prisons for the Poor: English Brideswells, 1555–1900.' In *Labour, Law and Crime. An Historical Perspective*, pp. 42–122. Edited by Francis Snyder and Douglas Hay, 1987

Innes, Joanna and Styles, John. 'The Crime Wave: Recent Writing on Crime and Criminal Justice in Eighteenth-Century England.' *Journal of British Studies* 25 (4, 1986): 380–435

Jenkins, Philip. 'From Gallows to Prison? The Execution Rate in Early-Modern England.' *Criminal Justice History* 7 (1986): 51–72

Jones, D.J.V. 'The Poacher: a Study in Victorian Crime and Protest.' *The Historical Journal* 22 (4, 1979): 825–60

Jones, David. *Crime, Protest, Community and Police in Nineteenth-Century Britain.* London, Boston: Routledge and Kegan Paul, 1982

— 'The New Police, Crime and People in England and Wales, 1829–1888.' *Transactions of the Royal Historical Society* 5th series 3 (1983): 151–168

Keeton, George W. *Lord Chancellor Jeffreys and the Stuart Cause.* London: MacDonald, 1965

Kent, J. *Elizabeth Fry.* London: B.T. Batsford, 1962

Kent, Joan R. 'The English Village Constable, 1580–1642: The Nature and Dilemmas of the Office.' *Journal of British Studies* 20 (2, 1981): 26–49

— *The English Village Constable 1580–1642.* Oxford: Clarendon Press, 1986

Kiernan, V.G. *The Duel in European History: Honour and the Reign of Aristocracy.* Oxford: Oxford University Press, 1988

King, P.J.R. 'Decision-Makers and Decision-Making in the English Common Law 1750–1800.' *Historical Journal* 27 (1, 1984): 25–58

— 'Newspaper Reporting, Prosecution Practice and Perceptions of Urban Crime: The Colchester Crime Wave of 1765.' *Continuity and Change* 2 (3, 1987): 423–54

— ' "Illiterate Plebians, Easily Misled": Jury Composition, Experience, and Behavior in Essex, 1735–1815.' In *Twelve Good Men and True: The Criminal Trial Jury in England, 1200–1800*, pp. 254–304. Edited by J.S. Cockburn and Thomas A. Green, 1988

— 'Prosecution Associations in Eighteenth-Century Essex.' In *Policing and Prosecution in Britain 1750–1850*. Edited by Douglas Hay and Francis Snyder, 1989

King, Walter J. 'Leet Jurors and the Search for Law and Order in Seventeenth-Century England: Galling Persecution or Reasonable Justice?' *Histoire sociale/Social History* 13 (26, 1980): 305–24

— 'Vagrancy and Local Law Enforcement: Why be a Constable in Stuart Lancashire?' *Historian* 17 (1980): 264–83

Knafla, L.A. 'Crime and Criminal Justice: A Critical Bibliography.' In *Crime in England 1550–1800*, pp. 270–98. Edited by J.S. Cockburn, 1977

—, ed. *Crime and Criminal Justice in Europe and Canada.* Waterloo: Wilfrid Laurier Press, 1981; rev. ed., 1985

— ' "Sin of All Sorts Swarmeth": Criminal Litigation in an English County in the Early Seventeenth Century.' In *Law, Litigants and the Legal Profession.* Edited by E.W. Ives and A.H. Manchester. London, 1983

Landau, Norma. *The Justices of the Peace, 1679–1760.* Berkeley: University of California Press, 1984

Landsman, Stephan. 'The Rise of the Contentious Spirit: Adversary Procedure in Eighteenth-Century England.' *Cornell Law Review* 75 (3, 1990): 497–609

Langbein, John H. 'The Origins of Public Prosecution at Common Law.' *American Journal of Legal History* 17 (1973): 313–35

— *Prosecuting Crime in the Renaissance.* Cambridge, MA: Cambridge University Press, 1974

— 'The Historical Origins of the Sanction of Imprisonment for Serious Crime.' *Journal of Legal Studies* 5 (1, 1976): 35–60

— *Torture and the Law of Proof: Europe and England in the Ancient Regime.* Chicago, IL: University of Chicago Press, 1977

— 'The Criminal Trial Before the Lawyers.' *University of Chicago Law Review* 45 (2, 1978): 263–316

— 'Understanding the Short History of Plea Bargaining.' *Law and Society Review* 13 (2, 1979): 261–72

— 'Albion's Fatal Flaws.' *Past and Present* 98 (1983): 96–120

— 'Shaping the Eighteenth-Century Criminal Trial: A View from the Ryder Sources.' *University of Chicago Law Review* 50 (1, 1983): 1–136

Lawson, Peter. 'Lawless Juries? The Composition and Behaviour of Hertfordshire Juries 1573–1624.' In *Twelve Good Men and True: The Criminal Trial Jury in England, 1200–1800*, pp. 117–57. Edited by J.S. Cockburn and Thomas A. Green, 1988

— 'Property Crime and Hard Times in England, 1559–1624.' *Law and History Review* 4 (1, 1986): 95–128

Lenman, Bruce and Parker, Geoffrey. 'The State, the Community and the Criminal Law in Early Modern Europe.' In *Crime and the Law: the Social History of Crime in Western Europe Since 1500*. Edited by V.A.C. Gatrell, Bruce Lenman and Geoffrey Parker, 1980

Linebaugh, Peter. 'The Tyburn Riot Against the Surgeons.' In *Albion's Fatal Tree*, pp. 65–118. Edited by Douglas Hay, Peter Linebaugh and E.P. Thompson, 1975

— 'The Ordinary of Newgate and his "Account." ' In *Crime in England, 1550–1800*, pp. 246–69. Edited by J.S. Cockburn, 1977

— 'All the Atlantic Mountains Shook.' *Labour/Le Travailleur* 10 (1982): 87–121

— '(Marxist) Social History and (Conservative) Legal History.' *New York University Law Review* 60 (1985): 101–32

Little, C. and Sheffield, C. 'Frontiers and Criminal Justice: English Private Prosecution Societies and American Vigilantism in the 18th and 19th Centuries.' *American Sociological Review* 48 (1983): 796–808

Lowe, W.J. 'The Lancashire Constabulary 1845–1870: The Social and Occupational Function of a Victorian Police Force.' *Criminal Justice History* 4 (1983): 41–62

Lucas, Paul. 'Blackstone and the Reform of the Legal Profession.' *English Historical Review* 77 (July, 1962): 456–89

— 'A Collective Biography of Students and Barristers of Lincoln's Inn 1680–1804: A Study of the 'Aristocratic Resurgence' of the Eighteenth Century.' *Journal of Modern History* 46 (2, 1974): 227–61

MacDonald, Michael. 'The Secularization of Suicide in England 1660–1800.' *Past and Present* 111 (May, 1986): 50–100

Macfarlane, Alan. *The Justice and the Mare's Ale: Law and Disorder in Seventeenth-Century England.* Oxford: Basil Blackwell, 1981

Malcolmson, R.W. 'Infanticide in the Eighteenth Century.' In *Crime in England 1550–1800.* Edited by J.S. Cockburn, 1977

Malcolmson, Robert ' "A Set of Ungovernable People'': The Kingswood Colliers in the Eighteenth Century.' In *An Ungovernable People*, pp. 85–127. Edited by John Brewer and John Styles, 1980

Manton, J. *Mary Carpenter and the Children of the Streets.* London: Heinemann Educational, 1976

Margarey, Susan. 'The Invention of Juvenile Delinquency in Early Nineteenth-Century England.' *Labour History* 34 (1978)

Martin, Ged., ed. *The Founding of Australia: The Argument About Australia's Origins.* Sydney: Hale and Iremonger, 1978

Mather, F.C. *Public Order in the Age of the Chartists.* Manchester: Manchester University Press, 1959

Mathews, Nancy L. *William Sheppard, Cromwell's Law Reformer.* Cambridge: Cambridge University Press, 1984

May, Margaret. 'Innocence and Experience: The Evolution of the Concept of Juvenile Delinquency in the Mid-Nineteenth-Century.' *Victorian Studies* 17 (1, 1973): 7–30

May, M. 'Violence in the Family: An Historical Perspective.' In *Violence and the Family*, pp. 135–68. Edited by J.P. Martin. New York: John Wiley and Sons, 1979

McConville, S. *A History of English Prison Administration*, Vol. 1: *1750–1877*. London: Routledge and Kegan Paul, 1981

McEldowney, John. 'Crown Prosecutions in Nineteenth-Century Ireland.' In *Policing and Prosecution in Britain 1750–1850*. Edited by Douglas Hay and Francis Snyder, 1989

McGowen, Randall. 'The Image of Justice and Reform of the Criminal Law in Early Nineteenth-Century England.' *Buffalo Law Review* 35 (1983): 89–125

— 'A Powerful Sympathy: Terror, the Prison, and Humanitarian Reform in Early Nineteenth-Century Britain.' *Journal of British Studies* 25 (3, 1986): 312–34

— 'The Body and Punishment in Eighteenth-Century England.' *Journal of Modern History* 59 (4, 1987): 651–79

— 'He Beareth not the Sword in Vain: Religion and the Criminal Law in Eighteenth-Century England.' *Eighteenth-Century Studies* 21 (2, 1987–8): 192–211

— 'The Changing Face of God's Justice: The Religious Dimension of the Debate over the Criminal Law.' *Criminal Justice History* 9 (1988): 63–98

McMullan, John L. 'Criminal Organization in Sixteenth and Seventeenth-Century London.' *Social Problems* 29 (3, 1982): 311–23

— *The Canting Crew: London's Criminal Underworld 1550–1700.* New Brunswick, NJ: Rutgers University Press, 1984

Melossi, D. and Pavarini, M. *The Prison and the Factory: Origins of the Penitentiary System.* London: Macmillan, 1981

Midwinter, E.C. *Law and Order in Early Victorian Lancashire.* York: St. Anthony's Press, 1968

— *Social Administration in Lancashire 1830–1860: Poor Law, Public Health and Police.* Manchester: Manchester University Press, 1969

Miller, Wilbur R. 'Police Authority in London and New York City, 1830–70.' *Journal of Social History* 8 (2, 1975): 81–101

— *Cops and Bobbies: Police Authority in New York and London 1830–1870.* Chicago: Chicago University Press, 1977

— 'London's Police Tradition in a Changing Society.' In *The British Police*, pp. 14–23. Edited by Simon Holdaway. London: Edward Arnold, 1979

Moir, Esther. *The Justices of the Peace.* Harmondsworth: Penguin, 1969

— Esther. *Local Government in Gloucestershire 1775–1800: A Study of Justices of the Peace. Publications of the Bristol and Gloucestershire Archaeological Society, Records Section* 8 (1969)

Morand, Richard. *Knowing Right from Wrong.* London: Collier Macmillan, 1981

Morgan, Kenneth. 'The Organization of the Convict Trade to Maryland: Stevenson, Randolph & Cheston, 1768–1775.' *William and Mary Quarterly* 3rd series 42 (1, 1985): 201–27

Morgan, R. 'Divine Philanthropy: John Howard Reconsidered.' *History* 62 (206, 1977)

Munger, F. 'Suppression of Popular Gatherings in England, 1800–1830.' *American Journal of Legal History* 25 (1981): 111–40

Munsche, P.B. 'The Game Laws in Wiltshire, 1750–1800.' In *Crime in England 1550–1800*, pp. 210–28. Edited by J.S. Cockburn, 1977

— 'The Gamekeeper and English Rural Society 1660–1830.' *Journal of British Studies* 20 (2, 1981): 82–105

— *Gentlemen and Poachers: The English Game Laws 1671–1831.* Cambridge: Cambridge University Press, 1981

Neeson, J.M. 'The Opponents of Enclosure in Eighteenth-Century Northamptonshire.' *Past and Present* 105 (1984)

Nippel, W. ' "Reading the Riot Act": The Discourse of Law Enforcement in Eighteenth-Century England.' *History and Anthropology* 1 (1985): 401–26

Oldham, James. 'Origins of the Special Jury.' *University of Chicago Law Review* 50 (1, 1983): 137–213

— 'On Pleading the Belly: A History of the Jury of Matrons.' *Criminal Justice History* 6 (1985): 1–64

— 'The Jury: Perspectives on Thomas Andrew Green's "Verdict According to Conscience." ' *Criminal Justice History* 8 (1987): 163–180

Paley, Ruth. 'An Imperfect, Inadequate and Wretched System? Policing London Before Peel.' *Criminal Justice History* 10 (1989): 95–130

— 'Thieftakers in London in the Age of the McDaniel Gang, c. 1745–1754.' In *Policing and Prosecution in Britain 1750–1850*. Edited by Douglas Hay and Francis Snyder, 1989

Palmer, Stanley H. *Police and Protest in England and Ireland, 1780–1850*. Cambridge: Cambridge University Press, 1988

Phifer, J.R. 'Law, Politics and Violence: The Treason Trials Act of 1696.' *Albion* 12 (1980): 235–56

Philips, David. 'The Black Country Magistracy, 1835–60.' *Midland History* 3 (3, 1976): 161–90

Philips, David. *Crime and Authority in Victorian England*. London: Croom Helm, 1977

— ' "A New Engine of Power and Authority": The Institutionalization of Law Enforcement in England 1780–1830.' In *Crime and the Law: The Social History of Crime in Western Europe Since 1500*, pp. 155–89. Edited by V.A.C. Gatrell, Bruce Lenman and Geoffrey Parker, 1980

— 'A Just Measure of Crime, Authority, Hunters and Blue Locusts: The 'Revisionist' History of Crime and the Law in Britain, 1780–1850.' In *Social Control and the State*, pp. 50–74. Edited by Stanley Cohen and Andrew Scull. Oxford: Martin Robertson, 1983

— ' "Good Men to Associate and Bad Men to Conspire": Associations for the Prosecution of Felons in England, 1760–1860.' In *Policing and Prosecution in Britain 1750–1850*. Edited by Douglas Hay and Francis Snyder, 1989

Phillipson, C. *Three Criminal Law Reformers: Beccaria, Bentham, Romilly*. London: Dent, 1923. Reprinted Montclair, NJ, P. Smith, 1970

Pinchbeck, Ivy and Hewitt, Margaret. *Children in English Society*. London: Routledge and Kegan Paul, 1973. 2 vols

Platt, Anthony. *The Child Savers: The Invention of Delinquency.* Chicago: University of Chicago Press, 1972

Pollock, Otto. *The Criminality of Women.* New York: Barnes, 1950

Prall, Start. *The Agitation for Law Reform During the Puritan Revolution.* The Hague: Martinus Nijhoff, 1966

Prest, Wilfrid, ed. *Lawyers in Early Modern Europe and America.* London: Croom Helm, 1981

—, ed. *The Professions in Early Modern England.* London: Croom Helm, 1987

— *The Rise of the Barristers: A Social History of the English Bar 1590–1640.* Oxford: Clarendon Press, 1987

Priestley, Philip. *Victorian Prison Lives: English Prison Biography, 1830–1914.* London, New York: Methuen, 1986

Pue, Wesley. 'The Criminal Twilight Zone: Pre-Trial Procedures in the 1840s.' *Alberta Law Review* 21 (2, 1983): 335–63

— 'Exorcising Professional Demons: Charles Rann Kennedy and the Transition to the Modern Bar.' *Law and History Review* 5 (1, 1987): 135–74

Pugh, R.B. *Imprisonment in Medieval England.* London: Cambridge University Press, 1968

Quinault, R. and Stevenson, J., eds. *Popular Protest and Public Order.* London: Allen and Unwin, 1978

Radzinowicz, Leon (Sir). *A History of English Criminal Law and its Administration Since 1750,* Vol. 1: *The Movement for Reform.* London: Stevens and Sons, 1948

— *A History of English Criminal Law and its Administration from 1750,* Vol. 2: *The Clash between Private Inititiative and Public Interest in the Enforcement of the Law.* New York: Macmillan, 1957

— *A History of English Criminal Law and its Administration from 1750.* Vol. 3: *Cross Currents in the Movement for the Reform of the Police.* New York: Macmillan, 1957

— *A History of English Criminal Law and its Administration from 1750.* Vol. 4: *Grappling for Control.* London: Stevens, 1968

Radzinowicz, Leon (Sir) and Hood, Roger. A History of English Criminal Law and its Administration Since 1750. Vol. 5: *The Emergence of Penal Policy.* London: Stevens and Sons, 1986

Reiner, Robert. *The Politics of the Police.* Brighton: Wheatsheaf Books, 1985

Reith, Charles (Sir). *The Police Idea: Its History and Evolution in England in the Eighteenth Century and After*. London, Toronto: Oxford University Press, 1938

— *British Police and the Democratic Ideal*. London: Oxford University Press, 1943

— *A New Study of Police History*. Edinburgh: Oliver and Boyd, 1956

Reith, Charles (Sir). *The Blind Eye of History: A Study of the Origins of the Present Police Era*. Montclair, N.J.: Patterson Smith, 1975

Rezneck, Samuel. 'The Statute of 1696: A Pioneer Measure in the Reform of Judicial Procedure in England.' *Journal of Modern History* 2 (1, 1930): 5–26

Richardson, Ruth. *Death, Dissection and the Destitute*. London: Routledge and Kegan Paul, 1987

Roberts, Stephen K. 'Juries and the Middling Sort: Recruitment and Performance at Devon Quarter Sessions.' In *Twelve Good Men and True: The Criminal Trial Jury in England, 1200–1800*, pp. 182–213. Edited by J.S. Cockburn and Thomas A. Green, 1988

Robinson, Cyril. 'The Deradicalization of the Policeman: A Historical Analysis.' *Crime and Delinquency* 24 (2, 1978): 129–51

— 'Ideology as History: A Look at the Way Some English Police Historians Look at the Police.' *Police Studies* 2 (2, 1979): 35–49

Robson, R. *The Attorney in Eighteenth-Century England*. Cambridge: Cambridge University Press, 1959

Rogers, Nicholas. 'Popular Protest in Early Hanoverian London.' *Past and Present* 79 (1978): 70–100

— 'Riot and Popular Jacobitism in Early Hanoverian England.' In *Ideology and Conspiracy: Aspects of Jacobitism, 1689– 1759*, pp. 70–88. Edited by Evelyn Cruikshanks. Edinburgh: John Donald, 1982

Rose, Lionel. *Massacre of the Innocents: Infanticide in Great Britain, 1800–1939*. London: Routledge and Kegan Paul, 1986

Rose, R.B. 'The Priestley Riots of 1791.' *Past and Present* 18 (1960): 68–88

Rothman, David S. *The Discovery of the Asylum*. Boston: Little, Brown, 1971

— *Conscience and Convenience*. Boston: Little, Brown, 1980

Rudé, George. *Wilkes and Liberty: A Social Study of 1763–1774*. Oxford, Clarendon Press, 1962

— *The Crowd in History: A Study of Popular Disturbances in France and England, 1730–1848*. New York: Wiley, 1964

— *Paris and London in the Eighteenth Century: Studies in Popular Protest*. London: Collins, 1970

— *Protest and Punishment: The Story of the Social and Political Protesters Transported to Australia 1788–1868*. Oxford: Oxford University Press, 1978

— *Criminal and Victim: Crime and Society in Early Nineteenth-Century England*. Oxford: Oxford University Press, 1985

Rule, John. 'Wrecking and Coastal Plunder.' In *Albion's Fatal Tree*, pp. 167–88. Edited by Douglas Hay, Peter Linebaugh and E.P. Thompson, 1975

— 'Social Crime in the Rural South in the Eighteenth and Early Nineteenth Centuries.' *Southern History* 9 (1979): 135–54

Rusche, Georg and Kirchheimer, O. *Punishment and Social Structure*. New York: Columbia University Press, 1939

Samaha, Joel. *Law and Order in Historical Perspective. The Case of Elizabethan Essex*. New York: Academic Press, 1974

— 'Hanging for Felony: The Rule of Law in Elizabethan Colchester.' *Historical Journal* 21 (4, 1978): 763–82

— 'The Recognisance in Elizabethan Law Enforcement.' *American Journal of Legal History* 25 (1981): 189–204

Sauer, R. 'Infanticide and Abortion in Nineteenth-Century Britain.' *Population Studies* 32 (1, 1978): 81–94

Scull, Andrew. *Museums of Madness: The Social Organization of Insanity in Nineteenth-Century England*. London: A. Lane, 1979

Sellin, Thorsten. *Pioneering in Penology: The Amsterdam Houses of Correction in the Sixteenth and Seventeenth Centuries*. Philadelphia: University of Pennsylvania Press, 1944

Shapiro, Barbara J. ' "To a Moral Certainty": Theories of Knowledge and Anglo-American Juries, 1600–1850.' *Hastings Law Journal* 38 (1, 1986): 153–93

— *Probability and Certainty in Seventeenth-Century England. A Study of the Relationships between Natural Science, Religion, History, Law and Literature*. Princeton: Princeton University Press, 1983

Sharp, Buchanan. *In Contempt of all Authority: Rural Artisans and Riot in the West of England 1586–1660*. Berkeley: University of California Press, 1980

Sharpe, J.A. 'Crime and Delinquency in an Essex Parish 1600–1640.' In *Crime in England, 1550–1800*, pp. 90–109. Edited by J.S. Cockburn. London: Methuen, 1977

— *Defamation and Sexual Slander in Early Modern England: The Church Courts at York*. Borthwick Papers 58 (1980)

— 'Enforcing the Law in the Seventeenth-Century English Village.' In *Crime and the Law*, pp. 97–119. Edited by V.A.C. Gatrell, Bruce Lenman and Geoffrey Parker, 1980

— 'Domestic Homicide in Early Modern England.' *Historical Journal* 24 (1, 1981): 29–48

— 'The History of Crime in Late Medieval and Early Modern England: A Review of the Field.' *Social History* 7 (2, 1982): 187–203

— *Crime in Seventeenth-Century England. A County Study*. New York: Cambridge University Press, 1983

— *Crime in Early Modern England 1550–1750*. New York: Longman, 1984

— 'The History of Violence in England: Some Observations.' *Past and Present* 108 (1985): 206–15

— ' "Last Dying Speeches": Religion, Ideology and Public Execution in Seventeenth-Century England.' *Past and Present* 107 (1985): 144–67

— 'The History of Crime in England, c. 1300–1914: An Overview of Recent Publications.' *British Journal of Criminology* 28 (2, 1988): 124–37

Shaw, A.G.L. *Convicts and the Colonies*. London: Faber, 1966

Sheehan, W.J. 'Finding Solace in Eighteenth-Century Newgate.' In *Crime in England, 1550–1800*, pp. 229–45. Edited by J.S. Cockburn, 1977

Shubert, Adrian. 'Private Initiative in Law Enforcement: Associations for the Prosecution of Felons, 1744–1856.' In *Policing and Punishment in Nineteenth-Century Britain*, pp. 25–42. Edited by Victor Bailey, 1981.

Silver, Allan. 'The Demand for Order in Civil Society: A Review of Some Themes in the History of Urban Crime, Police and Riot.' In *The Police: Six Sociological Essays*, pp. 1–24. Edited by David J. Bordua. New York: John Wiley and Sons, 1967

Silverthorne, Elizabeth, ed. *Deposition Book of Richard Wyatt, J.P., 1767–1776*. Surrey Record Society 30 (1978)

Simpson, Anthony E. 'Dandelions on the Field of Honour: Duelling, the Middle Classes and the Law in Nineteenth-Century England.' *Criminal Justice History* 9 (1988)

Sindall, R. 'Middle-Class Crime in Nineteenth-Century England.' *Criminal Justice History* 4 (1983): 23–40

Slack, Paul, ed. *Rebellion, Popular Protest, and the Social Order in Early Modern England.* Cambridge: Cambridge University Press, 1984

Smith, Abbott E. *Colonists in Bondage: White Servitude and Convict Labor in America, 1607–1776.* Gloucester: P. Smith, 1947

Smith, David. 'The Demise of Transportation: Mid-Victorian Penal Policy.' *Criminal Justice History* 3 (1982): 21–46

Smith, Philip Thurmond. *Policing Victorian London: Political Policing, Public Order, and the London Metropolitan Police.* Westport, Conn.: Greenwood, 1985

Snyder, Francis and Hay, Douglas, eds. *Labour, Law and Crime: An Historic Perspective.* London: Tavistock, 1987

South, Nigel. 'Law, Profit and 'Private Persons': Private and Public Policing in English History.' In *Private Policing*, pp. 72–109. Edited by C.D. Shearing and Philip C. Stenning. Beverly Hills, Ca.: Sage, 1987

Spierenburg, Pieter. *The Spectacle of Suffering. Executions and the Evolution of Repression from a Preindustrial Metropolis to the European Experience.* New York: Cambridge University Press, 1984

Stack, J.A. 'Deterrence and Reformation: Early Victorian Social Policy: The Case of Parkhust Prison, 1838–1864.' *Historical Reflections* 6 (2, 1979): 387–404

Steedman, Carolyn. *Policing the Victorian Community: The Formation of English Provincial Police Forces, 1856–1880.* London: Routledge and Kegan Paul, 1984

Stephen, James Fitzjames (Sir). *A History of the Criminal Law of England.* London: Macmillan, 1883. 3 vols. Reprint ed. New York: B. Franklin, 1964

Stevenson, John. *Popular Disturbances in England 1700–1870.* New York: Longman, 1979

Stevenson, John and Quinault R., eds. *Popular Protest and Public Order: Six Studies in British History, 1790–1920.* London: Allen and Unwin, 1974

Stevenson, S.J. 'The Rise of Suicide Verdicts in South-East England, 1530–1590: The Legal Process.' *Continuity and Change* 2 (1, 1987): 37–76

— 'Social and Economic Contributions to the Pattern of 'Suicide' in South-East England, 1530–1590.' *Continuity and Change* 2 (2, 1987): 225–262

Stockdale, Eric. *A Study of Bedford Prison, 1660–1877.* London: Phillimore, 1977

Stone, Lawrence. 'Interpersonal Violence in English Society, 1300–1980.' *Past and Present* 101 (1983): 22–33

— 'A Rejoinder.' *Past and Present* 108 (1985): 216–24

Storch, Robert. 'The Plague of Blue Locusts: Police Reform and Popular Resistance in Northern England 1840–1857.' *International Review of Social History* 20 (1, 1975): 61–90

— 'The Policeman as Domestic Missionary: Urban Discipline and Popular Culture in Northern England, 1850–1880.' *Journal of Social History* 9 (4, 1976): 481–509

— 'Police Control of Street Prostitution in Victorian London.' In *Police and Society*, pp. 49–72. Edited by D.H. Bayley. Beverly Hills, CA: Sage Publications, 1977

— 'Policing Rural Southern England before the Police: Opinion and Practice, 1830–1856.' In *Policing and Prosecution in Britain 1750–1850*. Edited by Douglas Hay and Francis Snyder, 1989

Styles, John. ' "Our Traitorous Money Makers": The Yorkshire Coiners and the Law, 1760–83.' In *An Ungovernable People*, pp. 172–249. Edited by John Brewer and John Styles, 1980

— 'An Eighteenth-Century Magistrate as Detective: Samuel Lister of Little Horton.' *Bradford Antiquary* New Series 47 (1982): 98–117

— 'From an Offence between Men to an Offence against Property? Industrial Pilfering and the Law in the Eighteenth Century.' In *Manufacture in Town and Country Before the Factory*, pp. 173–205. Edited by M. Berg, P. Hudson and M. Sonenscher. Cambridge: Cambridge University Press, 1983

— 'Sir John Fielding and the Problem of Criminal Investigation in Eighteenth-Century England.' *Transactions of the Royal Historical Society* 5th Series 33 (1983): 127–150

— 'The Emergence of the Police – Explaining Police Reform in Eighteenth and Nineteenth-Century England.' *British Journal of Criminology* 27 (1, 1987): 15–22

— 'Print and Policing: Crime and Advertising in Eighteenth-Century Provincial England.' In *Policing and Prosecution in Britain 1750–1850*. Edited by Douglas Hay and Francis Snyder, 1989

Sugarman, David and Rubin, G.R. 'Towards a New History of Law and Material Society in England 1750–1914.' In *Law, Economy and*

Society: Essays in the History of English Law 1750–1914, pp. 1–123. Edited by David Sugarman and G.R. Rubin. Abingdon: Professional Books, 1984

Sweeney, C. *Transported in Place of Death*. Melbourne: Macmillan, 1981

Swift, Roger. 'Urban Policing in Early Victorian England, 1835–86: A Reappraisal.' *History* 73 (238, 1988): 211–37

— *Police Reform in Early Victorian York, 1835–56*. York: University of York, Borthwick Papers, 1988

Thompson, E.P. 'The Moral Economy of the English Crowd in the Eighteenth Century.' *Past and Present* 50 (1971): 76–132

— ' Rough Music'': Le Charivari anglais,' *Annales: Economies, Societes, Civilisations* 27 (2, 1972): 285–312

— 'The Crime of Anonymity.' In *Albion's Fatal Tree*, pp. 255–308. Edited by Douglas Hay, Peter Linebaugh and E.P. Thompson, 1975

— *Whigs and Hunters: The Origin of the Black Act*. London: Allen Lane, 1975

Tilly, Charles. 'Collective Violence in European Perspective.' In *Violence in America*, pp. 4–44. Edited by H.D. Graham and Ted Robert Gurr. Toronto: Bantam, 1969

Tobias, J.J. *Crime and Industrial Society in the Nineteenth Century*, 1967; reprinted as *Urban Crime in Victorian England*. New York: Shocken, 1972

— *Crime and Police in England, 1700–1900*. New York: St. Martin's, 1979

Tomes, N. 'A 'Torrent of Abuse': Crimes of Violence between Working-Class Men and Women in London, 1840–1875.' *Journal of Social History* (3, 1978): 328–45

Tomlinson, M. Heather. ' ''Prison Palaces'': a Reappraisal of Early Victorian Prisons, 1835–77.' *Bulletin of the Institute of Historical Research* 51 (1978)

— 'Penal Servitude 1846–1865: A System in Evolution.' In *Policing and Punishment in Nineteenth-Century Britain*, pp. 126–149. Edited by Victor Bailey, 1981

Twining, William. *Theories of Evidence: Bentham and Wigmore*. London: Weidenfeld and Nicolson, 1985

Underdown, David. *Revel, Riot, and Rebellion: Popular Politics and Culture in England 1603–1660*. Oxford: Clarendon Press, 1985

Veall, Donald. *The Popular Movement for Law Reform, 1640–1660*. Oxford: Clarendon Press, 1970

Walker, Nigel. *Crime and Insanity in England*, Vol. 1: *The Historical Perspective*. Edinburgh: Edinburgh University Press, 1968

Walkowitz, Judith R. *Prostitution and Victorian Society: Women, Class, and the State*. New York: Cambridge University Press, 1980

Walsh, John. 'Methodism and the Mob in the Eighteenth Century.' In *Popular Belief and Practice: Studies in Church History*, Vol. 8, pp. 213–28. Edited by G.J. Cuming and D. Barker. Cambridge: Cambridge University Press, 1972

Walter, John and Wrightson, Keith. 'Dearth and the Social Order in Early Modern England.' *Past and Present* 71 (1976): 22–42

Webb, Sidney and Webb, Beatrice. *English Local Government from the Revolution to the Municipal Corporation Act*. Vol. I: *The Parish and the County*. London: Longmans, Green, 1906

— 'English Prisons under Local Government.' *English Local Government* 6. London: Longmans Green, 1922. Reprint ed. London: Frank Cass, 1963

Weinberger, Barbara. 'The Police and the Public in Mid-Nineteenth-Century Warwickshire.' In *Policing and Punishment in Nineteenth-Century Britain*, pp. 65–93. Edited by Victor Bailey, 1981

Weisberg, D. Kelly, ed. *Women and the Law*. Cambridge, Mass.: Schenkman, 1982. 2 vols

Welby, Glynne. *Rulers of the Countryside: The Justices of the Peace in Nottinghamshire 1775–1800*. Thoroton Society Transactions 78 (1974)

Whiting, J.R.S. *Prison Reform in Gloucestershire, 1776–1820: A Study of the Work of Sir George Onesiphrus Paul, Bart*. London: Phillimore, 1975

Wiener, C.Z. 'Sex-roles and Crime in Late Elizabethan Hertfordshire.' *Journal of Social History* 8 (4, 1975): 38–60

Williams, Dale E. 'Were Hunger Rioters Really Hungry? Some Demographic Evidence.' *Past and Present* (71, 1976): 70–75

— 'Morals, Markets and the English Crowd in 1766.' *Past and Present* 104 (1984): 56–73

Wilson, C.H. 'Convicts, Commerce and Sovereignty: The Forces Behind the Early Settlement of Australia.' In *Business Life and Public Policy: Essays in Honour of D.C. Coleman*, pp. 79–97. Edited by N. McKendrick and R.B. Outhwaite. Cambridge: Cambridge University Press, 1986

Winslow, Cal. 'Sussex Smugglers.' In *Albion's Fatal Tree*, pp. 119–66. Edited by Douglas Hay, Peter Linebaugh and E.P. Thompson, 1975

Wrightson, Keith. 'Two Concepts of Order: Justices, Constables and Jurymen in Seventeenth-Century England.' In *An Ungovernable People. The English and their Law in the Seventeenth and Eighteenth Centuries,* pp. 21–46. Edited by John Brewer and John Styles, 1980

— 'Infanticide in European History.' *Criminal Justice History* 3 (1982): 1–20

Zaller, Robert. 'The Debate on Capital Punishment During the English Revolution.' *American Journal of Legal History* 31 (2, 1987): 126–44

Zangerl, Carl H.E. 'The Social Composition of the County Magistracy in England and Wales.' *Journal of British Studies* 11 (1, 1971): 113–25

Zell, M. 'Suicide in Pre-Industrial England.' *Social History* 11 (3, 1986): 303–17

2

The History of Canadian Criminal Justice, 1750–1920

Jim Phillips

Introduction

Any review of the historiography of Canadian criminal justice must begin with an *apologia* and an acknowledgment of the limitations of the field. Canadian criminal justice history remains one of the most underdeveloped areas of Canadian history, and is also very much the poor relation in the burgeoning international family of studies in the history of crime and punishment. No general texts exist, even at the provincial level, although there are some anthologies (Friedland, 1984; MacLeod, 1988) and an excellent annotated bibliography (Smandych et al, 1987: see also the less useful one compiled by Knafla, 1979). There are also no holistic accounts of institutional developments such as police organization or prison policy, and the few scholarly monographs that have been produced deal with specific issues such as the making of the *Criminal Code* (Brown, D.H., 1989), a particular famous case (Friedland, 1985), the North West Mounted Police (NWMP) (MacLeod, 1976A), or the early years of Kingston Penitentiary (Beattie, 1977). There are a rather larger number of non-scholarly monographs about particular cases, but as populist and, indeed, often sensationalized accounts they find no place in this review.

It is largely because of this lack of general works in the field that this essay is constructed as an examination of the field in general rather than as an analysis of a limited number of major contributions. A preponderance of the best work is scattered throughout a disparate article literature in history, law, political science and criminology, and criminal justice themes are, indeed, often subsumed within writing that is primarily focused on some other issue. Hence the presence of some 300 references in what I consistently term a neglected field. These references include unpublished theses and papers. Some of the most interesting work is in this form, but I have included only a small number in this review because of the obvious difficulties of obtaining them.

The historiography to date therefore, while often of high quality, leaves many issues unexplored and many questions unanswered. It also evinces an unfortunate tendency in some authors to adopt wholesale and uncritically interpretive frameworks initially formulated for explaining English or American developments, with the result that the role of criminal law and criminal justice in *Canadian* social, economic and political development is inadequately explored. This is a crucial shortcoming, for the central purpose of historical study is to examine change over time within a particular society.

These inadequacies have their explanations. In part one can point to the lack of interest in general Canadian legal history prior to the 1980s (Flaherty, 1981). To some extent the problem derives from the relatively late date at which the new social history, which has contributed so much to the development of English and American criminal justice history and which is partly explored in the paper by John Beattie in this volume, became a part of the writing of Canadian history. The nature of the records also creates difficulties, for there are few great contemporary compilations to compare with, for example, the reports of the English parliament produced during the nineteenth-century debates over the death penalty, transportation, and the prison system. It would be unwise to make too much of this last point, however, for Canadian sources are available and in many cases have simply never been utilized by historians. Finally, it is worth noting that the problems of producing general studies of criminal justice history are the same as the problems of writing a synthetic history of anything Canadian: two European linguistic traditions, substantial differences in the social composition and in the timing of significant developments among the various colonies/provinces, and a federal-provincial split in responsibilities for different aspects of the system – all have contributed to a historiographic balkanization in this area as in many others.

Having said this, it should be noted that the last decade or so has seen the production of enough work to make a study of this kind feasible and useful. I should make it clear that I conceive of criminal justice history, and indeed of legal history generally, as being very broadly-rooted. It covers not only the obvious institutional areas such as substantive criminal law, courts, prisons, and policing, but much of what is more typically thought of as social, political, cultural and intellectual history, especially histories of social reform, labour unrest, popular culture and political disaffection.

This review at times affords greater coverage to some issues than others. The reason is simply the uneven production of solid work. We know much more about some themes, regions and periods than about others: examples of well-explored topics include the NWMP/RCMP, the early colonial penitentiaries, aspects of women's experience with the criminal justice system, the use of the criminal law to control labour unrest, and the motivations for and effect of the decision to introduce the English criminal law into post-conquest Quebec. But even given the gaps in knowledge, it is still possible to construct a periodization of institutional developments, and this is what part one of this review will provide. It will examine changes in the substantive criminal law, the courts, punishment, policing and prosecution; this will be done with reference, where possible, to broader considerations of societal criminality, political culture, social reform and attitudes to deviance and disorder. Historians' concerns are always centered on time and specific social context, and part one will accordingly be ordered both chronologically and, within the chronology, by topics and jurisdictions.

There are really three principal stages to this chronology. The first, examined in sections A (i) and A (ii) of part one, from c. 1750 until c. 1840, involves the ways in which the unreformed criminal justice system inherited from Britain was transplanted and partially adapted to local conditions. The second period, from c. 1840 to Confederation and covered in section A (iii) of part one, saw developments such as the consolidation of colonial criminal codes, changing attitudes to and practices in the newly- founded penitentiaries, the early history of Canadian policing, and the emerging role of institutions of urban social control. In section B of part one I discuss the third period, from Confederation to 1920, looking at new political arrangements, the profound changes wrought by industrialization, and the effect of western settlement.

The second part of this review examines a number of thematic issues in criminal justice history across the entire period from 1750 to 1920 and also across the disparate provinces and regions of the country. The unifying theme in this part is the role played by criminal justice in social life, social ordering, and the maintenance of political authority. This part is at times prescriptive and critical as well as being a descriptive guide to reading, for I argue in many places that much more work needs to be done before these issues can be said to have been fruitfully explored.

The reader will detect some overlap between the various themes discussed in part two, and between parts one and two. This is inevitable, for no simple scheme of ordering will ever permit complete isolation of one topic from another. Moreover, such overlap is a necessary concomitant of writing history. Despite my insistence that criminal justice history should contain much more than accounts of the development of its institutions (what the American legal historian Robert Gordon (1975) would call 'in the box legal history'), I do not believe that these themes can be considered as separable from the general historical trends discussed in part one. For example, while it is instructive to study the ways in which the criminal justice system has treated women, a full understanding of that cannot be achieved without bearing in mind the different ways in which criminal justice has affected Canadian history before and after industrialization, before and after Confederation, in peace and war, in town and country, in one province and another. Dealing with the complex interaction of theory and empirical evidence, of general trends and aberrations, is the great challenge of writing and understanding history.

The terminal dates have been chosen for good reason. The mid-eighteenth century was selected as a starting point because it represents the beginnings of substantial English settlement in what became, after the American revolution, British North America. While there exists an impressive body of literature on criminal justice in New France (see Smandych *et al*, 1987, *passim*), the administration of criminal justice in New France underwent a substantial transformation with the introduction of English criminal law and procedure after the conquest. This historical discontinuity renders that earlier history less instructive than it might otherwise be. At the other end of the chronology I chose to end at 1920 for two reasons. First, too little work has been done on more recent decades to make it useful to include the years after World War One. Second, to discuss the work that does exist, particularly that dealing with the years after 1945, would involve overlapping with many of the other essays in this volume, which deal with the modern international, including Canadian, literature.

Part One: Overview of Institutional Developments

A) PRE-CONFEDERATION

i) *The Unreformed System in the Maritimes and Upper Canada Before c. 1840*

The period before about 1840 was one in which the criminal justice systems of the Canadian colonies were based on, and to a large extent mirrored, the unreformed English system of the eighteenth and early nineteenth centuries, described by Beattie elsewhere in this volume. It ended with major reforms in the substantive law of crime and punishment, with the introduction of a new form of punishment – the penitentiary – and with changes in criminal procedure. All of these postdated similar reforms in England by a few years.

The introduction of criminal justice systems into the British North American colonies took place either as an aspect of the wider process of creating institutions for new colonies of English settlement in the second half of the eighteenth century (New Brunswick in 1784, Nova Scotia in 1749, Prince Edward Island in 1773, and Upper Canada in 1791) or as the result of conquest (Quebec in 1759–60). This is a distinction of fundamental importance, and I have therefore chosen to deal separately with English and French Canada.

All of the English Canadian colonies received the eighteenth-century English criminal law initially (Bell, 1979, 1980; Cote, 1964, 1977; Riddell, 1931B; Sherwood, 1977; Talbot, 1983), although all also enacted local criminal statutes (Barnes, 1984; Blackwell, 1980–81, pp. 528–9; Knafla and Chapman, 1983, pp. 249–50). These early colonial statutes primarily reproduced aspects of English common and statute law; although minor changes were made, no wholesale reformulation of the criminal law to suit distinctly different societies, as occurred in the colonies to the south, took place (Greenberg, 1982; Hindus, 1981; Hirsch, 1982; Kealey, L. 1986; Preyer, 1982). Because we have no systematic studies of the workings of the courts and the prosecutorial process it is unclear whether these colonial 'codes' and local practices effectively repealed by exclusion all other English criminal law. One account states that this happened from very early on, noting in particular that the oppressive English game laws were not enforced (Knafla and Chapman, 1983, p.249). It is one thing to say that certain laws were not enforced, however, and quite another to state that they were not *in force*, for local conditions may simply have rendered their application unnecessary, and this was likely true for the example given. My as yet unpublished research suggests that English law was wholly implanted in Nova Scotia and widely accepted as being in force for much of the eighteenth century; the series of local statutes passed from 1758 were merely declaratory of parts of the received law. There is, however, substantial evidence that as the nineteenth century advanced it became increasingly accepted that local statutes had wholly supplanted English statutory law by express repeal or by exclusion, and had also modified the common law (Murdoch, 1832, vol.4, pp. 116–207; Phillips, 1987). Conversely, this probably did not occur in Upper Canada before the clear adoption of an exclusive local code with the reforms of 1833 (Blackwell, 1980–81, pp. 531–3; McMahon, 1988).

Along with English criminal law the colonies received a system of law enforcement and courts very much like the English. It was based largely on private prosecution supported in some measure by crown attorneys, with apprehension of suspected criminals the responsibility of local justices of the peace, sheriffs and constables. There are only a few piecemeal accounts of the operation of prosecutorial systems in English Canada (Archibald, 1989; Jones, J.E. 1924; especially Stenning, 1986, ch. 2), and not much more than that on the general work of the justice of the peace (Aitchison,

1949A, 1953; Lewthwaite, 1987). Courts of criminal jurisdiction comprised the justices of the peace in Petty and Quarter Sessions, which in practice dealt largely with minor offences, and higher courts for trying serious crime, called King's Bench in Upper Canada, Supreme Court in Nova Scotia, New Brunswick, and Prince Edward Island. There are some purely institutional histories of the sessions courts (Banks, 1983; Oxner, 1984; Talbot, 1983; Tubrett, 1967) and of the higher courts (Banks, 1983; Cahill, 1988; Hett, 1973; Townshend, 1899; Tubrett, 1967); they reveal that the latter performed the roles of the English Courts of Assize, Oyer and Terminer and Gaol Delivery on circuit, although it was also not unusual to have cases tried by special commission in outlying areas of the often thinly-settled new colonies.

Unfortunately there are no detailed studies of the working of any one of these colonial courts. Claims such as those made by Knafla and Chapman (1983, pp. 252–3) that the higher courts in the Maritimes were more careful about procedures, more solicitous of the accused, and more attuned to particular community values than were their English counterparts therefore represent largely unevidenced generalizations. Generally one must glean information about the work of the courts – their procedures, workload and personnel – from a plethora of now largely outdated and at times idiosyncratic accounts of a particular trial or trials (Chisholm, 1940; Cruickshank, 1929; Elliott, 1931; Jones, J.E. 1924; Patterson, 1935; Phelan, 1976; Riddell, 1916A, 1916B, 1917A, 1917B, 1920A, 1920B, 1920C, 1923, 1925A, 1925B, 1928, 1931A, 1932; Sherwood, 1977), although more modern work can be revealing of a broader social context and attitudes (Blackwell, 1980–81; Brode, 1989A; Hutchinson, L. 1989; McMahon, 1988; Teatero, 1979; Vincent, 1977).

The English colonies also inherited English ideas about the form and function of imprisonment and its place in the pantheon of criminal sanctions. As explained by Beattie elsewhere in this volume, prisons played but a minor role in the punishment of crime in England before the mid-nineteenth century, and the English system was largely replicated in early Canada. Local jails held pre-trial detainees, and they and more substantial institutions such as the Halifax 'House of Correction,' or Bridewell, were also employed for short-term incarcerations as punishment for minor criminal offenders and for those who contravened the elaborate vagrancy laws (Baehre, 1981, 1990; Ekstedt and Griffiths, 1984, ch. 1; Kirkpatrick, 1964; Levy, 1979; Talbot, 1983; Weaver, 1986). From the later eighteenth century all these institutions became the subject of increasing criticism because of poor food and material conditions, the brutality of warders, and a chronic lack of security. They were also villified for the practice of congregate confinement of debtors, serious criminals awaiting trial, and minor offenders and vagrants, which was one reason why they were largely ineffective as reforming institutions (Baehre, 1977, 1990; Beattie, 1977, pp. 13–14; Ekstedt and Griffiths, 1984, ch. 1; Kroll, 1972; Weaver, 1986).

Attacks on prison conditions and proposals that they should be used to reform as well as to punish went hand in hand with a broader critique of the system of criminal punishments. As in England, capital punishment was, at least in theory, the principal method of criminal sanction: in Nova Scotia, for example, over 50 offences carried the death penalty by local statute in 1800 (Phillips, 1987). The gallows was supplemented by lesser penalties such as fines, imprisonment, the availability of benefit of clergy (usually branding) for some first-time offenders in crimes nominally capital, the pillory and whipping (Baehre, 1990; Beattie, 1977; Phillips, 1987). But by the early nineteenth century this system was condemned for its many inefficiencies and inconsistencies. Capital punishment did not deter criminals, contemporaries argued, so much as it deterred prosecutors and juries from respectively bringing capital charges to court or convicting accuseds on the full charge if it was brought. Even when offenders were convicted they might receive benefit of clergy or the royal pardon (Beattie, 1977; Phillips, 1989). With transportation to penal colonies generally unavailable to Canadian authorities because of its expense (Baehre, 1990), those pardoned were either entirely set free, made to join the armed forces, or banished from the colony (Blackwell, 1980–81; Phillips, 1989). Overall the system seemed to many contemporary critics to be irrational and inconsistent; it was also increasingly viewed as inhumane and inappropriate in its over-reliance on the death penalty. Although little has been written about them (Anderson, 1973; Beattie, 1977; Blackwell, 1980–81; Chandler, 1976; McMahon, 1988; Phillips, 1987), it is clear that all the English colonies witnessed successful campaigns in the 1820s and 1830s to radically alter the substantive law of punishments and to provide effective alternative punishments for serious crimes that would both deter and rehabilitate.

The substantive law was reformed beginning in 1833 in Upper Canada, in 1841 in Nova Scotia, in 1831 in New Brunswick, and in 1836 in Prince Edward Island. Along with this went changes in criminal procedure, notably permitting defendants in felony cases to be fully represented by counsel, and the upgrading of existing carceral institutions or the building of modern penitentiaries. Much has been written about the latter, especially about the construction of Kingston, finished in 1836 (Baehre, 1977, 1989, 1990; Beattie, 1977; Bellomo, 1972; Palmer, 1980; Splane, 1965; Taylor, 1979; Weaver, 1986). This work makes it abundantly clear that at least part of the motivation for this development was the dissatisfaction with the existing system described above, and that the penitentiary movement was also fuelled by a concern about social order. It is, moreover, evident that

Kingston at least was constructed as 'moral architecture,' as a structure designed to awe both inhabitants and the wider society into leading upright and moral lives (see especially Taylor, 1979).

Somewhat less convincing have been attempts to explain the Canadian colonial penitentiary movements as responses to social crises brought on by industrialization. This interpretation, which sets penitentiary building within a larger framework of the establishment of new, disciplining 'total' institutions such as schools, factories and asylums, has been employed with varying degrees of success for Europe, England and the United States in this period (Foucault, 1978; Ignatieff, 1978; Rothman, 1971, 1972), although its critics have forced a partial recantation from one of these authors (Ignatieff, 1983). While the traditional view that early English Canadian society, especially Upper Canadian society, was peaceful and law-abiding is increasingly being undermined (see especially Matthews, 1987A), this more general thesis about penitentiaries, social order and industrial discipline seems to fit the Canadian colonial experience imperfectly, despite some valiant attempts to mould it (Baehre, 1977, 1989; Brown, T.E., 1984; Taylor, 1979, in part; see also the discussion by Whittingham, 1985, and the partial refutation by Smandych, 1982). Both Upper Canada and Nova Scotia, sites of the first two penitentiaries, were largely agricultural and partly commercial societies at the time. In the former fear of social disorder certainly seems to have been a factor motivating the construction of the penitentiary, but that disorder was not the outraged protest of a new urban proletariat, nor was the fear that of a new industrial middle class. Rather, Irish and other immigration and ethnicity seem to have been at the heart of both social misbehaviour and of indigenous fears about its effects (Bleasdale, 1981; Cross, 1973; Weaver, 1986). In Nova Scotia there was not even a general concern about violence and disorder; it appears to have been assumed that a penitentiary was a necessary part of criminal justice reform and the debate centered on disputes between Halifax and the rest of the colony over who was to bear the major cost of the new institution (Baehre, 1990; Phillips, 1987). In short, the penitentiary movement in Canada before c. 1840 appears to have been the product of received ideologies about social order and social reform, not the product of industrialization and a concomitant desire to enhance labour discipline.

ii) *Quebec/Lower Canada, 1760 – c. 1840*

The history of the old regime in Quebec (Lower Canada from 1791) displays both similarities and differences with the English Canadian colonies. On the one hand the post-conquest period saw the establishment of Sessions Courts and of a higher court, King's Bench, for trying all cases according to English laws and procedures (Knafla and Chapman, 1983, pp. 258 *et seq*; Hay, 1981). In addition to its being one aspect of the general policy of assimilation, this decision was also rooted in a particular belief in the superiority of English laws and procedures over the French inquisitorial process, with its use of judicial torture representing for the English the epitome of continental 'barbarity' (Edwards, 1984; Hay, 1981, pp. 77–81; Johnson, 1934; L'Heureux, 1970; Morel, 1960, 1978A; Neatby, 1937, ch. 12; Smith, W., 1920; Soward, 1924). Private prosecution and justices of the peace were the linchpins of law enforcement until well into the nineteenth century, although it does appear that under the peculiar circumstances of the French-English split (see below) public prosecution played a larger role sooner in Lower Canada than it did elsewhere (Stenning, 1986, ch. 2). As usual, the death sentence was the centrepiece of the punitive regime (Boyer, 1966; Desaulniers, 1977; Morel, 1978A). As in the English colonies, dissatisfactions with all aspects of the system were manifested by a movement for reform (Boyer, 1966; especially Desaulniers, 1977; Morel, 1978B) which led to a massive reduction in the number of capital offences in the 1830s, a process completed in 1841, and the construction of a new prison in Montreal in 1836 (Borthwick, 1886; Lefebvre, 1954).

Only barely concealed by the similarities with the English colonies, however, are a host of significant differences, all related to the fact that English criminal law and criminal trial procedures were imposed and operated by an alien conqueror. Although the literature on the social and political role of the criminal law in post-conquest Quebec is not much greater in volume than that for English Canada in the same period, it does demonstrate that *habitants* viewed the system with substantial, indeed near overwhelming, suspicion. Hay (1981) shows that the English-run institutions, especially the Court of King's Bench, were largely ignored by the new French subjects, who generally refused to prosecute in them. French-Canadians could not sit as judges nor act as justices of the peace because of the religious disability laws. They could not often understand the laws or, in particular, the complicated trial procedures because of the language barrier. Most importantly, even when they knew the system, it was culturally alien to them. Indeed, many of the features which English commentators most lauded clashed with socio-cultural preconceptions. For example, public trial by jury ran up against the French fear of ignominy, reflected in the fact that while French criminal procedure was private and inquisitorial and French punishments correspondingly 'managed ... to make the fullest possible use of public shame and punishment' (Hay, 1981, p.80).

Similar evidence about the Canadian reaction to the English system to that discovered by Hay is presented in Morel (1978A), although the lessons he draws from it are less imaginative and sophisticated. In another study

Morel (1960) argues that the *habitants* adopted a strategy of what he calls 'passive resistance.' Many employed private arbitration rather than use the civil courts, and while they do not seem to have done this in the criminal law area, they left many offences unprosecuted. Unfortunately we know rather more about the immediate post-conquest period than about the nineteenth century; presumably French Canadians adopted and adapted to both the form and underlying assumptions of the criminal justice system, and it is necessary to discover more about when and how that occurred. Fecteau (1985) provides a fascinating beginning, arguing that adaptation was crucially linked to state formation and transformation as Quebec entered the modern commercial world of the nineteenth century.

Before leaving the subject of Quebec under the unreformed system, three further points should be noted. First, as with the English colonies, we know little about the specifics of the movement to reform the criminal law and methods of punishment. Second, from its earliest days the English criminal justice system in Quebec was associated with the military. Martial law was in place until 1764, but even after the institution of civil government the fact that many justices of the peace were military officers, that the military was the colony's only effective police force, and that such a large percentage of the colony's English inhabitants (who comprised the majority of prosecutors in the criminal courts) were attached to the military, all combined to infuse the system in the eyes of the conquered with the trappings of military overlordship (Hay, 1981, pp. 98–9; Knafla and Chapman, 1983, pp. 258–63). Third, and this point is to some extent related to the second, when the social and political order was threatened, as it was with the 1837 rebellion crisis, authorities used and abused the criminal law in dealing with rebels. In the treason trials of the late 1830s military tribunals were employed and many of the usual procedural protections afforded defendants were dispensed with to ensure convictions (Greenwood, 1988).

iii) *Urbanization, Adaptation and Modernization in the Maritimes and the Province of Canada, 1840 to 1867*

Two themes dominate the published literature on Canadian criminal justice history between the end of the unreformed system and Confederation. There should be more than two, but many obvious topics have not been studied at all, a point I will return to at the end of this section when I sketch briefly where future work could most usefully be concentrated.

The first major theme is represented by accounts of the evolution of penitentiary policy. The penitentiaries built in the 1830s and early 1840s all were ushered in on high hopes that the new institutions would be effective in their primary function of reformation of individuals and their secondary aim of acting as guides to general social order. The former was to be achieved by regimes of (more or less) solitary confinement, order, discipline and labour. Though the precise organization of each penitentiary was different, they were all based in one way or another on the trinity of work, discipline and order (Baehre, 1977, 1990; Beattie, 1977; Bellomo, 1972; Chunn, 1981; Edmison, 1976; Ekstedt and Griffiths, 1984, pp. 34 *et seq*; Shoom, 1966). In fact all of the new institutions turned out to be major disappointments. Congregate confinement continued to be practised, recidivism rates were high, prison labour encountered objections from artisans and craftsmen and was only intermittently used (Chunn, 1981; Palmer, 1980), prison authorities at times resorted to physical cruelties reminiscent of the worst of the old regime, and though various experiments were undertaken with different methods of prison organization and reward systems, the high hopes of the founders were largely unfulfilled. Asylums, also a feature of the mid-nineteenth-century expansion of the administrative state, were no more successful (Francis, 1977; Verdun-Jones and Smandych, 1981).

Nowhere was the failure of the penitentiary more spectacular than in Kingston's early decades, a period which Shoom (1966, p.220) calls 'perhaps [the] most degrading chapter in the history of Canadian penal institutions.' An investigation by the Brown Commission in 1849 revealed that corruption and cruelty had been widespread under the regime of warden Henry Smith. According to Beattie (1977, p.30) not only had Smith failed to lead convicts to better, morally upright life, but under his administration 'the brutalizing effects of capital punishment and the brutalizing effects of the penitentiary had both served to harden men's hearts and had both contributed to the rise of crime.' Changes were inaugurated, particularly a move to a modified separate system, provisions for inspection and the establishment of a separate facility for juvenile offenders at Penetanguishene (Ekstedt and Griffiths, 1984, pp. 38–41; Shoom, 1972); such tinkering with prison regimes was typical of mid-nineteenth-century penal policy (Baehre, 1990; Tremblay and Normandeau, 1986). But these initiatives achieved little: indeed the mid to late nineteenth-century Canadian penitentiary evolved into primarily a method of removing offenders from the community and punishing them by incarceration. Lip service continued to be paid to the goals of reform and rehabilitation, but the reality was a record of failures caused in part by administrative inertia and frugality. Beattie (1977, p.35) concludes his study by noting that 'the dilemma posed by the attempt to punish *and* reform criminals has yet to be solved.'

The second major theme from this period is that of the development of urban institutions to deal more effectively with the problems of crime in the new, growing, anonymous cities of the various colonies. Visible social disorder included the drunkenness and immorality of the new urban 'underclass' (Fingard, 1982, 1984, 1989A; Houston, 1972B; 1974), and the occasional explosion into riot (Armstrong, 1963; Bleasdale, 1981; Cross, 1971; Eadie, 1976; Foster, J. 1951; Wright, J.A. 1974). The development of middle and upper class responses is most obviously seen by the establishment and growth of municipal police forces from the old institutions of constables and 'watches,' and this has been described in a number of books and articles (Addington, 1980; Boritch, 1988; Campbell, 1970; Lefebvre, 1952; Marquis, 1982, 1986, 1988A; Phillips, 1990; Rogers, 1984; Senior, 1988; Shanes, 1975; Stenning, 1983, ch. 3; Turmel, 1971). But urban authorities' solutions to the perceived crime problem also came in a variety of new attitudes and other institutions. The necessity of regulating urban populations, of encouraging their lawful behaviour through social reform movements (Cross, 1984; Fingard, 1982, 1989A; Houston, 1974; Phillips, 1990; Weaver, 1986), and of providing machinery for dealing with the recalcitrant meant that the criminal justice system was at the forefront of nineteenth-century developments in civic government. Reformatories, asylums, and expanded local jails were built, and, most importantly, urban courts, run by either local elected officials or by stipendiary magistrates, became a feature of the landscape. Marquis (1987A) has termed this 'the rise of urban justice,' and it has been examined in a disparate number of articles. (In addition to those already cited see Acheson, 1985, pp. 30–42; Aitchison, 1949; Akins, 1895, pp. 170–1; Betts, 1976; Craven, 1983; Girard, 1988; Oxner, 1984; Weaver and Doucet, 1984).

It should be noted that this review of the years between 1840 and 1867 reveals that much remains to be done on criminal justice history during a formative period in Canadian history, a period that saw the coming of responsible government, the Union of the Canadas, the railway boom, and early industrialization and urbanization. As for the unreformed period discussed above, there are no broad-based studies of crime and society. There are few examinations of obvious particular developments, such as the continued reform of the substantive law of crime and punishment (Chandler, 1976: Desaulniers, 1977), the evolution of criminal court procedure (although see Verdun-Jones, 1981) in a period when it was becoming increasingly 'professionalized' in England as the lawyers took over, the effect of Canadian union on Canadien perceptions of criminal justice, the policing of labour gangs on railways, canals and other public works, and the effect of the transportation revolution on crime and on responses to it. Finding out more about all of this is a large but necessary agenda for Canadian criminal justice historians.

B) POST-CONFEDERATION

i) *The Institutional Effects of Confederation*

Confederation altered the structure of political responsibilities for crime and punishment, and it therefore represents a significant watershed in the institutional evolution of criminal justice. Changes in overall political authority for the criminal justice system can nevertheless be quickly disposed of in this review, for historians have not considered them worthy of much attention as an issue in federal-provincial relations. This is probably a wise choice: although criminal justice has since 1867 been influenced by both levels of government, there have been few issues on which fundamental conflict between governments has emerged. The only exception is represented by an immediate post-Confederation dispute between Victoria and Ottawa over the powers of the British Columbia Supreme Court (Bowker, 1986; Foster, H. 1983, 1986; Williams, 1977, 1986).

Under the new constitutional arrangements the federal government was made responsible for the substantive criminal law and for criminal procedure, and was also granted control of the appointment of superior court judges (those that tried serious crime) and the management of penitentiaries. The provinces retained the authority that their colonial predecessors had had over 'public and reformatory prisons in and for the province,' the appointment of judges to lower courts which included justices of the peace, and the administration of justice within the province, which included the organization and composition of all courts (Friedland, 1984, ch. 2; Hogg, 1985, pp. 397–9; Stenning, 1986). The distinction between the federal control over 'penitentiaries' and provincial authority for 'public and reformatory prisons' has evolved into the well-known distinction between sentences of more or less than two years, although that dividing line was employed decades earlier in the province of Canada in the decision on whether to send a convict to Kingston (Needham, 1980).

Only two institutional developments springing from the new political arrangements have been examined by historians. The first is changes in the substantive law of crime and punishment. Although provincial criminal laws remained in force until effectively repealed by new federal statutes, the federal parliament was quick to bring about two reformulations of the laws. The first was represented by a series of statutes, passed from 1869 onwards, dealing with many areas of the criminal law and codifying criminal procedure. The latter has remained the basis of criminal procedure (absent changes wrought by the Charter of Rights) to this day (Mewett, 1967).

Uniformity across the country was largely achieved through this process by 1892, but throughout the quarter century since 1867 discussions had also continued sporadically regarding a second reformulation, the enactment of a consolidated criminal code, which was achieved in 1892. Proposals for codification have a long history in the common law world and have usually been intimately connected to democratization, modernization and simplification of the law. Supporters of a criminal code insisted on the need for this area of the law, if no other, to be moulded to local conditions and to be as accessible to all as possible. In the end, however, as the fairly full accounts of the process that are available demonstrate (Brown, D.H. 1989; Friedland, 1981; Parker, 1981), the Code that passed in 1892 was neither particularly local nor especially accessible. It was based on English models (although England never enacted a code) and was essentially a consolidation of existing law rather than a reformulation. No further substantial changes were made in the criminal law until 1953 (MacLeod, 1978; Mewett, 1967, p.728).

Penitentiary management also changed with Confederation. The three existing colonial penitentiaries (Kingston, Halifax and Saint John) were brought under central government control and this was followed by construction of new prisons at Montreal, Stony Mountain (Man.), New Westminster (B.C.) and Dorchester (N.B.); when the last-named was opened the institutions at Saint John and Halifax were closed down (Baehre, 1982, 1990; Ekstedt and Griffiths, 1984, p.41). Federal Penitentiary Acts also created an inspectorate but it is difficult to discern any sharp innovations in penal practice. Punishment, deterrence, reformation and rehabilitation continued as the watchwords for federal policy, and the system went on underfunded and only half-heartedly committed to serious efforts at rehabilitation (Calder, 1979; 1981). Calder's (1981) published study of the federal penitential regime argues that the 'reality of penitentiary life was often far removed from the ideal enunciated by prison officials,' for 'convicts faced a harsh institutional environment with a punitive thrust and reformative pretensions.' It has been argued that not until after the Second World War was there a clear move to more humane and progressive penal policy in Canada (Johnstone and Henheffer, 1964). A consequence, perhaps, of the failure in the early years was the various crises that have afflicted the federal penitentiary system in the twentieth century and which appear to bedevil it to this day (Ekstedt and Griffiths, 1984).

ii) *Crime and Society: General*

The years between Confederation and the First World War were marked by the most profound social and economic changes in Canadian history and by efforts to use the criminal law and other methods of official intervention to solve the consequent social problems. As industrialization, urbanization, and western settlement brought political disaffection and social dislocation, Canada changed from a collection of rural and commercial eastern colonies populated largely by people of British and French origin or descent to a continental nation of many ethnic groups which, while still significantly rural and resource-oriented in its economic base, underwent substantial industrialization (Kealey, G.S. 1980; Finlay and Sprague, 1984, chs. 12–14). It is best to divide an analysis of how all this implicated criminal justice into three parts: criminal law and social reform, developments in urban institutions such as policing and prisons, and the problem of violence and disorder in labour relations.

In the eastern towns and cities, and to a lesser extent in the new urban centres of the west, the industrial age saw increased concerns among the upper and middle classes about immorality, drunkenness, and vice, evils generally attributed to the social and family breakdown consequent on the rapid destruction of old communities and traditional ways of life. They responded in various ways, often collected by historians under the umbrella of late nineteenth-century social reform. It is impossible to adequately summarize this reform movement here, for it had numerous strands of both inspiration and policy, or even to offer the reader more than a brief selection of the major works (Allen, R. 1968; 1971; Cook, R. 1985; Fingard, 1989B; Fraser, 1988; Pitsula, 1979: Rutherford, 1971; 1974). What is important for present purposes is to stress that in part the social reformers turned to the criminal law to achieve their goals.

One aspect of this was change in the substantive law itself. The best-known example is, of course, the temperance/prohibition campaigns. Temperance has a long history in Canada (Barron, 1980; Chapman, J. 1954; Garland and Talman, 1974; Houston, 1974), and received many new adherents in the late nineteenth century as drink was marked out as a significant cause of urban crime and poverty. Substantial efforts were expended through the criminal justice system to enforce either drinking regulations or, in some places at certain times, outright prohibition (Allen, R. 1969; Burnet, 1974; Decarie, 1972, 1974; Dick, 1981; Forbes, 1971; Gray, 1972; Hallowell, 1972; Tennyson, 1963). Along with alcohol regulation came the first Canadian attempts, in the early twentieth century, to regulate drug use. Though much good work has been written on this topic (Boyd, 1984; Chapman, T.L. 1976, 1979; Cook, S. 1969; Green, 1979; Green and Solomon, 1982; Murray, 1987; Trasov, 1962), it was not as significant for contemporaries as the substantial literature might suggest. In fact, many of these investigations were carried out as part of the research of the Le Dain Commission of Inquiry into drugs; it therefore tells as much about the sociology of knowledge in one corner of the academic profession in the 1970s as it does about attitudes toward crime and morality in the late nineteenth and early twentieth centuries.

More significant than concerns about drugs were those relating to prostitution, which brought into sharp focus the link between crime and social order. Prostitution was not only a crime, it also signalled a decline in religious and family values and negated the emerging Victorian myth of woman as the domestic bedrock of society. McLaren (1986, 1987) has charted in detail the evolution of prostitution laws in this period. Another aspect of change in substantive law was the 'invention' of juvenile delin- quency (Bennett, 1986, 1988; Coulter, 1982; Houston, 1972A, 1982; Jones, A. 1978; Rooke and Schnell, 1982A, 1982B, 1983; Tremblay and Norman- deau, 1986), which saw the evolution of special laws, courts and carceral institutions, as concern about a breakdown of family and community values became focused on delinquency.

In addition to making new laws and changing old ones, the middle classes also responded to the perceived social crisis by more vigorous enforcement of the law. This was certainly the case with prostitution (Backhouse, 1986; McLaren, 1987, 1988, 1990; Price, 1990), and with the vagrancy laws (Phillips, 1990; Pitsula, 1980). Religious and other forms of riot, marches and demonstrations were also subjected to vigorous efforts at suppresion (Kealey, G.S. 1970; Morton, 1970, 1980; Pariseau, 1973).

The second manifestation of a desire for more effective crime control in this period was change in urban institutions. Most urban petty crime was processed through magistrates' courts which met daily and dealt with offenders in a summary, almost perfunctory manner. Studies of these courts suggest that urban authorities may not have been prepared to pump substantial resources into the system, but they were equally unwilling to allow visible signs of disorder such as drunkenness, begging and prostitu- tion to go unpunished (Craven, 1983; Homel, 1981; Price, 1990; Thorner and Watson, 1984). The new importance of enforcing the law can also be seen in the development of city police forces during this period. A number of studies demonstrate that police numbers were augmented and that efforts were made to 'professionalize' the police, to render them more effective as (as you wish) either neutral forces for social order or agents of the middle and upper classes in their campaigns to discipline the lower orders. Policing was made into a career, and police forces into disciplined cadres of men (and a few women) infused with professional pride and distinctiveness (Boritch, 1988; Marquis, 1982, 1987, 1988, 1989; McGahan, 1988A, 1988B, 1989B, 1989C, 1989D; Phillips, 1990; Rawling, 1988; Rogers, 1984; Stenning, 1983, ch. 3; Talbot et al, 1983). In addition the final years of the period under review saw the establishment of provincial police forces in Ontario, Saskatchewan and Alberta (Anderson, 1972; Campbell, 1970; Kavanaugh, 1973; Robertson, D.F. 1978).

Another institution affected was the prison. Provincial politicians variously established new institutions, including ones for women only in Ontario (Strange, 1985) and Quebec (Lefebvre, 1954), and/or attempted to tighten up discipline and the labour requirement in existing ones in order that those responsible for threatening the social order could not avoid its guiding precepts of work, discipline and morality even when removed from it (Baehre, 1989; Tremblay and Normandeau, 1986). Faith in the (theoretical) rehabilitative goal stayed strong, even as it died in the United States (Wetherell, 1979). However, as with the federal system, success was very limited. Conditions were at times appalling, discipline was severe (Oliver, 1988), existing buildings were not adequate to allow for non-congregate confinement, free labour objected to the competition from prisoners, and the standard of administrative competence and inspection was very low (see also Ekstedt and Griffiths, 1984, pp. 43–8; Phillips, 1990).

The final aspect of developments in the relationship between crime and society that should be noted was the increased use of the criminal justice system to deal with labour disputes. Although this period saw the decriminalization of conspiracies to raise wages (Chartrand, 1984; Ostry, 1960; but see Craven, 1984), and of breach of employment contracts by workers (Craven, 1981), many aspects of the strike regime, particularly picketing, were made effectively subject to the criminal law (Chartrand, 1984). More importantly, authorities were rarely shy about using the police, the military and the criminal law to control and break strikes in a period which saw substantial labour disaffection and the rise of new and powerful labour organizations (Jamieson, 1979; Kealey, G.S. and Palmer, 1987; Morton, 1970; Palmer, 1987; Pariseau, 1973; Silverman, 1970).

iii) *The West: Long Distance Justice, European Settlement and the North West Mounted Police*

After industrialization the most important aspect of Canadian history between 1867 and 1920 was the expansion of western settlement. This development posed numerous challenges to federal and local politicians, and many of those challenges and some of the solutions involved the criminal justice system. Mediating the relations between white settlers and other intruders and the native peoples of the plains, for example, brought tight liquor control policies into the new territories as well as forcing a confrontation between European and native ideas of land-holding. Building the railroad required control of large gangs of migrant labour, and that involved both issues of general social disorder as well as labour-management conflict. Lastly, the new European settlers and settlements on the frontier had to be generally regulated – courts established and policing made available – with the experience of the 'lawless' American west to the forefront of the policy-makers' minds.

Each of these major themes, and others, has tended to be seen in the literature through the medium of studies of the NWMP (Royal Canadian Mounted Police from 1919). This section will reflect that general tendency, in that a substantial part of it will be devoted to the NWMP. But it will also examine broader aspects of late nineteenth and early twentieth-century western Canadian criminal justice history. I will begin, however, with a review of the literature on the pre-Confederation period.

There are two excellent recent summaries of the institutional development of criminal justice in the west, by Knafla (1986) and, especially, Foster, H. (1990). They reveal that prior to the mid-nineteenth century there existed considerable jurisdictional confusion and an often substantial gap between theory and practice. Before Confederation the southern prairies (Rupert's Land) were under the jurisdiction of the Hudson's Bay Company pursuant to its Royal Charter, with the criminal law that of England. The remainder of the west was 'Indian territory,' not formally under the jurisdiction of any British authority. However, because neither area supported legal institutions there was little practical difference between the two. There were some attempts in the late eighteenth century to deal with violent competition between rival fur traders by having serious crimes tried by the Quebec/Lower Canadian courts. This 'long-distance justice' (Foster, H. 1990, p.2) proved ineffective when doubts were raised about the legality of the procedures. The result was an imperial statute of 1803 which gave jurisdiction to the courts of Upper and Lower Canada.

Legal wrangling over the scope of the 1803 statute, particularly concerning whether it ousted Hudson's Bay Company jurisdiction in the Red River colony founded by Lord Selkirk in 1811 (Brown, D.H. 1979; Foster, H. 1990, pp. 19–30; Gressley, 1979), meant that it did not provide an adequate solution. Further reforms were undertaken in 1821, by the British parliament, and in 1822, by the Hudson's Bay Company (Foster, H. 1990, pp. 32 et seq; Knafla, 1986, pp. 36–7). Nevertheless the 'first formal legal system in the West' (Knafla, 1986, p.37) was not established until 1835. Magistrates, constables, and a higher criminal court composed of the governor and council of Assiniboia were established, a gaol was built at Fort Garry, the colony was organized into judicial districts, and a penal code promulgated which purported to receive the criminal law of England as of 1837 (Bindon, 1981; Knafla, 1986; F. Read, 1937; Stubbs, 1967). Some of the more famous cases involving serious crimes in the west in the first half of the nineteenth century are examined in Foster, H. (1990).

British Columbia, which was part of the 'Indian territory' and did not come under the Hudson's Bay Company's Charter until the 1820s, enters the story in the early 1840s. In 1843 the Company established a trading post at what is now Victoria to block northward American expansion, and in 1849 Vancouver Island became a crown colony. English law, justices of the peace, and, from 1853, a Supreme Court, were established (Farr, 1967; Foster, H. 1983; Herbert, 1954; Knafla, 1986). The mainland also became a crown colony in 1858 following the Pacific gold rush of 1857–58 (the two colonies were united in 1866). There are a number of good accounts of the ways in which the immigrant gold-miners operated systems of criminal and civil justice brought by them from other prospecting regions (Foster, H. 1983; Gough, 1975; Williams, 1986), and of the imposition of centralized criminal justice after 1858 (Foster, H. 1986; Hatch, 1955; Knafla, 1986; Williams, 1977).

The Confederation period saw the acquisition by the new Dominion of the provinces of Manitoba in 1870, British Columbia in 1871, and the area now comprising Alberta and Saskatchewan in 1869, on surrender by the Hudson's Bay Company of its Charter. In all areas the criminal law was, of course, that of Canada (Brown, D.H. 1975), and in British Columbia and Manitoba the laws were enforced by justices of the peace and superior criminal courts; in British Columbia this meant the Supreme Court and a system of County Courts, and in Manitoba the Supreme Court until 1872, the Court of Queen's Bench thereafter. The fascinating late nineteenth-century struggles within British Columbia and between Victoria and Ottawa over judicial status and authority impinged only tangentially on criminal justice, but the fine recent work on them is required reading for an under-standing of the court system (Foster, H. 1983, 1986; Williams, 1986). In the newly-acquired ex-Hudson's Bay Company territory, now called the North West Territories, enforcement at all levels was handed over to stipendiary magistrates and to the NWMP, whose members acted as justices of the peace as well as police officials. The governor and council could sit as a court but rarely did. The post-Confederation period also saw the expansion of existing prisons and the building of new institutions by territorial, provincial and federal governments (Ekstedt and Griffiths, 1984, ch. 2; James, 1978; Skinner et al, 1981).

Two topics dominate the field of post-Confederation western Canadian criminal justice history – the Riel trial and the NWMP. The former has been the subject of much debate relating to the law of treason, the general fairness of its procedures, and the insanity defence issue in particular

(Bingaman, 1972, 1975; Brown, D.H. 1975; Flannagan, 1983: Flannagan and Watson, 1981; Morton, 1974; Stanley, 1960; Thomas, 1977). The latter was traditionally represented by an historiography that bordered on hagiography, containing little but praise for the fair and fearless representatives of law and justice who brought the rule of law and a love for order to a harsh and potentially volatile environment (Atkin, 1973; Denny, 1939; Fetherstonhaugh, 1938; Haydon, 1971; Kelly and Kelly, 1973; Turner, 1950: these are but a few of the many such books; for a review of more see Klassen, 1974; Smandych et al, 1987, ch. 1; Walden, 1982, 1984). More recent work on the force has produced a subtler picture even if generally a still favourable one (Horrall, 1973; MacLeod, 1976A), and it has been complemented by broader-based studies of the nature of early western society. Together these two strands of historical literature are forcing a reconsideration of the nature of the supposedly 'peaceful frontier.'

The NWMP was founded in 1873 by the conservative MacDonald administration, originally as a temporary force to 'pacify' the North West. That is, to protect European settlers and to regulate relations between white settlers and the plains natives. Their origin is often ascribed to the Cypress Hill massacre of 1873, when American whiskey traders murdered several Assiniboine Indians, but in fact the idea of such a force had been in MacDonald's mind for some years (Brown and Brown, 1973; Goldring, 1973; Horrall, 1972; Morton, 1977). Modern accounts agree that 'continentalism,' not the whiskey trade, was primarily responsible for its creation (MacLeod, 1976A; 1976B). The force was ordered strangely to modern eyes. It was 'para-military' in its organization and in the fact that most of the early recruits were ex-servicemen. Its policing techniques featured one-man outposts and regular patrols which spread with the expansion of settlement. The life was not easy (Getty, 1974), internal dissatisfaction with conditions of service ran high at times, and desertion was actually a continual problem (Morgan, 1973).

Before 1885 the force carried out two principal tasks. The first concerned the native peoples of the plains. It negotiated treaties conceding land in exchange for reserves and payments, it persuaded the inhabitants to abandon the hunt and settle on the reserves, and it enforced those laws that particularly concerned Indians – the treaties of cession and the liquor prohibitions (MacLeod, 1976A). It is frequently suggested that the failure of the plains Indians to join the 1885 rebellion is a testament to the respect and reputation for fairness earned by the force during this period. Its second task was to take over the enforcement of the criminal law, and the application of much of the civil regulations, throughout the North West. The NWMP was not a 'mere' police force in the modern sense of the word. It was a general 'colonial' administrative service as well, carrying out fire prevention, quarantine enforcement, land registration, map-making, postal services, relief provision in bad times, and crop-reporting (Beahen, 1981; Getty, 1974; MacLeod, 1976B).

The function of the force changed somewhat after 1885. The completion of the CPR meant many more settlers and an increased rate of urbanization. The force became more regularly and purely identified with law enforcement, to its detriment as far as its responsibility for enforcing prohibition was concerned (Horrall, 1974). It lost much of its 'judicial' role when, in 1886, the criminal justice system in the North West Territories was remodelled: a Supreme Court was established, which did most of its work on circuit and without juries, and the position of stipendiary magistrate abolished, although NWMP officers retained their right to convict of minor offences as justices of the peace (Harvey, 1934, 1935; Horrall, 1972; Knafla, 1986, pp. 48–53). Most importantly, however, the force was retained, despite its being originally conceived of as a temporary expedient to lay the groundwork for settlement. It survived in part because of its connections with conservative patronage (Horrall, 1973; MacLeod, 1976B), in part because it had played a significant role in the suppression of the 1885 rebellion, and in part because its non-police functions apparently made its members very popular with the rural settlers of the west (Betke, 1980). Above all, though, it seems to have owed its survival to its role as the major policy tool of central Canadian continental expansionism: western settlement was one prong of the National Policy, and the intention was to create a society distinct, profitable and orderly on the frontier. The NWMP had been crucial in the achievement of that goal (MacLeod, 1976B).

Thus despite the force's traditional connection to the conservatives and consequent fears that it would be disbanded with the accession of the Laurier liberals in 1896, it survived the change in government. Indeed the last years of the nineteenth and early years of the twentieth centuries saw expansion. When the plains were removed from direct federal control with the formation of the provinces of Saskatchewan and Alberta in 1905 the NWMP was not immediately replaced by provincial forces: the Saskatchewan and Alberta police forces were not founded until 1917 (Anderson, 1972; Kavanaugh, 1973), and even then primarily because the force announced that if prohibition were re-introduced it would not be comfortable trying to enforce such 'civil' regulations (Horrall, 1974). By the early twentieth century, therefore, the force was very much a 'regular' police force, and was also becoming increasingly concentrated in the towns as urbanization became a significant factor in the new west (Getty, 1974). In this role it supplemented the work of new municipal forces: see generally Talbot et al (1983) and for Calgary Gilkes and Symons (1975), for Edmonton Donaghey (1972), for Lethbridge Carpenter (1975), and for Winnipeg, Hutchinson R.

(1974). The NWMP nonetheless remained a rural force on the northern plains, and it was also used in the far north (Horrall, 1973; Morrison, 1974, 1985; Stone, 1979).

The major historical debates over the NWMP concern the related issues of, firstly, the extent to which it was 'neutral' in the various conflicts between different groups in the new west, and, secondly, the relationship between the force and the apparently largely peaceful new society that was created. What links these issues is a view of the 'Mounties' as independent, impartial, and upstanding enforcers of the law who by their actions and their example forged a new society without the birthpangs of disorder and frontier lawlessness associated with the American west. As noted above, a long hagiographic tradition has implanted this perception firmly in Canadian popular culture.

Recent scholarship has given us a very different picture, and can be characterized as of three types. First, a number of accounts have put forward a more guarded but still favourable view of the role of the NWMP. MacLeod (1976A; 1976B) will have none of the hero worship and places the force firmly in the economic and political context of early nation-building. He gives it qualified approval, and is not willing to blame it for the decisions of others: it was not the NWMP that confined plains Indians to reserves but the federal government. Nor is he prepared to heap obloquy on it for actions that only in retrospect invite disapproval: it took part in strike-breaking, but all militias and police forces did so in the late nineteenth and early twentieth centuries. Having placed the NWMP within the confines of contemporary political and economic structures, he is cautiously laudatory. Particular analyses of the treatment of the Doukhobours and other European and American immigrant groups such as the Mormons come to similar conclusions (Betke, 1974, 1980; Breen, 1974). Other accounts also argue that the force was primarily responsible for the lack of conflict between settler groups, for the relative order with which land claims were established and livestock protected from theft (Breen, 1974; Fetherstonhaugh, 1938; Jennings, 1975), and for the fact that the native peoples were generally treated 'fairly' and respectfully, shielded from liquor traders and their treaty rights to land upheld against illegal land grabbers (Horrall, 1973).

A second line of writing, however, denigrates the force in a variety of ways. Walden (1982, 1984), for example, points out that such peaceful acceptance of outsiders and such rapid adaptation of immigrants to a new land does not ring true. Morgan (1973) catalogues problems of lack of morale, inefficiency, and immorality among the members. The most scathing attack has come in a semi-populist work by Brown and Brown (1973), who make much of MacDonald's intention to create an imperial, para-military force to enforce the divestment of Indian land and protect the new Dominion's interest in the economic development of the west. That is, they adopt a critical stance toward MacDonald's continentalism and strive to establish that it was the NWMP which was responsible for moving the Indians to reserves and for contributing to the destruction of the native way of life (see also Barron, 1988). The same book chronicles the pro-government and pro-employer role played by the force in labour conflicts, particularly those related to the building and running of the Canadian Pacific Railway. It assisted by protecting strike-breakers and by using its full authority against strike leaders. Brown and Brown argue that the force was more than the derivative arm of government policy, but an active agent in the process of suppression. By the time of its most spectacular labour intervention, the 1919 Winnipeg General Strike, it was firmly established as a major political and military force of and for the right, rooting out 'seditious societies' and 'disturbing elements' such as the One Big Union and its leaders. Horrall (1980) also chronicles its role in Winnipeg, but with an interpretation more befitting of the RCMP's official historian.

The third line of recent scholarship on this question takes a somewhat different and broader tack by asking whether western Canadian society was as peaceful and law-abiding as popular culture believes, and if it was, whether the particular character of the NWMP and of the settlers had much to do with it. There are a number of studies of southern Alberta which indicate that transiency, labour problems, poverty, the unavailability of police, inadequate land registration procedures, and dispossesion of the native peoples led to a persistent crime 'problem' and periodic crime waves in the years between 1875 and the First World War (Thorner, 1975, 1979; Thorner and Watson, 1981). When Calgary appointed a new police magistrate in 1911, it did so in an atmosphere of profound fear about an 'onslaught of crime' (Thorner and Watson, 1984). The broad questions of 'order and disorder' on the Canadian frontier are still unresolved, and the comparison with the American west is also being rethought as it is being shown that lack of formal institutions to the south did not necesarily mean lack of 'legal' ways to resolve disputes (Foster, H. 1985; Reid, 1980). Morton (1977) provides an interesting twist on this debate by pointing out that, assuming that the settlement of western Canada was less violent than that of the United States, it was facilitated partly by the decade or so time lag between the arrival of the police and of settlers, partly by the fact that Canadian plains Indians knew from the fate of their southern counterparts that resistance was useless, and partly by the benevolent despotism with which the force operated. The nature of western society and the role of the NWMP in its creation is an issue which will doubtless continue to be explored.

Part Two: Themes in the History of Crime, State and Society

A) INTRODUCTION

This part is concerned with two inter-related topics: studies of the incidence of crime (particular crimes and crime rates) and the historiography of the social meaning of crime, by which I mean attitudes toward crime, definitions of what is criminal and what is not, and interpretations of the relationship between the criminal justice system, the economy and socio-political hierarchies. These topics should be considered inter-related simply because it is not possible to assess the social significance of crime and punishment without knowing its incidence. Furthermore, increases and decreases in the incidence of particular crimes or of crime in general, whether changes in crimes committed or criminals apprehended, have historically been the result of a variety of socio-economic factors: the state of the economy, social differentiation, war, politics and culture, all of which lead to changes in attitudes and policies in the areas of criminalization, policing, and sanctioning.

As a foil to the still limited Canadian historiography two seminal works on England should be noted. The first is a still highly influential article by Hay (1975) which spawned a revolution in the way in which English social historians looked at the criminal law. Hay argues that the supposedly irrational administration of the death sentence in eighteenth-century England in fact represented a finely balanced mechanism whereby the English propertied classes retained their hegemony over the propertyless without a police force or standing army. The system combined majesty, justice, and mercy to entrench the ideological hegemony of the ruling classes. While the content of Hay's argument has been subjected to a variety of criticisms (see Langbein, 1983, and the article by Beattie in this volume for additional references), he has encouraged his supporters and forced his detractors to consider the criminal law as an integral aspect of the socio-economic and political structure of a community. The second piece of work is a recent book by Beattie (1986) which provides a richly-detailed statistical and qualitative analysis of crime rates, court structures and procedures, policing, prosecution and punishment in two English counties over a century and a half. It is, quite simply, the best book written in the field of criminal justice history; it deserves that title for the way it combines detailed statistical compilations, analyses of official reactions, policies and practices, and an appreciation of the meaning of crime and the legitimacy of the criminal process for all levels of society.

Readers should see Beattie's essay in this volume for a more detailed analysis of the literature on England. I mention these two contributions, which represent rather different approaches to thinking about the subject, as much for a negative as for a positive purpose. That is, to make the point that there remains much that is unexplored for Canada. We have some knowledge of the incidence of crime, and the literature on this is reviewed in the section immediately following. We have a more impressive range of suggestions and hypotheses about the role of crime in society and politics, looked at below in section C of this part. These represent sound foundations, but they also reveal what more needs to be built.

B) CRIMES AND CRIME RATES

Arguably the largest gap in our knowledge concerns the general crime rate, for there are no pre-twentieth-century studies of crime in general over any lengthy period for any region or province. Thus it is not only impossible to make general statements about the meaning and nature of crime, but also to offer particular analyses of the effects of immigration, economic change, wars and political upheaval. Statements in the literature about crime rates are usually based on qualitative, not quantitative, evidence: for an example see Beattie (1977, p.1). There are some statistically-based studies of particular localities over limited periods of time, the best of which deal with southern Alberta in the late nineteenth century (Klassen, 1975; Thorner, 1975, 1979; Thorner and Watson, 1981), Quebec at the turn of the nine-teenth century (Fecteau, 1985), and Upper Canada in the 1830s and 1840s (Blackwell, 1980–81; Talbot, 1983; Weaver, 1986; see also Graff, 1977B and Graff, 1977A, on the possibilities of using the available prison records). Weaver is particularly worth reading. He shows, in part through a thorough study of court and prison records, how local authorities in one part of Ontario responded to perceived lawlessness by criminalising behaviour previously acceptable and by augmenting enforcement mechanisms. The criminal law was an important tool in disciplining an aberrant social group, in this instance newly-arrived Irish migrant construction labourers.

There are also some examinations of particular offences over time. Those involving women are discussed below; others include treason (Wright, 1986) and vagrancy (Phillips, 1990; Pitsula, 1980). This short list unfortunately does not include any systematic studies of the major offences such as murder and serious property crime; the only ostensibly academic book on the history of murder in Canada (Boyd, 1988) is hardly scholarly at all, though at times quite entertaining.

Apart from the work just mentioned the literature on crimes is of three kinds. The first is represented by a plethora of accounts of crimes and criminal trials that are merely descriptive, useful as sources and often entertaining as stories, but which do not offer the reader much beyond the titillation of a 'good read' that involves a fair amount of blood, guts, heroic police work and the possibility of an execution at the end of it (Anderson, 1973; Bowker, 1986; Bulmer, 1879; Elliott, 1931; Inglis, 1972; Jones, J.E. 1924; Phelan, 1976; Smith, J.F. 1975; Shortt, 1900; see also the work of Riddell listed in the references).

Rather more useful are a series of accounts drawn from anecdotal or qualitative evidence which demonstrate the range of criminal activity either generally within a region and period (Cross, 1973; Fingard, 1989A; Foster, H. 1983; McGahan, 1988A, 1988B, 1988C, 1989A, 1989B; Williams, 1986), or in relation to a particular kind of offence, such as sex crimes (Chapman, T. 1983, 1986: Gigeroff, 1966). This work is better at finding evidence of concern about crime, or contemporary assesments of its causes, than it is at establishing incidence.

The third *genre* comprises accounts of isolated offences such as, for example, riots (Armstrong, 1963; Cross, 1971; Eadie, 1976; Foster, J. 1951; Roy, 1976; Stanley, 1972; Sugimoto, 1972; Wright, J.A. 1974), or murder and treason trials (Friedland, 1985; Grant, 1983; Greenwood, 1980, 1984, 1988; Harring, 1989; Koester, 1972; Moyles, 1979; Read, C. 1982; Romney, 1975; Schuh, 1979), or miscellaneous topics such as an early nineteenth-century buggery trial (Hutchinson, L. 1989), or the debate over the extradition of escaped slaves who allegedly committed crimes in winning their freedom (Brode, 1980, 1989B). Although the quality of this work varies, this list contains some of the best writing in the area. At times it is very revealing about the workings of the full criminal justice system at a particular time (Friedland, 1985), or legal and social attitudes toward homosexuals (Hutchinson, L. 1989), or the cultural clash evidenced by the imposition on native society of European ideas about the criminal law (Harring, 1989), or the racial and political influences in *causes célèbres* that bordered on 'state trials' (Greenwood, 1980, 1984, 1988). No amount of fine treatments of isolated incidents can, however, substitute for the kinds of comprehensive analyses whose absence I have noted above.

C) CRIME, POLITICS AND AUTHORITY

i) *General*

For most criminal justice historians there is no question that 'the criminal law involves an array of social control and social ordering mechanisms' (Wright, J.B. 1988, p.245). Much more contentious is the nature of the historical relationship between crime and political authority. Does it represent a crucial tool in 'the maintenance of political power in society' (Wright, J.B. 1988, p.245) or is it the case that 'the criminal law is ... the wrong place to look for the active hand of the ruling classes,' that it 'occupies a place not much more central than the garbage collection system' (Langbein, 1983, p.117)? Comprehensive investigations of this question in Canadian history must await the kinds of general accounts of the criminal process noted in the preceding section.

As with crimes and crime rates, therefore, much of what we know comes from episodic studies. At the most obvious level they reveal that in times of crisis Canadian authorities have not hesitated to employ the criminal law as an aspect of legitimating the suppression of economic and political dissent. This is demonstrated, for example, in the reaction to the rebellions of the 1830s. Greenwood (1988, p.261) discusses 'the ideological functions of early Canadian treason trials,' and shows how the criminal process was utilized and manipulated not only to secure convictions but also to send a message that 'political neutrality, in troublous times, in itself amounted to treason' (p.262). Studies of other political trials in this period echo such themes (Greenwood, 1980, 1984; Wright, J.B. 1986). So do those of Riel's trial, orchestrated to highlight the machinations of the rebellion's leader and to downplay legitimate Metis grievances (see above in part one). The trials that followed the Winnipeg General Strike were similarly employed to demonstrate that it was all a Bolshevik plot (McCormack, 1977; Masters, 1950) and to make acceptable the use of sedition and other laws to deal with immediate post-World War One radicalism (McCormack, 1977; Roberts, 1988) To some extent the same policies can be detected in the labour history of the late nineteenth century (see the preceding section and Torrance, 1986) and in the response to Fenianism (Keshen, 1987; Neidhart, 1974).

ii) *Race and the Criminal Law*

Another set of writing examines the use of the criminal law and criminal justice institutions in ordering relationships between Canada's historically dominant and expansionist white European society and various non-white communities, be they black ex-slaves, Asian immigrants, or the native peoples of southern and northern Canada. There is little information on the first-named. Winks' (1971) general study of black history in Canada contains some information on black offenders, and Brode (1989B) has charted the course of one famous extradition proceeding, but that is all one can point to. Similarly, while we are now coming to a full appreciation of the place originally assigned to Japanese and Chinese immigrants in Canadian life and culture (see for example Ward, 1978), there is little information specifically on how the criminal justice system operated in relation to them. Accounts of anti-Asian riots (Roy, 1976; Sugimoto, 1972) give us a criminal law mirror through which to view societal attitudes to Asians, but there are no systematic studies of their treatment by the criminal process.

Within the general topic of race and the criminal law there is rather more information available on indigenous peoples. Although 'the area of native people and the justice system ... has been a neglected area of scholarly inquiry in Canada' (McCaskill, 1983, p.288), one can discern in studies of white-native relations in the Maritimes (Upton, 1979), in British Columbia (Fisher, 1977; Gough, 1978A, 1978B), in Upper Canada/Ontario (Barron, 1983; Surtees, 1983) and on the western plains (Allen, R.S. 1983; Spry, 1983; see also the work on the NWMP reviewed above) that institutions of criminal justice played a crucial role in the twin policies of reservation and assimilation that have dominated the Canadian approach to native peoples (McCaskill, 1983; Stanley, 1983; Tobias, 1983). They have not been allowed to retain their own laws and methods of dispute resolution, have not been well-protected from white depredations, and have often been restricted in their activities by game laws and the like. In addition, the full force of the criminal law was, as noted above, used to deal with the second Riel Rebellion, and the coming of settlement generally brought clashes over land and livestock ownership that frequently caused resort to the criminal justice system. That system, primarily the NWMP, was also employed to enforce a pass system following the 1885 rebellion: natives were to be confined to reserves and not allowed to travel outside without a pass, a process dubbed by one historian 'a form of local administrative tyranny' (Barron, 1988, p.25).

Work on criminal justice in the north tends to be concentrated on the modern period, particularly on the efforts of Judge Jack Sissons to mould the law and the courts to reflect native values (see Morrow, 1981; Sissons, 1968). These more recent developments were a reaction to earlier instrusions of European criminal justice into a society to which it was often highly alien, a process which did not begin until the last years of the nineteenth century (see generally Zaslow, 1971). The best study is that of Harring (1989), who presents a richly detailed account of the violence that accompanied the arrival of Canadian law and police in one area of the north, and shows how practices acceptable in Inuit law were given a very different slant by Canadians. Other accounts of these trials are offered by Moyles (1979) and Keddy (1954), and a broader survey of a number of murder trials, less analytical than Harring but still sensitive to the fundamental culture clash, appears in Schuh (1979). She makes the useful point that in great measure these trials, and the imposition of European criminal justice generally, served the significant political purpose of 'flag-planting,' in both a physical and ideological sense: they 'demonstrated Canadian power and justice (to white Canadians if not to native people) in a part of the country where they had never been heard of before' (p.111). This was a policy to which Canadian authorities held firm, despite the fact that 'culture contact of a highly dramatic kind took place when men with only the most limited conception of white society were arrested and taken perhaps thousands of miles away for trial in the white man's court' (p.74).

iii) *Women and the Criminal Law*

A third significant theme for this section is the relationship between women, the criminal law, and gender hierarchies. The last decade or so has witnessed an explosion of interest in and writing on the history of women generally, and feminist and other women's historians have presented a new and formidable challenge to traditional ways of thinking about social ordering in the past, which have tended to stress politics, economics and culture only. There are now a series of articles which address the ways in which the criminal justice system has helped to control female sexuality and maintain patriarchal gender relations. The literature can be subdivided into three categories: women as victims, women as offenders, and prostitution. The last should be placed into a category separate from the other two because, as with contemporary studies of the phenomenon, historians have found that it fits uneasily into the victim/offender dichotomy.

The literature on women as victims of the criminal law is largely about rape, although there is also some writing on other topics. The latter includes a brief and impressionistic account of spousal abuse in late nineteenth and early twentieth-century Alberta (Chapman, T.L. 1988), which is unfortunately all that there is devoted to this topic for Canada, and accounts of the laws relating to abortion and contraception generally in the nineteenth century (Backhouse, 1983B; McLaren, A. 1978: McLaren and McLaren, 1986; see also Parker, 1983). The work on abortion and contraception discusses the process by which such activities were increasingly criminalized in the nineteenth century: for Backhouse (1983B) at least these developments were crucially linked to lobbying by the male medical profession struggling to assert its monopoly control over this and other aspects of its practice. Here paternalism too raises its head, for later nineteenth-century social reform propagated an image of middle-class women as sexually pure (except for procreative activities), the chaste embodiment of domestic virtue. (For an unusual sidelight on this 'social purity' movement, readers should see Warsh (1988), a fascinating study of female commitments to asylums in Ontario which reveals that not a few were committed for some form or another of sexual 'misbehaviour').

Three articles only comprise the literature specifically on rape. There is an account of one particular trial (Teatero, 1979), a brief analysis of the law with some case histories (Olson, 1976), and a much more detailed examination of the offence in the nineteenth century by Backhouse (1983A). Backhouse combines legislative history and statistics on rape convictions with analyses of judicial decisions and comments about social attitudes toward women, and argues that the nineteenth century saw the evolution of rape laws from being almost wholly based on conceptions of the female as a species of male property to being partly based on a realization that 'women deserved protection from sexual abuse in their own right.' Nevertheless the 'predominant thrust' of this change was 'paternalistic,' an aspect of the movement to render women passionless and domesticated (Backhouse, 1983A, p.236).

Outside studies of prostitution, there are only a handful of accounts of female offenders, and none that match up to the work done on, for example, eighteenth-century England (Beattie, 1975). Fingard (1984, 1989A) does little more than provide richly-detailed accounts of the lives of consistent offenders, and is not concerned to talk about the broader meanings of her evidence. Three studies, one of late nineteenth-century Halifax (Price, 1990), one of Toronto in the century between 1859 and 1955 (Boritch and Hagan, 1989), and one of early twentieth-century Calgary (Langdon, 1986), variously offer analyses of the range of female crime, collective profiles of the offending population, and of societal efforts to come to terms with female deviance. All demonstrate the prevalence of public order and 'morals' offences in female crime, and women's relative lack of involvement in more serious criminal activity.

Two further articles examine infanticide alone (Backhouse, 1984; Wright, M.E. 1987), revealing that it was widespread in the nineteenth century and that its perpetrators were as much victims of the societal disapproval of illegitimacy or of their own poverty as they were true 'criminals.' Yet the reaction of male-dominated society to this crime was equivocal: acquittals were fairly frequent and the courts dealt rather leniently with those who were caught and convicted. This can be seen as a further example of paternalism, a recognition that the social order was not threatened by tempering the rigours of the law with a due display of mercy for the inevitably contrite, 'ruined' offender.

The final and most comprehensively-studied aspect of the literature on women and crime deals with prostitution. It includes two statistical studies of its incidence (Backhouse, 1986; Price, 1990), and numerous accounts of the ways in which communities generally and late nineteenth-century social reformers in particular reacted to it (Bedford, 1981; Brooking, 1976; Fingard, 1989B; Gray, 1986; Levesque, 1989; Nilson, 1980; Rotenberg, 1974). The best work is contained in a series of articles by McLaren, J.P. (1986, 1987, 1988, 1990) and a piece by Strange (1988). In the former attitudes to prostitution in theory are linked to the practicalities of enforcement and the social purity movement. In the latter, an argument is developed that contemporary social reformers 'saw no contradiction between sexual reform and the bureaucratic management of urban society,' because 'industrial capitalist development depended in part upon a harmonious work force that could be counted on to reproduce a stable supply of workers and consumers' (Strange, 1988, pp. 255–6).

Almost all of this work shows the equivocal nature of attitudes to prostitution. On the one hand the late nineteenth and early twentieth century saw a 'moral panic' among many urban reformers for whom 'the search for sexual order was central [to the] ... attempts to bring about a moral urban society' (Strange, 1988, p.255). On the other hand then, as now, little effort was made to attack the problem at its roots, either by addressing issues of female poverty or those of male demand. Moreover there is ample evidence that the concern for sexual order and social purity became primarily focused in efforts to make prostitution less visible, not necessarily to eradicate it, and to constrain the sexual appetites of 'respectable' women. In many cities, so long as prostitution was a crime of lower class women the social reformers' concern did not, ultimately, run very deep. The 'social evil' was also considered a necessary evil, to be kept away from tainting the middle classes and to be controlled and regulated but not eradicated. So long as other aspects of middle class female sexuality were kept under control, and women's chastity protected generally, prostitution could be accepted.

iv) *Some Concluding Thoughts and Prescriptions*

An appropriate epilogue to this section is a discussion of the relationship between criminal justice and socio-political authority at a deeper level of social thought and organization. There is much that can be revealed by charting the subtle, continuous relationship between crime, class and political authority, by examining the ways in which the ideology of criminal law and of the 'rule of law' was 'imbricated' (Thompson, 1975) within the social and cultural structure.

In addition to what we know about political dissent, labour unrest, race, and gender, it is now becoming clear, from a number of local studies, that the traditional view of Canadian society, especially Upper Canadian and early western society, as overwhelmingly peaceful and law-abiding presents a false image (Cross, 1971, 1973, 1979; Jamieson, 1979; McNaught, 1974, 1975A; Matthews, 1987A; Morton, 1970, 1980; Thorner 1975, 1979; Thorner and Watson, 1981; Torrance, 1986; Weaver, 1986). But while this represents a sound foundation, and while the literature reviewed in the preceding section conveys a sense of the variety and particularity of

Canadian historical studies of crime, it does not amount to a general thesis about the role of crime and the criminal law in Canadian society. In the pursuit of deeper understandings we could be asking, for example, about the effect that the Canadian 'Tory' tradition (Hartz, 1964, 1969; Horowitz, 1966; Parker, 1986; Wise, 1967, 1974) has had on criminal justice, an issue which is being substantially debated in relation to Canadian legal culture generally (Baker, 1985, 1986, 1988; Howes, 1985; Romney, 1984, 1986, 1987, 1988A, 1988B). It has been some time since McNaught (1975B) discussed the relationship between political trials and the Canadian political tradition, and only McMahon (1988) has explicitly related the debate about Toryism to the operation of the criminal law. He examines the grand jury addresses of Upper Canadian chief justice John Beverley Robinson and demonstrates that they were for him an opportunity to defend the established political order in a time of increasing dissension. Fecteau (1985) provides another hint of broader meaning in his attempts to relate poverty, crime and state social control in a Quebec emerging from the semi-feudalism of the seigneurial regime.

This is not to suggest that research projects should represent assiduous searches for evidence of class suppression, blind to other interpretations. Historians, indeed, need to take up Marquis' (1988) challenge and assess the extent to which the criminal law, criminal justice institutions and the ideology of the rule of law in fact represented genuine consensus values. But this should, if true, be demonstrated, not assumed: the interpretive process is not aided by decisions to study only seven individuals in order to argue that their criminality was the product of individual moral failings (Fingard, 1984).

A further but different kind of problem in the literature is that some historians, rather than developing interpretations linked specifically to Canadian conditions, have preferred to take on board ideas forged for other societies at other times and apply them to the limited Canadian evidence. As noted in the first section of this review, this has been done to explain the penitentiary movement and the rise of the administrative state in the nineteenth century. It has also occurred in a generally well- researched and useful article about the Toronto Police Court (Craven, 1983) in the later nineteenth century, on which is imposed an interpretive framework about the role of courts drawn from Hay's (1975) study of English Assizes in the eighteenth century. The author admits in conclusion that the thesis is not that transferable, but has little to offer in the way of alternative methods of thinking about Canada. This is especially ironic in the light of Hay's own (1981) study of Quebec, in which he argues that his thesis on the nature of the eighteenth-century English criminal law cannot be applied to immediate post-conquest Quebec; the criminal process was much less efficacious as a form of social control in a society unfamiliar with the social and political values that underlay the system in England.

Here I am, of course, returning to a point made in the introduction, that specific historical contexts matter. Just as imperial policy could not succeed in simply transplanting institutions and expecting them to work the same way in a community unfamiliar with their underlying assumptions, historians must be wary of a blind adherence to extra-jurisdictional theorising. Of course there were a host of cultural and institutional similarities between Britain, British North America, and the United States in the nineteenth century, and I am not suggesting that leading theories from other jurisdictions should not be tested against the Canadian evidence. When it is done it can reveal, as in the penitentiary example, cultural and ideological affinities that appear to transcend differences in the material base. As an example of what more could be learned by adaptation of general theories to the Canadian context, consider the operation of the unrefomed system in Nova Scotia, chosen as an illustration because it is the jurisdiction I know best! The colony was settled without an obvious 'landed class,' and by 1800 enjoyed a varied ethnic mix of loyalist ex-Americans, pre-revolutionary New Englanders, Acadians, German Protestants, and Irish and English settlers, most of them scattered around the province in numerous small communities. It was also, particularly in the eighteenth century, a society in which the military played a significant economic and political role: Phillips (1989) argues that it also played a crucial part in the pardon process. How was an imported criminal justice system moulded to suit these conditions and this social structure? One account argues that the system in the Maritimes before 1812 was much more 'democratic,' more concerned with procedural protections for the accused, not seen as an instrument of any class or interest group (Knafla and Chapman, 1983, pp. 253–4). While this may be true, the authors offer no evidence to support their contention. Such assertions will continue to be of little value until historians undertake the kinds of extensive research which marks out the work by Beattie discussed above.

Reading List

Acheson, T.W. *Saint John: The Making of a Colonial Urban Community.* Toronto: University of Toronto Press, 1985

Addington, C.H. *A History of the London Police Force.* London, Ont.: Phelps Publishing, 1980

Aitchison, J.H. 'The Court of Requests in Upper Canada.' *Ontario History* 41 (1949A): 125–32

— 'The Municipal Corporations Act of 1849.' *Canadian Historical Review* 30 (1949B): 107–22

— 'The Courts of Request in Upper Canada, 1780–1850.' Unpublished PHD thesis, University of Western Ontario, 1953

Akins, T.B. *History of Halifax City*. Halifax: Nova Scotia Historical Society, 1895

Allen, R. 'The Social Gospel and the Reform Tradition in Canada, 1890–1928.' *Canadian Historical Review* 49 (1968): 381–99

— 'The Triumph and Decline of Prohibition.' In *Documentary Problems in Canadian History*, Vol. 2: *Post-Confederation*, pp. 185– 214. Edited by J.M. Bumsted. Georgetown, Ont.: Irwin-Dorsey, 1969

— *The Social Passion: Religion and Social Reform in Canada, 1914– 1928*. Toronto: University of Toronto Press, 1971

Allen, R.S. 'A Witness to Murder: The Cypress Hills Massacre and the Conflict of Attitudes Towards the Native People of the Canadian-American West During the 1870s.' In *As Long as the Sun Shines and Water Flows: A Reader in Canadian Native Studies*, pp. 229–46. Edited by I.A. Getty and A.S. Lussier. Vancouver: University of British Columbia Press, 1983

Anderson, F.W. 'Prisons and Prison Reform in the Old Canadian West.' *Canadian Journal of Corrections* 2 (1960): 209–15

— *Saskatchewan's Provincial Police*. Calgary: Frontier Publishing, 1972

— *A Concise History of Capital Punishment in Canada*. Calgary: Frontier Publishing, 1973

Archibald, B. *Prosecuting Officers and the Administration of Criminal Justice in Nova Scotia*. Halifax: Study Paper No.6. Prepared for the Royal Commission on the Donald Marshall Inquiry, 1989

Armstrong, F.H. 'The York Riots of March 23, 1832.' *Ontario History* 55 (1963): 61–72

Atkin, R. *Maintain the Right: The Early History of the NWMP, 1873–1900*. Toronto: Macmillan, 1973

Backhouse, C. 'Nineteenth-Century Canadian Rape Law 1800–1892.' In *Essays in the History of Canadian Law*, Vol. 2, pp. 200–47. Edited by D. Flaherty. Toronto. University of Toronto Press and Osgoode Society, 1983A

— 'Involuntary Motherhood: Abortion, Birth Control and the Law in Nineteenth-Century Canada.' *Windsor Yearbook of Access to Justice* 3 (1983B): 61–130

— 'Desperate Women and Compassionate Courts: Infanticide in

Nineteenth-Century Canada.' *University of Toronto Law Journal* 34 (1984): 447–78

— 'Nineteenth-Century Canadian Prostitution Law: Reflections of a Discriminatory Society.' *Histoire Sociale/Social History* 18 (1986): 387–423

Baehre, R. 'Origins of the Penitentiary System in Upper Canada.' *Ontario History* 69 (1977): 185–207

— 'Paupers and Poor Relief in Upper Canada.' *Historical Papers* (1981): 57–80

— *The Prison System in Atlantic Canada before 1880.* Ottawa: Solicitor General, 1982

— 'The Prison as Factory, the Convict as Worker: A Study of the Mid-Victorian Saint John Penitentiary.' Unpublished paper, 1989

— 'From Bridewell to Federal Penitentiary: Aspects of Prisons in Nova Scotia to 1880.' In *Essays in the History of Canadian Law*, Vol. 3: *Nova Scotia*, pp. 163–99. Edited by P. Girard and J. Phillips. Toronto: University of Toronto Press and Osgoode Society, 1990

Baker, G.B. 'The Reconstitution of Upper Canadian Legal Thought in the Late-Victorian Empire.' *Law and History Review* 3 (1985): 219–92

— 'The Juvenile Advocate Society, 1821–1826: Self-Proclaimed Schoolroom for Upper Canada's Governing Classes.' *Historical Papers* (1986): 74–101

— 'So Elegant a Web: Providential Order and the Rule of Secular Law in Early Nineteenth-Century Upper Canada.' *University of Toronto Law Journal* 38 (1988): 184–205

Banks, M.A. 'The Evolution of the Ontario Courts 1788–1981.' In *Essays in the History of Canadian Law*, Vol. 2, pp. 492–572. Edited by D. Flaherty. Toronto: University of Toronto Press and Osgoode Society, 1983

Barnes, T.G. ' "As Near as May Be Agreeable to the Laws of this Kingdom": Legal Birthright and Legal Baggage at Chebucto, 1749.' In *Law in a Colonial Society: The Nova Scotia Experience*, pp. 1–23. Edited by T.G. Barnes et al. Toronto: Carswell, 1984

Barron, F.L. 'The American Origins of the Temperance Movement in Ontario, 1828–1850.' *Canadian Review of American Studies* 11 (1980): 131–50

— 'Alcoholism, Indians and the Anti-Drink Cause in the Protestant Indian Missions of Upper Canada, 1822–1850.' In *As Long as the Sun Shines and Water Flows: A Reader in Canadian Native Studies*, pp. 191–202.

Edited by I.A. Getty and A.S. Lussier. Vancouver: University of British Columbia Press, 1983

— 'The Indian Pass System in the Canadian West, 1882–1935.' *Prairie Forum* 13 (1988): 25–42

Beahen, W. 'Mob Law Could Not Prevail.' *Alberta History* 29 (1981): 1–7

Beattie, J.M. 'The Criminality of Women in Eighteenth-Century England.' *Journal of Social History* 8 (1975): 80–116

— *Attitudes Towards Crime and Punishment in Upper Canada, 1830–1850: A Documentary Study.* Toronto: Centre of Criminology, University of Toronto, 1977

— *Crime and the Courts in England, 1660–1800.* Princeton: Princeton University Press, 1986

Bedford, J. 'Prostitution in Calgary, 1905–1914.' *Alberta History* 29 (1981): 1–11

Bell, D.G. 'A Note on the Reception of English Statutes in New Brunswick.' *University of New Brunswick Law Journal* 28 (1979): 195–201

— 'The Reception Question and the Constitutional Crisis of the 1790s in New Brunswick.' *University of New Brunswick Law Journal* 29 (1980): 157–73

Bellomo, J.J. 'Upper Canadian attitudes Towards Crime and Punishment, 1832–1851.' *Ontario History* 64 (1972): 11–26

Bennett, P.W. 'Turning Bad Boys Into Good Citizens: The Reforming Impulse of Toronto's Industrial Schools Movement, 1883–1920s.' *Ontario History* 78 (1986): 209–32

— 'Taming Bad Boys of the Dangerous Class: Child Rescue and Restraint at the Victoria Industrial School, 1887–1935.' *Histoire Sociale/Social History* 21 (1988): 71–96

Betke, C. 'The Mounted Police and the Doukhobors in Saskatchewan, 1899–1909.' *Saskatchewan History* 27 (1974): 1–14

— 'Pioneers and Police on the Canadian Prairies, 1885–1914.' *Historical Papers* (1980): 9–32

Betts, G. 'Municipal Government and Politics, 1800–1850.' In *To Preserve and Defend: Essays on Kingston in the Nineteenth Century*, pp. 223–44. Edited By G. Tulchinsky. Montreal and Kingston: McGill-Queen's University Press, 1976

Bindon, K.M. 'Hudson's Bay Company Law: Adam Thom and the Institution of Order in Rupert's Land 1839–1854.' In *Essays in the History of Canadian Law*, Vol. 1, pp. 43–87. Edited by D. Flaherty. Toronto: Univerity of Toronto Press and Osgoode Society, 1981

Bingaman, S. 'The Trials of the White Rebels.' *Saskatchewan History* 25 (1972): 41–54

— 'The Trials of Poundmaker and Big Bear.' *Saskatchewan History* 28 (1975): 81–94

Blackwell, J.D. 'Crime in the London District: 1828–1837: A Case Study of the Effect of the 1833 Reform in Upper Canadian Penal Law.' *Queen's Law Journal* 6 (1980–81): 528–67

Bleasdale, R. 'Class Conflict on the Canals of Upper Canada in the 1840s.' *Labour/Le Travail* 7 (1981): 9–39

Boritch, H. 'Conflict, Compromise and Administrative Convenience: The Police Organisation in Nineteenth-Century Toronto.' *Canadian Journal of Law and Society* 3 (1988): 141–74

Boritch, H. and Hagan, J. 'Men, Women and a Century of Crime in Toronto: Gender, Class and Patterns of Social Control, 1859–1955.' Unpublished paper, 1989

Borthwick, J.D. *History of the Montreal Prison from 1784 to 1886.* Montreal: A. Periard, 1886

Bowker, W.F. 'The Sproule Case: Bloodshed at Kootenay Lake, 1885.' In *Law and Justice in a New Land: Essays in Western Canadian Legal History*, pp. 233–66. Edited by L.A. Knafla. Toronto: Carswell, 1986

Boyd, N. 'The Origins of Canadian Narcotics Legislation: The Process of Criminalisation in Historical Context.' *Dalhousie Law Journal* 8 (1984): 102–36

— *The Last Dance: Murder in Canada.* Scarborough, Ont.: Prentice Hall, 1988

Boyer, R. *Les crimes et les chatiments au Canada français du XVIIe au XXe siècle.* Montreal: Cercle du livre de France, 1966

Breen, D.H. 'The Mounted Police and the Ranching Frontier.' In *Men in Scarlet*, pp. 115–37. Edited by H.A. Dempsey. Calgary: McClelland and Stewart West, 1974

Brode, P. 'In the Matter of John Anderson: Canadian Courts and the Fugitive Slave.' *Law Society of Upper Canada Gazette* 14 (1980): 92–7

— 'Grand Jury Addresses of the Early Canadian Judges in an Age of Reform.' *Law Society of Upper Canada Gazette* 23 (1989A): 130–47

— *The Odyssey of John Anderson.* Toronto: University of Toronto Press and Osgoode Society, 1989B

Brooking, L.W. 'Prostitution in Toronto, 1911.' In *The Proper Sphere: Women's Place in Canadian Society*, pp. 241–249. Edited by R. Cook and W. Mitchinson. Toronto: Oxford University Press, 1976

Brown, D.H. 'The Meaning of Treason in 1885.' *Saskatchewan History* 28 (1975): 65–73

— 'Unpredictable and Uncertain: Criminal Law in the Canadian North West Before 1886.' *Alberta Law Review* 17 (1979): 497–512

— 'The Craftsmanship of Bias: Sedition and the Winnipeg General Strike.' *Manitoba Law Journal* 14 (1984): 1–33

— *The Genesis of the Canadian Criminal Code of 1892.* Toronto: University of Toronto Press and Osgoode Society, 1989

Brown, L. and Brown, C. *An Unauthorised History of the RCMP.* Toronto: James Lewis and Samuel, 1973

Brown, T.E. 'The Origins of the Asylum in Upper Canada, 1830–1839: Towards an Interpretation.' *Canadian Bulletin of Medical History* 1 (1984): 27–58

Bulmer, J.T. 'Trials for Treason in 1776–1777.' *Collections of the Nova Scotia Historical Society* 1 (1879): 110–118

Burnet, J.R. 'The Urban Community and Changing Moral Standards.' In *Studies in Canadian Social History*, pp. 298–325. Edited by B. Horn and R. Sabourin. Toronto: McClelland and Stewart, 1974

Cahill, J.B. 'Richard Gibbons' 'Review' of the Administration of Justice in Nova Scotia, 1774.' *University of New Brunswick Law Journal* 37 (1988): 35–58

Calder, W.A. 'The Federal Penitentiary System in Canada, 1867–1899.' Unpublished PHD thesis, University of Toronto, 1979

— 'Convict Life in Canadian Federal Penitentiaries, 1867–1900.' In *Crime and Criminal Justice in Europe and Canada*, pp. 297–318. Edited by L.A. Knafla. Waterloo: Wilfrid Laurier University Press, 1981

Campbell, M.F. *A Century of Crime: The Development of Crime Detection Methods in Canada.* Toronto: McClelland and Stewart, 1970

Carpenter, J.H. *The Badge and the Blotter: A History of the Lethbridge Police.* Lethbridge: Historical Society of Alberta, 1975

Chandler, D. *Capital Punishment in Canada: A Sociological Study in Repressive Law.* Toronto: McClelland and Stewart, 1976

Chapman, J. 'The Mid-Nineteenth-Century Temperance Movement in New Brunswick and Maine.' *Canadian Historical Review* 35 (1954): 43–60

Chapman, T.L. 'Drug Usage and the Victoria Daily Colonist: The Opium Smokers of Western Canada.' In *Proceedings of the Canadian Society for Legal History*, pp. 60–75. Edited by L.A. Knafla. Toronto: 1971

— 'Drug use in Alberta.' *Alberta History* 24 (1976): 18–27

— 'The Anti-Drug Crusade in Western Canada.' In *Law and Society in Canada in Historical Perspective*, pp. 89–115. Edited by D. Bercuson and L.A. Knafla. Calgary: University of Calgary Press, 1979

— 'An Oscar Wilde Type: The Abominable Crime of Buggery in Western Canada, 1890–1920.' *Criminal Justice History* 4 (1983): 97–118

— 'Male Homosexuality: Legal Restraints and Social Attitudes in Western Canada, 1890–1920.' In *Law and Justice in a New Land: Essays in Western Canadian Legal History*, pp. 277–92. Edited by L.A. Knafla. Toronto: Carswell, 1986

— ' "Till Death Do Us Part": Wife Beating in Alberta, 1905–1920.' *Alberta History* 36 (1988): 13–22

Chartrand, M. 'The First Canadian Trade Union Legislation: An Historical Perspective.' *Ottawa Law Review* 16 (1984): 267–96

Chisholm, J.A. 'Our First Trial for Murder: R. v. Peter Cartcel.' *Canadian Bar Review* 18 (1940): 385–89

Chunn, D. 'Good Men Work Hard: Convict Labour in Kingston Penitentiary, 1835–1850.' *Canadian Criminal Forum* 4 (1981): 13–22

Cook, R. *The Regenerators: Social Criticism in Late Victorian English Canada.* Toronto: University of Toronto Press, 1985

Cook, S.J. 'Canadian Narcotics Legislation, 1908–1923.' *Canadian Review of Sociology and Anthropology* 6 (1969): 36–46

Cote, J. 'The Reception of English Law into Alberta.' *Alberta Law Review* 3 (1964): 262–92

— 'The Reception of English Law.' *Alberta Law Review* 15 (1977): 29–92

Coulter, R. 'Not to Punish But to Reform: Juvenile Delinquency and the Children's Protection Act in Alberta, 1909–1929.' In *Studies in Childhood History: A Canadian Perspective*, pp. 167–84. Edited by P. Rooke and R. Schnell. Calgary: Detselig Enterprises, 1982

Craven, P. 'The Law of Master and Servant in Mid-Nineteenth-Century Ontario.' In *Essays in the History of Canadian Law*, Vol. 1, pp. 175–211. Edited by D. Flaherty. Toronto: University of Toronto Press and Osgoode Society, 1981

— 'Law and Ideology: The Toronto Police Court 1850–1880.' In *Essays in the History of Canadian Law*, Vol. 1, pp. 248–307. Edited by D. Flaherty. Toronto: University of Toronto Press and Osgoode Society, 1983

— 'Labour Conspiracies in Toronto 1854–1872.' *Labour/Le Travail* 14 (1984): 49–70

Cross, M.S. 'Stony Monday 1849: The Rebellion Losses Riots in Bytown.' *Ontario History* 63 (1971): 177–90

— 'The Shiners War: Social Violence in the Ottawa Valley in the 1830s.' *Canadian Historical Review* 54 (1973): 1–26

— 'Violence and Authority: The Case of Bytown.' In *Law and Society in Canada in Historical Perspective*, pp. 5–22. Edited by D. Bercuson and L.A. Knafla. Calgary: University of Calgary Press, 1979

— ' "The Laws are Like Cobwebs": Popular Resistance to Authority in Mid-Nineteenth-Century British North America.' In *Law in a Colonial Society: The Nova Scotia Experience*, pp. 103–23. Edited by T.G. Barnes et al. Toronto: Carswell, 1984

Cruickshank, E.A. 'John Beverley Robinson and the Trials for Treason in 1814.' *Ontario Historical Society Papers and Records* 25 (1929): 191–219

Decarie, M.G. 'Something Old, Something New: Aspects of Prohibitionism in Ontario in the 1890s.' In *Oliver Mowat's Ontario*, pp. 154–71. Edited by D. Swainson. Toronto: Macmillan, 1972

— 'Paved with Good Intentions: The Prohibitionists' Road to Racism in Ontario.' *Ontario History* 66 (1974): 15–22

Denny, C.E. *The Law Marches West*. Toronto: Dent, 1939

Desaulniers, J. 'Les peine de mort dans la Législation criminelle de 1760 à 1892.' *Revue générale de droit* 1 (1977): 141–84

Dick, E. 'From Temperance to Prohibition in Nineteenth-Century Nova Scotia.' *Dalhousie Review* 61 (1981): 530–52

Donaghey, S. *A History of the City of Edmonton Police Department: Blue, Red and Gold, 1892–1972*. Edmonton: City of Edmonton Police Department, 1972

Eadie, J.A. 'The Navvy Riots on the N.T.Q.' *Papers and Records of the Lennox and Addington Historical Society* 15 (1976): 127–9

Edmison, J.A. 'Some Aspects of Nineteenth-Century Canadian Prisons.' In *Crime and Its Treatment in Canada*, pp. 347–69. Edited by W.T. McGrath. Toronto: Macmillan, 1976

Edwards, J.Ll.J. 'The Advent of English (Not French) Criminal Law and Procedure into Canada: A Close Call in 1774.' *Criminal Law Quarterly* 26 (1984): 464–82

Ekstedt, J. and Griffiths, C. *Corrections in Canada: Policy and Practice*. Toronto: Butterworths, 1984

Elliott, J.K. 'Crime and Punishment in Early Upper Canada.' *Ontario Historical Society Papers and Records* 27 (1931): 335–40

Farr, M.L. 'The Organisation of the Judicial System in the Colonies of

Vancouver Island and British Columbia, 1849–1871.' *University of British Columbia Law Review* 3 (1967): 1–35

Fecteau, J-M. 'Régulation sociale et répression de la déviance au Bas-Canada au tournant du 19e siècle (1791–1815).' *Revue d'histoire de l'Amérique française* 38 (1985): 499–521

Fetherstonhaugh, R.C. *The Royal Canadian Mounted Police.* New York: Carrick and Evans, 1938

Fingard, J. *Jack in Port: Sailortowns of Eastern Canada.* Toronto: McClelland and Stewart, 1982

— 'Jailbirds in Mid-Victorian Halifax.' In *Law in a Colonial Society: The Nova Scotia Experience*, pp. 81–102. Edited by T.G. Barnes et al. Toronto: Carswell, 1984

— *The Dark Side of Life in Victorian Halifax.* Porter's Lake, N.S.: Pottersfield Press, 1989A

— 'Evangelical Social Work in Canada, 1890–1920.' In *Social Welfare 1850–1950: Australia, Argentina and Canada Compared*, pp. 206–40. Edited by D.C.M. Platt. Basingstoke: Macmillan, 1989B

Finlay, J.L. and Sprague, D.N. *The Structure of Canadian History.* Scarborough: 2nd ed. Prentice-Hall, 1984

Fisher, R. *Contact and Conflict: Indian-European Relations in British Columbia, 1774–1890.* Vancouver: University of British Columbia Press, 1977

Flaherty, D. 'Writing Canadian Legal History: An Introduction.' In *Essays in the History of Canadian Law*, Vol. 1, pp. 3–42. Edited by D. Flaherty. Toronto: University of Toronto Press and Osgoode Society, 1981

Flannagan, T. *Riel and the Rebellion: 1885 Reconsidered.* Saskatoon: Western Producer Prairie Books, 1983

Flannagan, T. and Watson, N. 'The Riel Trial Revisited: Criminal Procedure and the Law in 1885.' *Saskatchewan History* 34 (1981): 57–73

Forbes, E. 'Prohibition and the Social Gospel in Nova Scotia.' *Acadiensis* 1 (1971): 11–36

Foster, H. 'The Kamloops Outlaws and Commissions of Assize in Nineteenth-Century British Columbia.' In *Essays in the History of Canadian Law*, Vol. 2, pp. 308–64. Edited by D. Flaherty. Toronto: University of Toronto Press and Osgoode Society, 1983

— 'The Struggle for the Supreme Court: Law and Politics in British Columbia, 1871–1885.' In *Law and Justice in a New Land: Essays in*

Western Canadian Legal History, pp. 167–213. Edited by L.A. Knafla. Toronto: Carswell, 1986

— 'Shooting the Elephant: Historians and the Problem of Frontier Lawlessness.' Unpublished paper presented to the British Legal History Conference, 1985

— 'Long Distance Justice: The Criminal Jurisdiction of Canadian Courts West of the Canadas, 1763–1859.' *American Journal of Legal History* 34 (1990): 1–48

Foster, J. 'The Montreal Riots of 1849.' *Canadian Historical Review* 32 (1951): 61–65

Foucault, M. *Discipline and Punish: The Birth of the Prison.* New York: Pantheon Books, 1978

Francis, D. 'The Development of the Lunatic Asylum in the Maritime Provinces.' *Acadiensis* 6 (1977): 23–38

Fraser, B.J. *The Social Uplifters: Presbyterian Progressives and the Social Gospel in Canada, 1875–1915.* Waterloo: Wilfrid Laurier University Press, 1988

Friedland, M.L. 'R.S. Wright's Model Criminal Code: A Forgotten Chapter in the History of the Criminal Law.' *Oxford Journal of Legal Studies* 1 (1981): 307–46

— *A Century of Criminal Justice: Perspectives on the Development of Canadian Law.* Toronto: Carswell, 1984

— *The Case of Valentine Shortis: A True Story of Crime and Politics in Canada.* Toronto: University of Toronto Press and Osgoode Society, 1985

Garland, M.A. and Talman, J.J. 'Pioneer Drinking Habits and the Rise of the Temperance Agitation in Upper Canada Prior to 1840.' In *Aspects of Nineteenth-Century Ontario*, pp. 171–193. Edited by F.H. Armstrong. Toronto: University of Toronto Press, 1974

Getty, I. 'The Role of Mounted Police Outposts in Southern Alberta.' In *Men in Scarlet*, pp. 23–35. Edited by H.A. Dempsey. Calgary: McClelland and Stewart West, 1974

Gigeroff, A.K. 'The Evolution of Criminal Legislation with Respect to Homosexuality, Pedophilia and Exhibitionism.' *Criminal Law Quarterly* 8 (1966): 445–54

Gilkes, M. and Symons, M. *Calgary's Finest: A History of the City Police Force.* Calgary: Century Calgary Publications, 1975

Girard, P.V. 'The Rise and Fall of Urban Justice in Halifax, 1815–1886.' *Nova Scotia Historical Review* 8 (1988): 57–71

Goldring, P. 'The Cypress Hills Massacre: A Century's Retrospect.' *Saskatchewan History* 26 (1973): 81–102

Gordon, R.W. 'J. Willard Hurst and the Common Law Tradition in American Legal Historiography.' *Law and Society Review* 10 (1975): 44–55

Gough, B.M. 'Keeping British Columbia British: The Law and Order Question on a Gold Mining Frontier.' *Huntington Library Quarterly* 38 (1975): 269–80

— 'Official Uses of Violence Against Coast Indians in Colonial British Columbia.' In *Pacific Northwest Themes: Historical Essays in Honour of Keith A. Murray*, pp. 63–85. Edited by J.W. Scott. Bellingham, Wash.: Washington State University Press, 1978A

— 'Send a Gunboat: Checking Slavery and Controlling Liquor Traffic Among Coast Indians of British Columbia in the 1860s.' *Pacific Northwest Quarterly* 69 (1978B): 159–68

Graff, H. 'Crime and Punishment in the Nineteenth Century: A New Look at the Criminal.' *Journal of Interdisciplinary History* 7 (1977A): 477–91

— 'Pauperism, Misery and Vice: Illiteracy and Criminality in the Nineteenth Century.' *Journal of Social History* 11 (1977B): 245–68

Grant, B.J. *Six For the Hangman: Unforgettable New Brunswick Murders.* Fredericton: Fiddlehead Books, 1983

Gray, J.H. *Booze: The Impact of Whiskey on the Prairies.* Toronto: McClelland and Stewart, 1972

— *Red Lights on the Prairies.* Saskatoon: Western Producer Prairie Books, 1986

Green, M. 'A History of Canadian Narcotics Control: The Formative Years.' *University of Toronto Faculty of Law Review* 37 (1979): 42–79

Green, M. and Solomon, R. 'The First Century: The History of Non-Medical Opiate Use and Control Policies in Canada, 1870–1970.' *University of Western Ontario Law Review* 20 (1982): 307–36

Greenberg, D. 'Crime, Law Enforcement and Social Change in Colonial America.' *American Journal of Legal History* 26 (1982): 293–325

Greenwood, F.M. 'L'insurrection apprehendée et l'administration de la justice au Canada: Le point de vue d'un historien.' *Revue d'histoire de l'Amérique française* 34 (1980): 57–93

— 'The Chartrand Murder Trial: Rebellion and Repression in Lower Canada, 1837–1839.' *Criminal Justice History* 5 (1984): 129–59

— 'The General Court-Martial of 1838–1839 in Lower Canada: An Abuse of Justice.' In *Canadian Perspectives on Law and Society: Issues in Legal History*, pp. 249–90. Edited by W. Pue and J.B. Wright. Ottawa: Carleton University Press, 1988

Gressley, G.M. 'Lord Selkirk and the Canadian Courts.' In *Canadian History Before Confederation: Essays and Interpretations*, pp. 277–93. Edited by J.M. Bumsted. Georgetown, Ont.: Irwin-Dorsey, 1979

Hallowell, G. *Prohibition in Ontario, 1919–1923*. Ottawa: Ontario Historical Society, 1972

Harring, S.L. 'Rich Men of the Country: Canadian Law in the Land of the Copper Inuit.' *Ottawa Law Review* 21 (1989): 1–64

Hartz, L. *The Founding of New Societies: Studies in the History of the United States, Latin America, South Africa, Canada and Australia*. New York: Harcourt Brace, 1964

— 'Violence and Legality in the Fragment Cultures.' *Canadian Historical Review* 50 (1969): 123–40

Harvey, H. 'The Early Administration of Justice in the North West.' *Alberta Law Quarterly* 1 (1934): 1–15

— 'Some Further Notes on the Early Administration of Justice in the North West.' *Alberta Law Quarterly* 2 (1935): 171–94

Hatch, F.J. 'The British Columbia Police: 1858–1871.' Unpublished MA thesis, University of British Columbia, 1955

Hay, D. 'Property, Authority and the Criminal Law.' In *Albion's Fatal Tree: Crime and Society in Eighteenth-Century England*, pp. 17–63. Edited by D. Hay et al. London: Allen Lane, 1975

— 'The Meanings of the Criminal Law in Quebec, 1764–1774.' In *Crime and Criminal Justice in Europe and Canada*, pp. 77–110. Edited by L.A. Knafla. Waterloo: University of Wilfrid Laurier Press, 1981

Haydon, A.L. *The Riders of the Plains: A Record of the Royal North-West Mounted Police of Canada, 1873–1910*. Edmonton: Hurtig Publishers, 1971

Herbert, R.G. 'A Brief History of the Introduction of English Law into British Columbia.' *University of British Columbia Legal Notes* 2 (1954): 93–101

Hett, R. 'Judge Willis and the Court of King's Bench in Upper Canada.' *Ontario History* 65 (1973): 19–30

Hindus, M. *Prison and Plantation: Crime, Justice and Authority in Massachusetts and South Carolina, 1767–1878*. Chapel Hill: University of North Carolina Press, 1981

Hirsch, A. 'From Pillory to Penitentiary: The Rise of Criminal Incarceration in Early Massachusetts.' *Michigan Law Review* 80 (1982): 1179–1269

Hogg, P. *Constitutional Law of Canada*. 2nd ed. Toronto: Carswell, 1985

Homel, G.H. 'Denison's Law: Criminal Justice and the Police Court in Toronto, 1877–1921.' *Ontario History* 73 (1981): 171–86

Horowitz, G. 'Conservatism, Liberalism and Socialism in Canada: An Interpretation.' *Canadian Journal of Economics and Political Science* 32 (1966): 143–71

Horrall, S.W. 'Sir John A. MacDonald and the Mounted Police Force for the Northwest Territories.' *Canadian Historical Review* 53 (1972): 179–200

— *The Pictorial History of the Royal Canadian Mounted Police*. Toronto: McGraw Hill Ryerson, 1973

— 'A Policeman's Lot is Not a Happy One: The Mounted Police and Prohibition in the North-West Territories, 1874–1891.' *Transactions of the Historical and Scientific Society of Manitoba* 30 (1974): 5–16

— 'The Royal Northwest Mounted Police and Labour Unrest in Western Canada, 1919.' *Canadian Historical Review* 61 (1980): 169–90

Houston, S.E. 'Victorian Origins of Juvenile Delinquency: A Canadian Experience.' *History of Education Quarterly* 12 (1972A): 254–80

— 'Politics, Schools and Social Change in Upper Canada.' *Canadian Historical Review* 53 (1972B): 249–71

— 'The Impetus to Reform: Urban Crime, Poverty and Ignorance in Ontario, 1850–1875.' Unpublished PHD thesis, University of Toronto, 1974

— 'The 'Waifs and Strays' of a Late Victorian City: Juvenile Delinquents in Toronto.' In *Childhood and the Family in Canadian History*, pp. 129–42. Edited by J. Parr. Toronto: McClelland and Stewart, 1982

Howes, D. 'Property, God and Nature in the Thought of Sir John Beverley Robinson.' *McGill Law Journal* 30 (1985): 365–414

Hutchinson, L. ' "Not To Be Named Among Christians'': Buggery Trials in Saint John, N.B., 1806.' Unpublished paper, 1989

Hutchinson, R. *A Century of Service: A History of the Winnipeg Police Force, 1874–1974*. Winnipeg: City of Winnipeg Police Force, 1974

Ignatieff, M. *A Just Measure of Pain: The Penitentiary in the Industrial Revolution*. New York: Pantheon Books, 1978

— 'State, Civil Society and Total Institutions: A Critique of Recent Social Histories of Punishment.' In *Social Control and the State*, pp. 75–105.

Edited by S. Cohen and A. Scull. Oxford: Martin Robertson, 1983

Inglis, R.E. 'The Ox Case.' *Nova Scotia Historical Quarterly* 1 (1972): 31–40

James, J.T.L. 'Gaols and their Goals in Manitoba, 1870–1970.' *Canadian Journal of Criminology* 20 (1978): 34–42

Jamieson, B. 'Some Reflections on Violence and the Law in Industrial Relations.' In *Law and Society in Canada in Historical Perspective*, pp. 141–55. Edited by D.J. Bercuson and L.A. Knafla. Calgary: University of Calgary Press, 1979

Jennings, J.N. 'Policemen and Poachers: Indian Relations on the Ranching Frontier.' In *Frontier Calgary*, pp. 87–99. Edited by A.W. Rasporich and H.W. Klassen. Calgary: McClelland and Stewart West, 1975

Johnson, W.S. 'The Origins of the Law of the Province of Quebec.' *Revue du Droit* 13 (1934): 218–29

Johnstone, W.F. and Henheffer, B.W. 'History of Treatment in Canadian Penitentiaries.' In *Social Problems: A Canadian Profile*, pp. 449–54. Edited by R. Laskin. Toronto: McGraw-Hill, 1964

Jones, A. 'Closing Penetanguishene Reformatory: An Attempt to Deinstitutionalize Treatment of Juvenile Offenders in Early Twentieth-Century Ontario.' *Ontario History* 70 (1978): 227–44

Jones, J.E. *Pioneer Crimes and Punishments in Toronto and the Home District*. Toronto: George Morang, 1924

Katz, L. 'Some Legal Consequences of the Winnipeg General Strike.' *Manitoba Law Journal* 4 (1970): 39–52

Kavanaugh, K.W. 'The Alberta Provincial Police.' *RCMP Quarterly* 38 (1973): 28–31

Kealey, G.S. 'The Orange Order in Toronto: Religious Riot and the Working Class.' In *Essays in Canadian Working Class History*, pp. 13–34. Edited by G. Kealey and P. Warrian. Toronto: McClelland and Stewart, 1970

— *Toronto Workers Respond to Industrial Capitalism, 1867–1892*. Toronto: McClelland and Stewart, 1980

Kealey, G.S. and Palmer, B. *Dreaming of What Might Be: The Knights of Labour in Ontario, 1880–1900*. Toronto: New Hogtown Press, 1987

Kealey, L. 'Patterns of Punishment: Massachusetts in the Eighteenth Century.' *American Journal of Legal History* 30 (1986): 163–86

Keddy, E.R. 'A Remarkable Murder Trial: Rex v. Sinnisiak.' *University of Pennsylvania Law Review* 100 (1954): 48–75

Kelly, N. and Kelly, W. *The Royal Canadian Mounted Police: A Century of History, 1873–1973*. Edmonton: Hurtig Publishers, 1973

Keshen, J. 'Cloak and Dagger: Canada West's Secret Police, 1864–1867.' *Ontario History* 79 (1987): 353–81

Kirkpatrick, A.M. 'Jails in Historical Perspective.' *Canadian Journal of Corrections* 6 (1964): 405–18

Klassen, H.C. 'The Mounties and the Historians.' In *Men in Scarlet*, pp. 175–86. Edited by H.A. Dempsey. Calgary: McClelland and Stewart West, 1974

— 'Social Troubles in Calgary in the Mid-1890s.' *Urban History Review* 3 (1975): 8–16

Knafla, L.A. 'Crime, Criminal Law and Justice in Canadian History: A Select Bibliography, Origins to 1940.' In *Law and Society in Canada in Historical Perspective*, pp. 157–71. Edited by D.J. Bercuson and L.A. Knafla. Calgary: University of Calgary Press, 1979

— 'Aspects of the Criminal Law, Crime, Criminal Process and Punishment in Europe and Canada, 1500–1935.' In *Crime and Criminal Justice in Europe and Canada*, pp. 1–15. Edited by L.A. Knafla. Waterloo: Wilfrid Laurier University Press, 1981

— 'From Oral to Written Memory: The Common Law Tradition in Western Canada.' In *Law and Justice in a New Land: Essays in Western Canadian Legal History*, pp. 31–77. Edited by L.A. Knafla. Toronto: Carswell, 1986

Knafla, L.A. and Chapman, T.L. 'Criminal Justice in Canada: A Comparative Study of the Maritimes and Lower Canada 1760–1812.' *Osgoode Hall Law Journal* 21 (1983): 245–74

Koester, C.B. 'The Queen vs. George Bennett: Nicholas Flood Davin's Defence of George Brown's Assassin.' *Ontario History* 64 (1972): 221–38

Kroll, R.E. 'Confines, Wards and Dungeons.' *Collections of the Nova Scotia Historical Society* 40 (1972): 93–107

Langbein, J.H. 'Albion's Fatal Flaws.' *Past and Present* 98 (1983): 96–120

Langdon, M.E. 'Female Crime in Calgary, 1914–1941.' In *Law and Justice in a New Land: Essays in Western Canadian Legal History*, pp. 293–309. Edited by L.A. Knafla. Toronto: Carswell, 1986

Lefebvre, F. 'L'histoire du guet à Montréal.' *Revue d'histoire de l'Amérique française* 6 (1952): 263–73

— 'La vie à la prison de Montréal au XIXe siècle.' *Revue d'histoire de l'Amérique française* 7 (1954): 524–37

Levesque, A. 'Eteindre le red light: reformateurs et la prostitution à Montréal, 1865–1925.' *Urban History Review* 17 (1989): 191–201

Levy, J.C. 'The Poor Law in Early Upper Canada.' In *Law and Society in Canada in Historical Perspective*, pp. 23–44. Edited by D.J. Bercuson and L.A. Knafla. Calgary: University of Calgary Press, 1979

Lewthwaite, S. 'Keepers of the Peace: The Magistrates of Georgia Township, 1830–1850.' Unpublished MA thesis, University of Toronto, 1987

L'Heureux, J. 'L'organisation judiçaire au Quebec de 1764 à 1774.' *Revue générale de droit* 1 (1970): 266–331

MacLeod, R.C. 'The Mounted Police and Politics.' In *Men in Scarlet*, pp. 95–114. Edited by H.A. Dempsey. Calgary: McClelland and Stewart West, 1974

— *The NWMP and Law Enforcement, 1873–1905*. Toronto: McClelland and Stewart, 1976A

— 'Canadianising the West: The NWMP as Agents of the National Policy, 1873–1905.' In *Essays in Western History*, pp. 101–10. Edited by L.H. Thomas. Edmonton: University of Alberta Press, 1976B

— 'The Shaping of Canadian Criminal Law, 1892–1902.' *Historical Papers* (1978): 64–75

—, ed. *Lawful Authority: Readings on the History of Criminal Justice in Canada*. Toronto: Copp Clark Pitman, 1988

Marquis, G. 'The Police Force in Saint John, New Brunswick, 1860– 1900.' Unpublished MA thesis, University of New Brunswick, 1982

— 'A Machine of Oppression Under the Guise of the Law: The Saint John Police Establishment.' *Acadiensis* 16 (1986): 58–77

— 'The Contours of Canadian Urban Justice, 1830–1875.' *Urban History Review* 15 (1987): 126–73

— 'Working Men in Uniform: The Early Twentieth-Century Toronto Police.' *Histoire Sociale/Social History* 20 (1987): 259–277

— 'Enforcing the Law: The Charlottetown Police Force.' In *Gaslights, Epidemics and Vagabond Cows: Charlottetown in the Victorian Era*, pp. 86–102. Edited by D. Baldwin and T. Spira. Charlottetown: Ragweed Press, 1988

— 'The Toronto Police Institution, 1910–1940.' Unpublished PHD thesis, Queen's University, 1988

— 'Doing Justice to 'British Justice': Law, Ideology and Canadian Historiography.' In *Canadian Perspectives on Law and Society: Issues in Legal History*, pp. 43–69. Edited by W. Pue and J.B. Wright. Ottawa: Carleton University Press, 1988

— 'Police Unionism in Early Twentieth-Century Toronto.' *Ontario History* 81 (2, June 1989): 109–28

Masters, D.C. *The Winnipeg General Strike*. Toronto: University of Toronto Press, 1950

Matthews, W.T. 'The Myth of the Peaceable Kingdom: Upper Canadian Society in the Early Victorian Period.' *Queen's Quarterly* 94 (1987A): 384–401

— 'Local Government and the Regulation of the Public Market in Upper Canada, 1800–1860: The Moral Economy of the Poor.' *Ontario History* 79 (1987B): 297–326

McCaskill, D. 'Native People and the Justice System.' In *As Long as the Sun Shines and the Water Flows: A Reader in Canadian Native Studies*, pp. 288–298. Edited by I.A. Getty and A.S. Lussier. Vancouver: University of British Columbia Press, 1983

McCormack, R. *Reformers, Rebels and Revolutionaries: The Western Canadian Radical Movement, 1899–1919*. Toronto: University of Toronto Press, 1977

McGahan, P. *Crime and Policing in Maritime Canada: Chapters from the Urban Records*. Fredericton: Goose Lane, 1988A

— 'Crime and Policing in Charlottetown.' Halifax: Atlantic Institute of Criminology, 1988B. (Occasional Paper Series)

— *Reconstructing Patterns of Crime in Charlottetown, 1875–1900*. Digby, NS: n.p. 1988C

— 'Crime and Policing in Late Nineteenth and Early Twentieth Century Kings County, Nova Scotia.' Halifax: Atlantic Institute of Criminology, 1988D. (Occasional Paper Series)

— *Killers, Thieves, Tramps and Sinners*. Fredericton: Goose Lane, 1989A

— 'Crime and Policing in Late Nineteenth Century Halifax.' Halifax: Atlantic Institute of Criminology, 1989B. (Occasional Paper Series)

— 'The Reorganisation of the Halifax Police Force, 1893.' Halifax: Atlantic Institute of Criminology, 1989C. (Occasional Paper Series)

— 'Disciplining the Guardians: The Halifax Police Force 1905–1913.' Halifax: Atlantic Institute of Criminology, 1989D. (Occasional Paper Series)

McLaren, A. 'Birth Control and Abortion in Canada, 1870–1920.' *Canadian Historical Review* 59 (1978): 319–40

McLaren, A. and McLaren, A.T. *The Bedroom and the State: The Changing Practice and Politics of Contraception and Abortion in Canada, 1880–1980*. Toronto: McClelland and Stewart, 1986

McLaren, J.P. 'Chasing the Social Evil: Moral Fervour and the Evolution of Canada's Prostitution Laws, 1867–1917.' *Canadian Journal of Law and Society* 1 (1986): 125–65

— 'White Slavers: The Reform of Canada's Prostitution Laws and Patterns of Enforcement, 1900–1920.' *Criminal Justice History* 8 (1987): 53–119

— 'The Canadian Magistracy and the Anti-White Slavery Campaign, 1900–1920.' In *Canadian Perspectives on Law and Society: Issues in Legal History*, pp. 329–53. Edited by W. Pue and J.B. Wright. Ottawa: Carleton University Press, 1988

McLaren, J.P. and Lowman, J. 'Enforcing Canadian Prostitution Laws, 1892–1920: Rhetoric and Practice.' In *Securing Compliance*, pp. 21–78. Edited by M.L. Friedland. Toronto: University of Toronto Press, 1990

McMahon, D.J. 'Law and Public Authority: Sir John Beverley Robinson and the Purposes of the Criminal Law.' *University of Toronto Faculty of Law Review* 46 (1988): 390–423

McNaught, K. 'Violence in Canadian History.' In *Studies in Canadian Social History*, pp. 376–91. Edited by M. Horn and R. Sabourin. Toronto: McClelland and Stewart, 1974

— 'Collective Violence in Canadian History: Some Problems of Definition and Research.' In *Proceedings of the Workshop on Violence in Canadian Society*, pp. 165–77. Toronto: Centre of Criminology, University of Toronto, 1975A

— 'Political Trials and the Canadian Political Tradition.' In *Courts and Trials: A Multi-Disciplinary Approach*, pp. 137–61. Edited by M.L. Friedland. Toronto: University of Toronto Press, 1975B

Mewett, A. 'The Criminal Law, 1867–1967.' *Canadian Bar Review* 45 (1967): 726–740

Morel, A. 'La Réaction des Canadiens devant l'administration de la justice de 1764 à 1774.' *Revue de barreau* 20 (1960): 53–63

— 'La réception du droit criminelle Anglais au Québec (1760– 1892).' *Revue juridique Thémis* 13 (1978A): 449–541

— 'Les crimes et les peines: évolution des mentalités au Québec au 19ième siècle.' *Revue de droit de l'université de Sherbrooke*, 8 (1978B): 384–96

Morgan, E. 'The North-West Mounted Police: Internal Problems and Public Criticisms, 1874–1883.' *Saskatchewan History* 26 (1973): 41–62

Morrison, W.R. 'The North-West Mounted Police and the Klondike Gold Rush.' *Journal of Contemporary History* 9 (1974): 93–105

— *Showing the Flag: The Mounted Police and Canadian Sovereignity in the North, 1894–1925.* Vancouver: University of British Columbia Press, 1985

Morrow, W.G. 'Adapting Our Justice System to the Cultural Needs of Canada's North.' In *Crime and Criminal Justice in Europe and Canada*, pp. 257–71. Edited by L.A. Knafla. Waterloo: Wilfrid Laurier University Press, 1981

Morton, D. 'Aid to the Civil Power: The Canadian Militia in Support of Social Order, 1867–1914.' *Canadian Historical Review* 51 (1970): 407–25

—, ed. *The Queen v. Louis Riel.* Toronto: University of Toronto Press, 1974

— 'Cavalry or Police: Keeping the Peace on Two Adjacent Frontiers, 1870–1900.' *Journal of Canadian Studies* 12 (1977): 27–37

— 'Kicking and Complaining: Demobilisation Riots in the Canadian Expeditionary Force, 1918–1919.' *Canadian Historical Review* 61 (1980): 334–60

Moyles, R.G. *British Law and Arctic Men: The Celebrated 1917 Murder Trials of Sinnisiak and Uluksuk.* Saskatoon: Western Producer Prairie Books, 1979

Munro, J.A. 'British Columbia and the 'Chinese Evil': Canada's First Anti-Asiatic Immigration Law.' *Journal of Canadian Studies* 6 (1971): 42–51

Murdoch, B. *Epitome of the Laws of Nova Scotia.* Halifax: Joseph Howe, 1832

Murray, G.F. 'Cocaine Use in the Era of Social Reform: The Natural History of a Social Problem in Canada, 1880–1911.' *Canadian Journal of Law and Society* 2 (1987): 29–44

Neatby, H.M. *The Administration of Justice Under the Quebec Act.* Minneapolis: University of Minnesota Press, 1937

Needham, H.G. 'Historical Perspectives on the Federal-Provincial Split in Jurisdiction in Corrections.' *Canadian Journal of Corrections* 22 (1980): 298–306

Neidhart, W.S. 'The Fenian Trials in the Province of Ontario, 1866–1867: A Case Study of Law and Politics in Action.' *Ontario History* 66 (1974): 23–36

Nilsen, D. 'The 'Social Evil': Prostitution in Vancouver, 1900–1920.' In *In Her Own Right: Selected Essays in Women's History in British Columbia*, pp. 205–28. Edited by B. Latham and C. Lees. Victoria: Camosun College, 1980

Oliver, P. 'A Terror to Evil Doers: The Central Prison and the Criminal Class in Late Nineteenth-Century Ontario.' In *Patterns of the Past: Reinterpreting Ontario's History*, pp. 206–37. Edited by R. Hall et al. Toronto: Dundurn Press, 1988

Olson, R. 'Rape – An Un-Victorian Aspect of Life in Upper Canada.' *Ontario History* 66 (1976): 75–9

Ostry, B. 'Conservatives, Liberals and Labour in the 1870s.' *Canadian Historical Review* 41 (1960): 93–127

Oxner, S. 'The Evolution of the Lower Court of Nova Scotia.' In *Law in a Colonial Society: The Nova Scotia Experience*, pp. 59–79. Edited by T.G. Barnes et al. Toronto: Carswell, 1984

Palmer, B. 'Kingston Mechanics and the Rise of the Penitentiary, 1833–1836.' *Histoire Sociale/Social History* 13 (1980): 7–32

Palmer, B. 'Labour Protest and Organisation in Nineteenth-Century Canada, 1820–1890.' *Labour/Le Travail* 20 (1987): 1–45

Parker, G. 'The Origins of the Canadian Criminal Code.' In *Essays in the History of Canadian Law*, Vol. 1, pp. 249–280. Edited by D. Flaherty. Toronto: University of Toronto Press and Osgoode Society, 1981

— 'The Legal Regulation of Sexual Activity and the Protection of Females.' *Osgoode Hall Law Journal* 21 (1983): 187–244

— 'Canadian Legal Culture.' In *Law and Justice in a New Land: Essays in Western Canadian Legal History*, pp. 3–29. Edited by L.A. Knafla. Toronto: Carswell, 1986

Pariseau, J.J. *Disorders, Strikes and Disasters: Military Aid to the Civil Power in Canada, 1867–1933*. Ottawa: Department of National Defence History Directorate, 1973

Patterson, G.H. 'Old Court Records of Pictou County Nova Scotia.' *Canadian Bar Review* 13 (1935): 143–51

Phelan, J. 'The Tar and Feather Case: Gore Assizes, August 1827.' *Ontario History* 68 (1976): 17–24

Phillips, J. 'The Reform of Nova Scotia's Criminal Law, 1832–1841.' Unpublished paper, 1987

— 'The Royal Pardon in Nova Scotia, 1750–1800.' Unpublished paper, 1989

— 'Poverty, Unemployment and the Criminal Law: The Administration of the Vagrancy Laws in Halifax, 1864–1890.' In *Essays in the History of Canadian Law*, Vol. 3: *Nova Scotia*, pp. 128–62. Edited by P. Girard and J. Phillips. Toronto: University of Toronto Press and Osgoode Society, 1990

Pitsula, J.M. 'The Emergence of Social Work in Toronto.' *Journal of Canadian Studies* 14 (1979): 35–42

— 'The Treatment of Tramps in Late Nineteenth-Century Toronto.' *Historical Papers* (1980): 116–132

Preyer, K. 'Penal Measures in the American Colonies: An Overview.' *American Journal of Legal History* 26 (1982): 326–353

Price, B.J. 'Female Petty Crime in Halifax 1864–1890.' In *Essays in the History of Canadian Law*, Vol. 3: *Nova Scotia*, pp. 200–231. Edited by P. Girard and J. Phillips. Toronto: University of Toronto Press and Osgoode Society, 1990

Rawling, B. 'Technology and Innovation in the Toronto Police Force, 1875–1925.' *Ontario History* 80 (1988): 53–71

Read, C. *The Rising in Western Upper Canada, 1837–8: The Duncombe Revolt and After*. Toronto: University of Toronto Press, 1982

Read, F. 'Early History of the Manitoba Courts.' *Manitoba Bar News* 10 (1937): 451–5, 467–71, 482–84

Reid, J.P. *Law for the Elephant: Property and Social Behaviour on the Overland Trail*. San Marino: Huntington Library, 1980

Riddell, W.R. 'The First Reported Criminal Trial.' *Journal of Criminal Law* 7 (1916): 8–14

— 'Canadian State Trials: The King v. David McLane.' *Transactions of the Royal Society of Canada* 3 (1916): 321–37

— 'The First English Criminal Court in Canada.' *Journal of Criminal Law* 8 (1917): 8–15

— 'The First English Court in Canada on its Criminal Side.' *Journal of the American Institute of Criminal Law and Criminology* 8 (1917): 8–15

— 'Criminal Law in Upper Canada a Century Ago.' *Journal of the American Institute of Criminal Law and Criminology* 9 (1920A): 516–32

— 'A Criminal Circuit in Upper Canada a Century Ago.' *Canadian Law Times* 40 (1920B): 711–27

— 'Trial for High Treason in 1838.' *Ontario Historical Society Papers and Records* 18 (1920C): 50–8

— 'The Ancaster Bloody Assize of 1814.' *Ontario Historical Society Papers and Records* 20 (1923): 107–25

— 'When a Few Claimed Monopoly of Spiritual Functions: Canadian State Trials – The King Against Clark Burton.' *Ontario Historical Society Papers and Records* 22 (1925): 202–9

— 'Criminal Courts and the Law in Early Upper Canada.' *Ontario Historical Society Papers and Records* 17 (1925): 210–21

— *The Bar and the Courts of the Province of Upper Canada or Ontario.* Toronto: Macmillan, 1928

— 'First Legal Execution for Crime in Upper Canada.' *Ontario Historical Society Papers and Records* 27 (1931A): 514–16

— 'The Story of an Old Statute.' *Ontario Historical Society Papers and Records* 27 (1931B): 517–19

— 'Bygone Phases of Canadian Criminal Law.' *Journal of Criminal Law, Criminology and Police Science* 23 (1932): 51–66

Roberts, B. *Whence They Came: Deportation From Canada, 1900–1935.* Ottawa: University of Ottawa Press, 1988

Robertson, D.F. 'The Saskatchewan Provincial Police, 1917–1928.' *Saskatchewan History* 31 (1978): 1–11

Robertson, R.W.W. *The Law Moves West: The N.W.M.P. 1873–1878.* Toronto: McClelland and Stewart, 1970

Rogers, N. 'Serving Toronto The Good: The Development of the City Police Force, 1834–1884.' In *Forging a Consensus: Historical Essays on Toronto*, pp. 116–140. Edited by V.L. Russell. Toronto: University of Toronto Press, 1984

Romney, P. 'The Ordeal of William Higgins.' *Ontario History* 67 (1975): 69–89

— 'A Conservative Reformer in Upper Canada: Charles Fothergill, Responsible Government, and the 'British Party', 1824–1840.' *Historical Papers* (1984): 42–62

— *Mr. Attorney: The Attorney General for Ontario in Court, Cabinet and Legislature, 1791–1899.* Toronto: University of Toronto Press and Osgoode Society, 1986

Romney, P. 'From the Types Riot to the Rebellion: Elite Ideology, Anti-Legal Sentiment, Political Violence, and the Rule of Law in Upper Canada.' *Ontario History* 79 (1987): 113–44

— 'Very Late Loyalist Fantasies: Nostalgic Tory History and the Rule of Law in Upper Canada.' In *Canadian Perspectives on Law and Society:*

Issues in Legal History, pp. 119–47. Edited by W. Pue and J.B. Wright. Ottawa: Carleton University Press, 1988A

— 'Reinventing Upper Canada: American Immigrants, Upper Canadian History, English Law and the Alien Question.' In *Patterns of the Past: Interpreting Ontario's History*, pp. 78–107. Edited by R. Hall et al. Toronto: Dundurn Press, 1988B

Rooke, P. and Schnell, R. 'Childhood and Charity in Nineteenth-Century British North America.' *Histoire Sociale/Social History* 15 (1982A): 157–79

— 'Guttersnipes and Charity Children: Nineteenth-Century Child Rescue in the Atlantic Provinces.' In *Studies in Childhood History: A Canadian Perspective*, pp. 82–104. Edited by P. Rooke and R. Schnell. Calgary: Detselig Enterprises, 1982B

—, eds. *Discarding the Asylum: From Child Rescue to the Welfare State in English Canada, 1800–1959.* Lanham, Md.: University Press of America, 1983

Rotenberg, L. 'The Wayward Worker: Toronto's Prostitute at the Turn of the Century.' In *Women at Work: Ontario 1850–1939*, pp. 33–69. Edited by J. Acton et al. Toronto: Canadian Women's Educational Press, 1974

Rothman, D.J. *The Discovery of the Asylum: Social Order and Disorder in the New Republic.* Boston: Little Brown, 1971

— 'The Invention of the Penitentiary.' *Criminal Law Bulletin* 8 (1972): 555–86

Roy, P. 'The Preservation of the Peace in Vancouver: The Aftermath of the Anti-Chinese Riot of 1887.' *British Columbia Studies* 31 (1976): 44–59

Rutherford, P. 'Tomorrow's Metropolis: The Urban Reform Movement in Canada, 1880–1920.' *Historical Papers* (1971): 202–24

—, ed. *Saving the Canadian City: The First Phase, 1880–1920.* Toronto: University of Toronto Press, 1974

Schuh, C. 'Justice on the Northern Frontier: Early Murder Trials of Native Accused.' *Criminal Law Quarterly* 22 (1979): 74–111

Sealey, D.B. *The Mounties and Law Enforcement.* Agincourt, Ont.: Irwin Dorsey, 1980

Senior, E.K. 'The Influence of the British Garrison on the Development of the Police in Montreal, 1832–1853.' In *Lawful Authority: Readings on the History of Criminal Justice in Canada*, pp. 85–97. Edited by R.C. MacLeod. Toronto: McClelland and Stewart, 1988

Shanes, M.A. 'The Police Organisation as a Mechanism of Social Control in Nineteenth-Century Hamilton.' Unpublished MA thesis, McMaster University, 1975

Sherwood, R. 'The Laws of Pictou.' *Nova Scotia Historical Quarterly* 7 (1977): 101–9

Shoom, S. 'Kingston Penitentiary: The Early Decades.' *Canadian Journal of Corrections* 8 (1966): 215–20

— 'The Upper Canada Reformatory, Penetanguishene: The Dawn of Prison Reform in Canada.' *Canadian Journal of Corrections* 14 (1972): 260–7

Shortt, A. *Early Records of Ontario, Being Extracts from the Records of the Court of Quarter Sessions for the District of Mecklenburg with Introduction and Notes.* Kingston: Kingston Daily News, 1900

Silverman, P.G. 'Military Aid to the Civil Power in British Columbia: The Labour Strikes at Wellington and Steveston, 1890, 1900.' *Pacific Northwest Quarterly* 61 (1970): 156–61

Sissons, J.H. *Judge of the Far North.* Toronto: McClelland and Stewart, 1968

Skinner, S.J. et al. *Corrections: An Historical Perspective of the Saskatchewan Experience.* Regina: Canadian Plains Research Centre, University of Regina, 1981

Smandych, R.C. 'The Rise of the Asylum in Upper Canada: An Application of Scull's Macro-Sociological Perspective.' *Canadian Criminology Forum* 4 (1982): 142–8

Smandych, R.C., Matthews, C.J. and Cox, S.J. *Canadian Criminal Justice History: An Annotated Bibliography.* Toronto: University of Toronto Press, 1987

Smith, J.F. 'Cumberland County Hatchet Murder.' *Nova Scotia Historical Quarterly* 5 (1975): 117–29

Smith, W. 'The Struggle Over the Laws of Canada, 1763–1783.' *Canadian Historical Review* 1 (1920): 166–86

Soward, F.H. 'The Struggle Over the Laws of Canada, 1783–1791.' *Canadian Historical Review* 5 (1924): 314–35

Splane, R. *Social Welfare in Ontario, 1791–1893.* Toronto: University of Toronto Press, 1965

Spry, I.M. 'The Tragedy of the Loss of the Commons in Western Canada.' In *As Long as the Sun Shines and the Water Flows: A Reader in Canadian Native Studies,* pp. 203–28. Edited by I.A. Getty and A.S. Lussier. Vancouver: University of British Columbia Press, 1983

Stanley, G.F., ed. *The Birth of Western Canada: A History of the Riel Rebellions*. Toronto: University of Toronto Press, 1960

— 'The Caraquet Riots of 1875.' *Acadiensis* 2 (1972): 21–38

— 'As Long as the Sun Shines and the Water Flows: An Historical Comment.' In *As Long as the Sun Shines and the Water Flows: A Reader in Canadian Native Studies*, pp. 1–26. Edited by I.A. Getty and A.S. Lussier. Vancouver: University of British Columbia, 1983

Stenning, P. 'Trusting the Chief: Legal Aspects of the Status and Political Accountability of the Police in Canada.' Unpublished SJD thesis, University of Toronto, 1983

— *Appearing for the Crown: A Legal and Historical Review of Criminal Prosecutorial Authority in Canada*. Cowansville, Que.: Brown Legal Publications, 1986

Stone, T. 'The Mounties as Vigilantes: Perceptions of Community and the Transformation of Law in the Yukon.' *Law and Society Review* 14 (1979): 83–114

Strange, C. 'The Criminal and Fallen of their Sex: The Establishment of Canada's First Women's Prison, 1874–1901.' *Canadian Journal of Women and the Law* 1 (1985): 79–92

— 'From Modern Babylon to a City Upon a Hill: The Toronto Social Survey Commission of 1915 and the Search for Sexual Order in the City.' In *Patterns of the Past: Reinterpreting Ontario's History*, pp. 255–77. Edited by R. Hall et al. Toronto: Dundurn Press, 1988

Stubbs, R. St.G. *Four Recorders of Rupert's Land*. Winnipeg: Peguis Publishers 1967

Sugimoto, H.H. 'The Vancouver Riots of 1907: A Canadian Episode.' In *East Across the Pacific*, pp. 92–126. Edited by H. Conroy. Santa Barbara: Clio Press, 1972

Surtees, R.J. 'Indian Land Cessions in Upper Canada, 1815–1830.' In *As Long as the Sun Shines and Water Flows: A Reader in Canadian Native Studies*, pp. 65–84. Edited by I.A. Getty and A.S. Lussier. Vancouver: University of British Columbia Press, 1983

Talbot, C.K. *Justice in Early Ontario, 1791–1803: A Study of Crime, Courts and Prisons in Upper Canada*. Ottawa: Crimcare, 1983

Talbot, C.K. et al. *The Thin Blue Line: An Historical Perspective of Policing in Canada*. Ottawa: Crimcare, 1983

Taylor, C.J. 'The Kingston, Ontario Penitentiary and Moral Architecture.' *Histoire Sociale/Social History* 12 (1979): 385–408

Teatero, W. 'The Crown v. William Brass.' *Ontario History* 71 (1979): 139–56

Tennyson, B.D. 'Sir William Hearst and the Ontario Temperance Act.' *Ontario History* 55 (1963): 233–45

Thomas, L.H. 'A Judicial Murder – The Trial of Louis Riel.' In *The Settlement of the West*, pp. 63–84. Edited by H. Palmer. Calgary: University of Calgary Press, 1977

Thompson, E.P. *Whigs and Hunters: The Origin of the Black Act.* London: Allen Lane, 1975

Thorner, T. 'The Not So Peaceable Kingdom: Crime and Criminal Justice in Frontier Calgary.' In *Frontier Calgary*, pp. 100–13. Edited by A.W. Rasporich and H.C. Klassen. Calgary: McClelland and Stewart, 1975

— 'The Incidence of Crime in Southern Alberta 1878–1905.' In *Law and Society in Canada in Historical Perspective*, pp. 53–88. Edited by D.J. Bercuson and L.A. Knafla. Calgary: University of Calgary Press, 1979

Thorner, T. and Watson, N. 'Patterns of Prairie Crime: Calgary, 1875–1939.' In *Crime and Criminal Justice in Europe and Canada*, pp. 219–55. Edited by L.A. Knafla. Waterloo: Wilfrid Laurier University Press, 1981

— 'Keeper of the King's Peace: Colonel G.F. Sanders and the Calgary Police Magistrates Court.' *Urban History Review* 12 (1984): 45–55

Tobias, J.L. 'Protection, Civilization, Assimilation: An Outline History of Canada's Indian Policy.' In *As Long as the Sun Shines and Water Flows: A Reader in Canadian Native Studies*, pp. 39–55. Edited by I.A. Getty and A.S. Lussier. Vancouver: University of British Columbia Press, 1983

Torrance, J. *Public Violence in Canada, 1867–1982.* Kingston and Montreal: McGill-Queen's University Press, 1986

Townshend, C.J. 'History of the Courts of Judicature in Nova Scotia.' *Canadian Law Times* 19 (1899): 23–37, 58–72, 87–98, 142–57

Trasov, G. 'History of the Opium and Narcotic Drug Legislation in Canada.' *Criminal Law Quarterly* 4 (1962): 274–82

Tremblay, P. and Normandeau, A. 'L'économie pénale de la société Montréalaise, 1845 – 1913.' *Histoire Sociale/Social History* 19 (1986): 177–99

Tubrett, E. 'The Development of the New Brunswick Court System 1784–1803.' Unpublished MA thesis, University of New Brunswick, 1967

Turmel, J. *Police de Montreal: Historique de service*, Vol. 1: *1796–1909*. Montreal: Service de la Police de Montreal, 1971

Turner, J.P. *The North West Mounted Police, 1873–1893*. Ottawa: King's Printer, 1950. 2 vols

Upton, L.F.S. *Micmacs and Colonists: Indian-White Relations in the Maritime Provinces, 1713–1867*. Vancouver: University of British Columbia Press, 1979

Verdun-Jones, S.N. 'Not Guilty By Reason of Insanity: The Historical Roots of the Canadian Insanity Defence.' In *Crime and Criminal Justice in Europe and Canada*, pp. 179–218. Edited by L.A. Knafla. Waterloo: Wilfrid Laurier University Press, 1981

Verdun-Jones, S.N. and Smandych, R. 'Catch-22 in the Nineteenth Century: The Evolution of Therapeutic Confinement for the Criminally Insane in Canada, 1840–1900.' *Criminal Justice History*, (1981): 85–108

Vincent, T.B., ed. 'Jonathan Belcher: Charge to the Grand Jury, Michaelmas Term 1754.' *Acadiensis* 7 (1977): 103–9

Walden, K. *Visions of Order: The Canadian Mounties in Symbol and Myth.* Toronto: Butterworths, 1982

— 'The Great March of the Mounted Police in Popular Literature, 1873–1973.' *Historical Papers* (1984): 33–56

Ward, W.P. *White Canada Forever*. Montreal and Kingston: McGill-Queen's University Press, 1978

Warsh, C.K. 'The First Mrs. Rochester: Wrongful Confinement, Social Redundancy, and Commitment to the Private Asylum, 1883–1923.' *Historical Papers* (1988): 145–67

Weaver, J. 'Crime, Public Order and Repression: The Gore District in Upheaval, 1832–1851.' *Ontario History* 78 (1986): 175–207

Weaver, J. and Doucet, M. 'Town Fathers and the Community: The Roots of Community Power and Physical Form in Hamilton, Upper Canada, in the 1830s.' *Urban History Review* 13 (1984): 75–90

Wetherell, D.G. 'To Discipline and Train: Adult Rehabilitation Programmes in Ontario Prisons, 1874–1900.' *Histoire Sociale/Social History* 12 (1979): 145–65

Whittingham, M.D. 'Crime, Punishment, Correction and the Rise of the Administrative State in England and Upper Canada.' *Law Society of Upper Canada Gazette* 19 (1985): 201–9

Williams, D.R. *The Man for a New Country: Sir Matthew Baillie Begbie.* Sidney, B.C.: Gray's Publishing, 1977

— 'The Administration of Criminal and Civil Justice in the Mining Camps and Frontier Communities of British Columbia.' In *Law and Justice in a New Land: Essays in Western Canadian Legal History*, pp. 215–32. Edited by L.A. Knafla. Toronto: Carswell, 1986

Winks, R. *The Blacks in Canada*. Kingston and Montreal: McGill- Queen's University Press, 1971

Wise, S. F. 'Upper Canada and the Conservative Tradition.' In *Profiles of a Province: Studies in the History of Ontario*, pp. 111–36. Edited by E.G. Firth. Toronto: Ontario Historical Society, 1967

— 'Liberal Consensus or Ideological Battleground: Some Reflections on the Hartz Thesis.' *Historical Papers* (1974): 1–14

Wright, J.A. 'The Halifax Riot of 1863.' *Nova Scotia Historical Quarterly* 4 (1974): 299–310

Wright, J.B. 'The Ideological Dimensions of Law in Upper Canada: The Treason Proceedings of 1814 and 1838,' Working Paper of the Carleton University Jurisprudence Centre, 1986

— 'Issues in Criminal Law and Authority: Civil Liberties and Morality.' In *Canadian Perspectives on Law and Society: Issues in Legal History*, pp. 245–8. Edited by W. Pue and J.B. Wright. Ottawa: Carleton University Press, 1988

Wright, M.E. 'Unnatural Mothers: Infanticide in Halifax, 1830–1875.' *Nova Scotia Historical Review* 7 (1987): 13–29

Zaslow, M. *The Opening of the Canadian North, 1870–1914*. Toronto: McClelland and Stewart, 1971. 2 vols

3

Policing

Philip C. Stenning and Clifford D. Shearing

In this essay we identify what we consider to be significant issues in scholarly thinking on policing and the texts that, in our view, address them in useful and interesting ways. Thus, it is an introduction that gives salience to perspectives that we find congenial. Where possible books have been referred to in preference to journal articles.

Policing within liberal-democratic societies is typically an activity carried out by the state to 'preserve the peace.' This view establishes it both as the property of the state and an activity that promotes harmony. It identifies the state as a benevolent guarantor of order. Much police scholarship has accepted this way of seeing as its starting point (Cain, 1979). In doing so it has contributed to the legitimation of the state and its order maintenance activities (Ericson, 1987, 1989 for a discussion of the way in which meanings are ordered through the constitution of conceptual frameworks to create symbolic canopies that constrain, enable and motivate action).

This recognition of the constitutive features of police scholarship is not a call for an objective, neutral, non-constitutive framework. Police scholarship, like all scholarship, is constitutive of the world it seeks to describe. While this is not a cause for despair it does require scholars to be sensitive to the constitutive implications of their conceptions and to carefully select implications that can be defended on theoretical grounds (Shearing, 1989).

In response to the liberal view, alternative 'critical' conceptions have emerged which have challenged it by, for example, arguing that the state seeks to guarantee ways of doing things that sustain inequality rather than peaceful coexistence or by arguing that the state is not the only, or the most significant, guarantor of order. These challenges point to the value of a conception of policing that opens to empirical examination issues that the liberal conception settles by definition (Cain, 1979). In our view, the appropriate response to these problems is a conception of policing that allows for multiple guarantors of order and that does not legitimate some orders at the expense of others. Policing should be conceived of as guaranteeing a way of doing things within some space-time domain through both symbolic and behavioural strategies by any entity with the capacity and will to act as a guarantor (*The Canadian Encyclopedia*, 1988 on 'Police'; Shearing, 1989; Stenning, Shearing, Addario and Condon, 1990).

Those responsible for policing frequently seek to establish the order they endorse through the promulgation and enforcement of rules of conduct that promote a particular way of doing things. When such rules are authorized by public agencies such as parliaments, local legislatures or municipal governments, they are referred to as laws, and the maintenance of ways of doing things prescribed by them (commonly assigned to specialist public police forces) is frequently spoken of as 'law enforcement' (Bayley, 1985 on policing as it has developed in different societies; *The Canadian Encyclopedia*, 1988 on 'Police' and 'Law Enforcement').

In this form of policing, governments act as guarantors of order within the territories over which they exercise jurisdiction. When a government responds to threats to its status and capacity as a guarantor of order, its response is often called 'political policing' (Bunyan, 1976 and Turk, 1982 consider political policing in this sense; also Solomon, in this volume). While it is useful to distinguish between policing that responds to threats to an order guaranteed by a government (regular policing) and threats to the government as a guarantor of order (political policing) it is important to recognize that all policing by governments is essentially political because the definition of an order and its maintenance by government is an essentially political activity (Reiner, 1985 on these two meanings of the term 'political' as it is used in relation to policing). As a way of distinguishing between these two forms of policing without getting entangled in the various meanings of the word 'political' Brodeur (1983) distinguishes between 'low' and 'high' policing.

Law enforcement, that is policing of laws under the authority of a government, is only one form of policing. In practice, many communities and organizations that would not normally be considered 'governments,' seek to achieve and maintain the orderliness which they (or more precisely persons who speak for them) regard as desirable or necessary to their functioning. They use a variety of means and institutions to achieve this end (Henry, 1983 on the relationship between private and public ordering). The function of policing may be primarily assigned to a specialist body (a police or security force), or it may be performed by non-specialists as part of other jobs (such as apartment superintendents, or office receptionists) (Shearing and Stenning, 1989 on this distinction). In most communities the responsibility for policing is in practice shared in some way between public and private authorities, and between specialists and non-specialists, and sometimes by every member of the community (Critchley, 1978 on the medieval institution of frankpledge; Radcliffe and Cross, 1971). Not surprisingly, therefore, some of the most intense and long-standing debates about policing have been about how this sharing of responsibilities is most appropriately and effectively accomplished. A good example is the debate that took place in Britain over the establishment of The London Metropolitan Police ('Scotland Yard') in the early 1800s (Beattie in this volume; Reiner, 1985). This inevitably leads to questions about the relationships between 'the police' and 'the policed.' This issue is often discussed under the rubric of 'accountability' (Kinsey, Lea and Young, 1986; Reiner, 1985; South, 1988).

Scholars who have taken an interest in policing have tended to focus their attention on the most visible, public forms of policing, that is, on the work of state-sponsored, specialized, public police forces. As a result, policing has tended to become associated, both in the academic literature and in popular culture, with the activities, perspectives and methods of these forces (good examples are Bittner, 1970; Klockars, 1985). Until very recently, there has been much less appreciation or systematic examination of other, more private and less visible forms of policing (Cain, 1979; Draper, 1978; Marx 1988; Spitzer and Scull, 1977 for some early examples of this more expansive view). Because of this, our knowledge of the history and development of the policing function in different societies is still, despite an apparently voluminous literature on police and policing, very incomplete (Beattie in this volume).

Historically, great variety in the mix of public and private policing in different ages and in different societies is evident. In earlier times, policing was regarded in many societies as a communal responsibility, part of the day-to-day social obligations of every member of the community (Radzinowicz, 1956). With the birth and gradual evolution of the modern nation state, however, there was a growing trend toward the assumption of primary responsibility for public policing (i.e. the policing of publicly defined order in public places) by the state and its agents. This trend generated the creation, especially during the eighteenth and nineteenth centuries in Europe and North America, of specialized public police forces, organized, paid for, and responsible to, the state (Bayley, 1985; Rubinstein, 1973).

In the case of 'low' policing, such forces were typically established as quasi-military organizations and, through the adoption of distinctive uniforms, were designed to be highly visible in the community. They were deployed to patrol every part of the community in a systematic, routine fashion. The theory was that such a visible and routine presence would serve not only to increase the chances of detecting and responding to disorders of all kinds, but also to deter (and hence prevent) such disorders, especially those which the community regarded as 'crimes' (i.e. violations of the criminal laws of the state) (Radzinowicz, 1956; Rubinstein, 1973). There has, however, recently been considerable debate among historians about the motives behind the changes in the organization of policing and the interests served by them (Beattie, in this volume; Palmer, 1988; Reiner, 1985 reviews of 'traditional' and 'revisionist' histories).

In countries with a liberal-democratic tradition, laws protecting private property ownership and privacy have restricted routine patrols by state-sponsored police personnel to public streets. Only in exceptional circumstances have public police officers been given authorized access to private property without the consent of the owner or occupier (Reiss, 1987; Stinchcombe, 1963). Since most crimes and other disorders were both conceived and executed on private property the 'New Police' of the eighteenth and nineteenth centuries inevitably found themselves increasingly reliant on the general public who had access to such places to inform them about crimes and disorders which were being planned or had occurred, so that they could respond to them (Rubinstein, 1973 for a history of the impact of technology on public police reliance on citizens as a source of information). In this way, policing by public police forces has developed reactive features that involve them in responding to crimes and other disorders after they have occurred as a result of calls for assistance by affected citizens (Reiss, 1971 for a consideration of policing in the United States that argues that it is predominantly reactive; for an analysis based on Canadian data that samples cases more randomly than Reiss and concludes that policing is far more proactive than Reiss suggests see Ericson, 1982).

The intelligence difficulties faced by modern specialized public police forces have typically produced two reactions from them. On the one hand, they regularly ask for more intrusive powers that will allow them greater and more frequent access to private places. Debates around these demands, in which the appropriate scope and limits of the intrusive and coercive powers of the police are contested, have persisted throughout the history of modern public police forces (Baldwin and Kinsey, 1982). On the other hand, much of the effort of public police forces goes into exploring ways to improve their communication systems, the means through which citizens can make calls for police service, and into increasing the efficiency of police dispatch and patrol systems in responding to calls (Larson, 1972).

While undercover policing has always been essential to 'high' policing (Marx, 1988) it was the inadequacies of routine uniformed patrols by police officers to prevent disorder before it occurred that led public police forces in North America and England, in the latter half of the nineteenth century, to develop detective services. Unlike the patrol services, these detective services were designed to be less conspicuous and more covert in their operations. Their primary role was to develop sources of information (informants) within the communities they policed, and to investigate crimes which had been reported to the police or discovered by them (Ericson, 1981A).

This basic approach to 'low' policing, in which a majority of a force's resources are devoted to routine patrols of the area to be policed, while a small specialist group of officers concentrate on intelligence gathering and investigative work supported by records, communications and dispatch systems, was well established within most public police forces by the end of the nineteenth century. Reform of public policing by these agencies during the twentieth century has largely focused on making improvements to this basic approach. Thus, reform efforts concentrated on such matters as improving records, communications and dispatch systems, reducing the time within which the police are able to respond to calls for assistance, and generally improving the selection, recruitment and training of police officers with a view to achieving an increased 'professionalism' in their work (Fogelson, 1977; Goldstein, 1977; Rubinstein, 1973).

Such reforms have not infrequently spawned new problems for the police, however. As they have striven to become more efficient and 'professional,' for instance, they have become increasingly separated from the communities they serve. Not only are they boxed away in their police cruisers for more and more of their working day, and occupationally dependent upon staying close to their police radios – thus making it physically more difficult for them to mingle with the communities they serve – but their growing struggle for recognition as 'professionals' has been accompanied by a claim to specialized expert knowledge about what is required for effective police work, which in turn has tended to make the police less receptive to lay community input into decision-making about their performance of their function (Alderson, 1979 for a critique of these developments from within the public police community). The result all too often has been deteriorating police-community relations, a problem which has been exacerbated during the last thirty years by the enormous changes which have occurred, especially in the ethnic composition of urban communities, which have not been adequately reflected in changed police recruitment, training and personnel policies (Banton, 1964; Bayley, 1985). Police-community relations, accountability and control of the police, and how to detect and prevent police deviance, are the topics that have dominated public debates about the public police during the latter half of the twentieth century (Kinsey, Lea and Young, 1986; Punch, 1983; Shearing, 1981).

This interest in police accountability prompted considerable research on police decision-making. Examinations of public police decision-making have tended to focus on the issue of the equality of police treatment of various groups. This research indicates that police officers do not respond equally to different categories of persons (Black, 1980). There has been considerable argument as to the reasons for this and the degree to which responsibility for this should rest with the police and be attributed to police prejudice. This debate has led to an examination of a wide range of influences affecting police conduct. These include the law itself (Ericson, 1981B; McBarnet, 1979), the organizational environment within which the police work including differences between police officers in their responses to their work (Ericson, 1981A; Reiner, 1985); the police occupational culture (Reuss-Ianni and Ianni, 1983; Shearing and Ericson, forthcoming, 1991); the maintenance of social relations central to the police role, such as their authority vis-à-vis the public (Piliavin and Briar, 1965); external sources of influence, such as the wishes of persons who mobilize the police by calling them (Black, 1980); and, finally, political influence (Fogelson, 1977).

Apart from an understandable defensiveness over such matters, the main response of public police agencies to these developments has been to try to find ways to put the police officer back in touch with the community. 'Community policing' and 'preventive policing' have thus become the new official desiderata within police circles, and have spawned a variety of innovative, experimental approaches to the delivery of police services. Many of these reflect an apparent return to more traditional ideas about how the task of public policing can most effectively be accomplished, such as the renewed interest in foot patrols and 'community service officers' (Alderson, 1979). This reform movement has coincided with, and to a large degree been rendered imperative by, a growing fiscal pressure on public police forces, if not actually to reduce their expenditures, at least to settle for much smaller budgetary increases, and to use their resources more economically and efficiently.

These difficulties which public police forces have faced in the postwar era, have provided the context for another significant development in the evolution of policing. We refer here to the burgeoning growth, during the last thirty years, of an increasing variety of private policing services (Shearing and Stenning, 1989 for comparative figures on growth in Canada and the United States). Broadly, these can be categorized in two ways. In the first place, a distinction can be made between 'contract' policing services, and proprietary or 'in-house.' Contract services are policing services which are provided to multiple clients, on a fee-for-service basis, by an entrepreneur. In-house services, on the other hand, are policing services which a corporation or other organization develops and maintains exclusively to service its own internal policing needs (South, 1988).

The other distinction which is useful in describing the modern private policing sector is that between labour-intensive services (such as guard services and private detective agencies) and mechanically-based, hardware-intensive services (which include a whole array of more or less technologically sophisticated protective, surveillance and investigative devices and equipment). Recent research indicates that the growth of the various industries which provide this policing hardware has been outstripping the growth of more labour-intensive policing services both in the private and the public sectors, a trend which has been seen as signifying an important shift in the nature of policing and the way it is accomplished (South, 1988).

Private security initiatives are often significantly different from their public police counterparts in ways other than their organization. While the activities of the public police are, for the most part, ostensibly focused on crime and its control through the criminal justice system, private police organizations often operate in accordance with broader definitions of the policing task. Because most of these organizations are employed by industrial or commercial corporations, the most common focus of their policing efforts tends to be the protection of profit and the prevention and control of loss, regardless of whether the losses which are of concern to them are a result of crime or of other hazards. This largely preventive focus on loss, rather than crime, influences the way policing is organized and carried out. Responsibilities which are not usually given priority in the modern public police mandate – such as control of health and safety hazards, regulation of workforce behaviour, and the prevention of natural disasters from fire or flooding – consequently figure prominently in the mandate of private policing organizations (Shearing and Stenning, 1989).

While public sector policing has, for the most part, been assigned to specialists (that is, to people for whom policing is their principal or exclusive occupation), private sector policing, where the guarantor of order is located within the private sphere, is characterized to a much greater extent by assigning policing tasks to those whose main occupation is not policing. This 'embedding' of policing in other functions and occupations enables policing to be accomplished effectively and cheaply in many situations (especially in the workplace and the marketplace) and hearkens back to the days before the establishment of the modern public police forces, when public policing was regarded as the responsibility of all citizens, whatever their status or occupation (Critchley, 1978). Modern efforts by public police authorities to promote 'community-based' policing is a similar attempt to make policing once more a community responsibility.

Many private policing organizations (of both the contract and in-house kinds) are in the service of large multi-national corporations, whose interests transcend national economies and borders. Unlike most public policing agencies which operate primarily within national or sub-national boundaries, therefore, many private policing organizations are organized and function internationally. This feature of much private policing leads to additional problems concerning their public accountability which do not so frequently arise in the case of public policing agencies (Cunningham and Taylor, 1985; South, 1988).

It seems likely that, within the foreseeable future, policing will remain a joint endeavour involving not only public and private police organizations, but also, to a greater or lesser degree, the public more generally. Exactly what this mix of responsibilities and roles will be, and what will be the implications for the nature of social control and individual freedom will constitute the critical questions for the modern generation of scholars and other observers of policing.

Reading List

Alderson, John. *Policing Freedom: A Commentary on the Dilemma of Policing in Western Democracy*. Plymouth: MacDonald and Evans, 1979
A book by a former Chief Constable in England is a good example of moves from within the police community to develop 'new policing emphases and styles' in response to changes in the policing environment, such as the difficulties police departments have in persuading governments to increase the resources at their disposal. Alderson is regarded as a progressive force within the police community as he is arguing for 'a new model for policing a free, permissive, participatory democracy.'

Baldwin, Robert and Kinsey, Richard. *Police Powers and Politics*. London: Quartet Books, 1982
Like Alderson's book Baldwin and Kinsey ask, what kind of police and policing is appropriate for Britain? In answering they respond to the suggestions of commentators from within the police community. This is one of a growing number of books written by British criminologists on the reform of policing and its control structures.

Banton, Michael P. *The Policeman in the Community*. London: Tavistock, 1964
Banton's book is one of the earliest books by an academic on the reform of the police in Britain. It is intended as a text for police officers on police-minority relations.

Bayley, David H. *Patterns of Policing: A Comparative International Analysis*. New Brunswick, NJ: Rutgers University Press, 1985
Bayley provides a conceptual framework for examining policing that recognizes public and private, political and ordinary, and specialized and non-specialized policing. This is used to undertake a comparative analysis of the history, forms and control of policing.

Bittner, Egon. *The Functions of the Police in Modern Society.* Chevy Chase, MD: National Institute of Mental Health, Center for Studies of Crime and Delinquency, 1970
An enormously influential book, especially in North America, in establishing the conceptual framework in which policing has been examined. It focuses attention on the public police and their access to physical force.

Black, Donald J. *The Manners and Customs of the Police.* New York: Academic Press, 1980
Black draws upon and goes beyond some earlier work on police decision-making. The effects of the way law is expressed in interaction are explored, and what traces these interactions produce, such as crime rates. One of the key features of Black's research is a recognition of the reactive character of police work and the associated importance of complainants' preferences to the outcomes of police-citizen encounters.

Brodeur, Jean-Paul. 'High Policing and Low Policing: Remarks about the Policing of Political Activities.' *Social Problems* 30 (5, June 1983): 507–20
Brodeur directs attention to the significance of political policing in this article, and examines the analytic consequences of focusing primarily on ordinary policing for the way political policing has been conceived theoretically.

Bunyan, Tony. *The History and Practice of the Political Police in Britain.* London: Julian Friedman, 1976
One of the early scholarly pieces draws attention to the importance of political policing and criticizes the tendency in early police scholarship to view policing in functional terms that stressed its civilizing influence as opposed to its role in conflict and struggle.

Cain, Maureen. 'Trends in the sociology of police work.' *International Journal of the Sociology of Law* 7 (2, May 1979): 143–67
Cain provides a very useful review of the scholarly frameworks that have been used in defining and analyzing policing and identifies theoretical issues and dimensions that require further examination.

The Canadian Encyclopedia. 2nd ed. Edmonton: Hurtig Publishers, 1988.
The articles on 'Police' and 'Law Enforcement' provide a brief introduction to policing in Canada

Critchley, Thomas Alan. *A History of the Police in England and Wales.* rev. ed. London: Constable, 1978
This provides a good illustration of the 'conventional' history of the police criticized by writers like Bunyan and Reiner.

Cunningham, William and Taylor, Todd. *Private Security and Police in America: The Hallcrest Report.* Portland, OR: Chancellor Press, 1985

Findings of the most recent and comprehensive research on private policing in the United States are reported. Most aspects of private policing organizations are touched on in the report, which contains many recommendations for improving the performance and accountability of private policing, as well as enhancing the relationship between private and public police organizations.

Draper, Hilary. *Private Police*. Harmondsworth, Middlesex: Penguin, 1978
Draper provides, as far as we know, the earliest examinations of the scope and activities of private policing in Britain.

Ericson, Richard V. *Making Crime: A Study of Detective Work*. Toronto: Butterworths, 1981A
Police detective work in Canada is examined to show how police act to create and constitute the social reality of crime. The study takes up and explores ideas considered earlier by Black and others on the production of crime rates.

Ericson, Richard V. *Reproducing Order: A Study of Police Patrol Work* Toronto: Published in Association with the Centre of Criminology, University of Toronto by the University of Toronto Press, 1982
Ericson examines the patrol work of police officers in Canada using data collected from the same department as his work on detectives. He shows how patrol officers and detectives interact and calls into question some long accepted assumptions about the reactive character of police patrol work.

Ericson, Richard V. 'Rules for Police Deviance.' In *Organizational Police Deviance*, pp. 83–110. Edited by Clifford D. Shearing. Toronto: Butterworths, 1981B
In this paper Ericson develops the idea first put forward by McBarnet that rules which at first glance may appear to be constraints on the police may in fact operate to enable police to act in ways that are at odds with the apparent intent of the rules.

Ericson, Richard V., Baranek, Patricia M. and Chan, Janet B.L. *Negotiating Control: A Study of News Sources*. Toronto: University of Toronto Press, 1989
This study examines the struggle that takes place between news sources and news media over what will be presented as 'the news' as part of the process of symbolic ordering through which both events and subjectivities are constituted.

Ericson, Richard V., Baranek, Patricia M. and Chan, Janet B.L. *Visualizing Deviance: A Study of News Organization*. Toronto: University of Toronto Press, 1987
A sophisticated, yet wonderfully clear and readable examination of the way in which the news media contribute to the policing of the symbolic world of meanings that shape action and hence order.

Fogelson, Robert M. *Big-City Police*. Cambridge, MA: Harvard University Press, 1977
The author, a political scientist, studies the history of policing in several municipal police departments in the United States. The interplay between political parties and lobby groups is examined, and the development of American policing in terms of waves of reform.

Goldstein, Herman B. *Policing a Free Society*. Cambridge, MA: Ballinger, 1977
Goldstein seeks to influence policy about public policing within the United States by moving behind the issues that occupy public attention. He sets an agenda for police reform that covers such issues as police accountability, police allocation of resources and police training.

Henry, Stuart. *Private Justice: Towards Integrated Theorizing in the Sociology of Law*. Boston: Routledge and Kegan Paul, 1983
Private Justice seeks to re-think conceptions of law by insisting that 'to understand law in society it is necessary to understand the nature of [the] interdependence between public and private, the formal and the informal, the part and the whole.' The book draws upon and seeks to develop notions of legal pluralism.

Kinsey, Richard, Lea, John and Young, Jock. *Losing the Fight Against Crime*. New York: Basil Blackwell, 1986
An agenda for police reform is set that seeks to respond to the 'the failure of Mrs. Thatcher's law and order programme' in Britain. It seeks to develop a position they refer to as 'left realism' that recognizes the reality of crime in Britain which prompted the law and order programs of the Conservative government and that provides a 'realistic' program to deal with it from the perspective of the left.

Klockers, Carl B. *The Idea of Police*. Beverly Hills, Calif.: Sage Publications, 1985. (Law and Criminal Justice Series, Vol. 3)
A good example of the conception of police and policing generated by the theoretical framework developed by Bittner.

Larson, Richard C. *Urban Police Patrol Analysis*. Cambridge, MA: MIT Press, 1972
This book illustrates the technologically oriented reform of the police that was generated within the police community by a focus on improved technology, rather than a change in philosophy as the answer to improving public policing.

Marx, Gary T. *Undercover: Police Surveillance in America*. Berkeley, CA: University of California Press, 1988
Marx examines the surreptitious activities engaged in by the state as part of its ordering activities.

McBarnet, Doreen J. 'Arrest: The Legal Context of Policing.' In *The British*

Police, pp. 24–40. Edited by Simon Holdaway. London: Edward Arnold, 1979

McBarnet questions the validity of the prevailing theoretical assumption that police deviations from the ideas associated with the rule of law were the result of informal processes that undermined the directions provided by law. She argues that in fact it is the law itself that very often directs police to act in ways that are counter to the rhetoric of law.

Palmer, Stanley H. *Police and Protest in England and Ireland, 1780–1850*. Cambridge; New York: Cambridge University Press, 1988

A recently published and thorough, scholarly examination of a critical period of policing history in England and Ireland. The book, like Radzinowicz's (1956) treatment of this topic, is based on a thorough examination of contemporary papers and media accounts. Current conceptions of this historical period are reviewed in the light of this study.

Piliavin, Irving and Briar, Scott. 'Police Encounters with Juveniles.' *American Journal of Sociology* 70 (1965): 206–14

An example of the early North American scholarship on the police which raises an issue that has become an established part of police scholarship, namely, the importance of signs of respect for police authority as a determinant of police action.

Punch, Maurice, ed. *Control in the Police Organization*. Cambridge, MA: MIT Press, 1983

A collection of essays, by both North American and European writers, canvasses a variety of views on the control of the police organization and the constraints that make this difficult.

Radcliffe, Geoffrey R. Y. and Cross, Geoffrey N. *The English Legal System*. 5th ed. London: Butterworths, 1971

The early chapters provide a useful summary of the early development of policing and criminal justice in England.

Radzinowicz, Leon (Sir). *A History of Criminal Law and its Administration from 1750*. London: Stevens and Sons, 1956. (Vol. 2, The Clash between Private Initiative and Public Interest in the Enforcement of the Law)

Volume two (of a five-volume work that provides an incredibly detailed account of the development of criminal justice in England) examines the debate and jockeying that took place in the eighteenth and early nineteenth century about the role of the state and private interests in the maintenance of order.

Reiner, Robert. *The Politics of the Police*. Brighton, Sussex: Wheatsheaf Books, 1985

This is an important scholarly book on policing that stands apart from the policy debate over policing that has so dominated British writing on the police. Reiner examines the debates between conventional and revisionist historians and the arguments over police accountability. He provides a very interesting analysis of the police occupational culture as well as the public culture of the police.

Reiss, Jr., Albert J. 'The Legitimacy of Intrusion into Private Space.' In *Private Policing*, pp. 19–44. Edited by Clifford D. Shearing and Philip C. Stenning. Newbury Park, Calif.: Sage, 1987. (Sage Criminal Justice System Annuals, Vol. 23)

In this paper Reiss develops his interest in the institutions of privacy and their consequences by examining the implications of the restrictions that provide for privacy in public and private policing as well as the citizens affected by these activities.

Reiss, Jr., Albert J. *The Police and the Public*. New Haven: Yale University Press, 1971

Reiss' book is an early scholarly analysis that focuses attention on the routine day-to-day activities of the public police and identifies police dependence on citizens as a source of information about breaches of order that occurs when police respect the institutions of privacy which characterize democratic societies.

Reuss-Ianni, Elizabeth and Ianni, Francis A. J. 'Street Cops and Management Cops: The Two Cultures of Policing.' In *Control in the Police Organization*, pp. 251–74. Edited by Maurice Punch. Cambridge, MA: MIT Press, 1983

This paper provides a useful analysis of the established views of the police culture and its influence on police decision-making.

Rubinstein, Jonathan. *City Police*. New York: Farrar, Straus and Giroux, 1973

An excellent analysis of early American policing that examines the daily activity of policing in different periods and explores how at different times the gathering of information and the supervision of police officers changed.

Shearing, Clifford D. 'Decriminalizing Criminology: Reflections on the Literal and Tropological Meanings of the Term.' *Canadian Journal of Criminology* 31 (2, April 1989): 169–78

Ordering is identified in this paper as criminology's most fundamental phenomenon.

Shearing, Clifford D., ed. *Organizational Police Deviance*. Toronto: Butterworths, 1981

A collection of essays that examines police rule breaking carried out in the interests of order maintenance.

Shearing, Clifford D. and Ericson, Richard V. 'Culture as Figurative Action.' *British Journal of Sociology* 42 (forthcoming, 1991)

A critique of the conventional conception of police culture that draws attention to its narrative and figurative features.

Shearing, Clifford D. and Stenning, Philip C., eds. *Private Policing*. Newbury Park, Calif.: Sage, 1987. (Sage Criminal Justice System Annuals, Vol. 23)

This collection of essays defines private policing very generally to include a variety of forms of order maintenance undertaken by authorities and agents other than the public police.

Shearing, Clifford D. and Stenning, Philip C. 'Private Security and Social Control.' In *Crime in the Streets and in the Suites*, pp. 384–402. Edited by Doug A. Timmer and Stanley Eitzen. Boston, MA: Allyn and Bacon, 1989

An essay that explores the growth, nature and philosophy of corporate policing and its implications for the development of order maintenance.

South, Nigel. *Policing for Profit: The Private Security Sector*. London: Sage, 1988

This book provides an excellent review of the literature on private policing and explores the development of this phenomenon in Britain, with an emphasis on public policy questions.

Spitzer, Steven and Scull, Andrew T. 'Privatization and Capitalist Development: The Case of the Private Police.' *Social Problems* 25 (1, October 1977): 18–29

An important early essay drawing attention to the significance of private policing that identifies stages in its development and examines the reasons for its pattern of development.

Stenning, Philip C., Shearing, Clifford D., Addario, Susan M. and Condon, Mary G. 'Controlling Interests: Two Conceptions of Ordering Financial Markets.' In *Securing Compliance: Seven Case Studies*, pp. 88–119. Edited by Martin L. Friedland. Toronto: University of Toronto Press, 1990

An exploration of symbolic and behavioural ordering in financial markets.

Stinchcombe, Arthur L. 'Institutions of Privacy in the Determination of Police Administrative Practice.' *American Journal of Sociology* 96 (2, 1963): 150–60

A classic essay drawing attention to the implications of privacy for the organization of social life and its consequences for public policing and police-citizen relations.

Turk, Austin T. *Political Criminality: The Defiance and Defense of Authority*. Beverly Hills, CA: Sage Publications, 1982

A recent North American exploration of political criminality and political policing.

4

Penology

Richard V. Ericson

Traditionally, penology is the study of the disposition of criminal offenders. The field therefore includes study of sentencing by the courts, and of the policies and practices involved in dealing with criminal offenders under sentence. As such, penology has drawn on liberal political theory, and its articulation in legal discourse, for its inspiration and framework (Ashworth, 1983; Heath, 1963; Honderich, 1976; Richards, 1981).

Penologists are concerned with justifications for punishing criminal offenders, including for example whether an offender's behaviour is deserving of denunciation and/or retaliation, and whether punishing the person's behaviour has utilitarian value, such as inhibiting the person from doing it again (specific deterrence), or discouraging others from doing similar things (general deterrence). Social scientists have taken up these questions, as framed by liberal legal discourse, to ascertain whether criminal sanctions serve particular purposes. The evaluation of penal measures (Wilkins, 1969) focuses upon whether some sanctions compared to others are more likely to have general deterrent effects (Blumstein, Cohen and Nagin, 1978; Zimring and Hawkins, 1973) or specific deterrent effects (Lerman, 1975; Walker, 1980; Waller, 1974).

Research on specific deterrence has proliferated in the context of the notion that particular penal sanctions, properly administered, can have 'rehabilitative' effects and prevent recidivism (re-offending). Research has consistently failed to show the superiority of particular 'rehabilitative' measures over other penal sanctions. Moreover, the concept of rehabilitation has been sharply criticized for being vague and amorphous. Some deem the concept vacuous except as a powerful justification for taking more power over the offender's life than would have been taken if the person was punished in just proportion to the seriousness of his offence (American

Friends Service Committee, 1971; Von Hirsch, 1976). Nevertheless, arguments in favour of the rehabilitative ideal continue, as do sanctions justified in the name of rehabilitation and evaluations of these sanctions (Allen, 1981; Cullen and Gilbert, 1982). Many penologists persist in debating rehabilitation and just punishment as a binary opposition, while the penal system persists in absorbing this discourse into its panoply of sanctions and practices (Christie, 1982).

In addition to studying how criminal sanctions can be used to prevent crime and reproduce order in civil society, penologists have analyzed the maintenance of order in penal settings, especially the prison. In the context of trying to understand prison riots and disturbances, or major shifts in the characteristics and concerns of inmates, social scientists have been called upon to study the social organization of the prison (Bottoms and Light, 1987; Canadian Journal of Criminology, 1984; Carlen, 1983; Cohen and Taylor, 1972; Desroches, 1983; Goffman, 1961; Jacobs, 1977; Mathiesen, 1964; Sykes, 1958). Furthermore, in the context of increased legalism in society generally, legal analysts have focused on how bringing the rule of law to penal settings might help to order relations there (Jackson, 1983; Jacobs, 1980; MacGuigan, 1977).

The ascendancy of legalism – with its assertions about the importance of the rule of law, equality and just proportion – has also resulted in a renewed concern for the control of official discretion. Hence penologists have increasingly been called upon to undertake analyses of the discretion available to judges (Hogarth, 1971), prison officials (Jackson, 1983), and parole authorities (McNaughton-Smith, 1976; Nuffield, 1982) as such analyses yield signs of arbitrariness, inequality and injustice. In turn, policy recommendations are advanced to abolish some of the more arbitrary and unjust measures, such as parole, and to structure and circumscribe the discretion of officials, such as judges deciding upon sentences (Canadian Sentencing Commission, 1987).

Conceived in the above terms, penology is technocratic, pragmatic and administrative. It is a technical arm of the state for the better rationalization and administration of penal sanctions. It is inherently ideological since the very question of 'effectiveness' begs answers that are infused with particular values and interests. It is inevitably reformist, involved in a perpetual search for improved, if not perfected, means of deciding upon and administering penal sanctions.

While technocratic penology remains dominant, the field has been substantially broadened and enhanced in the past two decades through a heightened interest in the subject by historians and sociologists. Among historians, a number of 'revisionists' (Foucault, 1977; Ignatieff, 1978; Rothman, 1971) challenged traditional accounts of punishment that took the liberal legal framework for granted and depicted the evolution of punishment as a sustained march of progress from bad to good practices, from blind barbarism to enlightened humanism. Instead of taking the official reform agenda for granted and doing Whig history in its terms, revisionist historians study penal reform as the primary object of inquiry. In particular, they focus on the origins of the penitentiary, and other segregative institutions such as the asylum and the poor house, to ascertain why these institutions became seen as the way forward for dealing with the depraved and deprived members of society. Revisionist historians analyse macro structures (e.g. economic, political, cultural), and their relation to social problems (e.g. changes in employment, demographics, and fear of crime and disorder) as these may have contributed to the construction of segregative institutions. They also analyse the early operation of penal institutions and how they were transformed into something very different from what reformers had conceived initially. In doing so they show that penal reforms are perpetually in need of reform, and that the reform process is as much a part of the penal system as are the penal mechanisms and penal agents themselves.

The work of revisionist historians, especially Foucault (1977), has had a major impact on the field. Historians have moved on to analyse penal reform processes in the late nineteenth and early twentieth centuries. They have shown that in this period penology, criminology and other human sciences were increasingly drawn upon to inform penal policy and practice. They have also shown how this period was characterized by the development of 'progressive' measures in the name of rehabilitation, which in turn fostered the 'welfare sanction,' enhanced official discretion, and bolstered the strong state (Chunn, forthcoming; Garland, 1985; Rothman, 1980).

Sociologists studying the contemporary penal system are also under the strong influence of Foucault (1977) and other revisionist historians. Sociologists focus on contemporary reform efforts to raise similar questions about why particular penal reforms arise, their unintended consequences, and how they feed into a perpetual program of reform (Ericson, 1987). In particular, there has been extensive research on the 'decarceration' or community-based corrections movement, including explanations of its origins in economic, political and ideological terms, and documentation of how it has brought more people within the confines of additional penal sanctions while failing to lessen the use of imprisonment (Chan and Ericson, 1981; Cohen, 1985; Scull, 1984; for counter evidence, see McMahon, forthcoming).

For sociologists, analysis of penal reform is part of a broader project of linking the study of penal sanctions to social and political theory (Garland, 1990). There is a concern, again following Foucault (1977), to see penal institutions as part of a broader inter-institutional network in society, which is in turn shaped by the political economy and culture. This concern places imprisonment and various non-carceral sanctions in the societal context of policing and social control. In the modern apparatus of 'penality' (Garland and Young, 1983), there is inter-changeability of dependent populations across welfare, health and penal institutions (Lowman, Menzies and Palys, 1987); various professional interests entrenched both inside and outside penal establishments (Cohen, 1985); an increasing use of surveillance and information gathering devices for penal control, enhanced by scientific and legal technologies that are embedded in community-based social control systems (Lowman, Menzies and Palys, 1987) and, as a result of all of the above, a substantial involvement by various private-sector organizations in the business of administering penal sanctions and formulating policies about them (Ericson, McMahon and Evans, 1987; Lowman, Menzies and Palys, 1987; Melossi, 1989; Ryan and Ward, 1989).

These developments have entailed a blurring of the boundaries between penology and basic disciplines, especially sociology, political science and history. While research has penal reforms and penal practices as a substantive focus, it increasingly takes its problematics from one or more of the basic disciplines. Increasingly scholars focus on the penal system for the understanding it can provide about basic issues in social and political theory, such as the role of the state; the dimensions of professionalization and bureaucratization in society; how the penal institution intersects with other institutions in the constitution of society; and the contemporary political significance of punishment in relation to the moral sensibilities it evokes and the level of protection it invokes.

Sparked by this broader range of academic interest, penology is a vibrant field. As with any vibrant field, there is no settled orthodoxy, but rather active research agendas and programs from a range of perspectives. The excessive claims of revisionist historians are themselves undergoing revision as a result of reflection by their own members (Ignatieff, 1981; Rothman, 1981), as well as through painstaking empirical research (Beattie, 1986). Similarly, sociologists who have over-stated singular causes and over-emphasized negative consequences of contemporary penal reforms, have engaged in self-reflection (Scull, 1984), and are being challenged through theoretical refinements (Garland, 1990) and empirical research (Downes, 1988; Lowman, Menzies and Palys, 1987; McMahon, forthcoming; Young, forthcoming). There are many signs of intellectual ferment in penology, a field that promises to make significant contributions to knowledge and public policy deliberations in the years to come.

Reading List

Allen, Francis A. *The Decline of the Rehabilitative Ideal*. New Haven, CT: Yale University Press, 1981
An essay on rehabilitation as a component of penal policy, including a review of recent criticisms of the concept, and arguments for the refinement of the concept and its continued use in penal theory and practice.

American Friends Service Committee. *Struggle for Justice: A Report on Crime and Punishment in America*. New York: Hill and Wang, 1971
A critical analysis of the penal system and the interests that sustain it, with particular focus on how practices in the name of 'rehabilitation' intensify punishment and sustain inequities.

Ashworth, Andrew. *Sentencing and Penal Policy*. London: Weidenfeld and Nicolson, 1983
A comprehensive legal and social policy analysis of sentencing and punishment, covering the justifications of punishment, judicial discretion, special categories of offenders, the symbolic dimensions of punishment, and issues in sentencing and the administration of various punishments.

Beattie, John M. *Attitudes Toward Crime and Punishment in Upper Canada, 1830-50: A Documentary Study*. J.M. Beattie with the assistance of L.M. Distad. Toronto: Centre of Criminology, University of Toronto, 1977. (Working paper of the Centre of Criminology, University of Toronto)
An essay on crime and punishment in Upper Canada during the period when the first penitentiary was founded at Kingston, with copies of documents from the period addressing capital punishment, local gaols, the founding of the penitentiary and the early operation of the penitentiary.

Beattie, John M. *Crime and the Courts in England, 1660-1800*. Princeton, NJ: Princeton University Press, 1986
A definitive empirical study of crime and the administration of justice in England between 1660 and 1800, with excellent chapters on the operation and impact of transportation and the emergence of imprisonment which challenge and modify the accounts of revisionist historians.

Blumstein, Alfred, Cohen, Jacqueline and Nagin, Daniel, eds. *Deterrence and Incapacitation: Estimating the Effects of Criminal Sanctions on Crime Rates*. Washington, DC: National Academy of Sciences, 1978
A comprehensive review of research on the incapacitative effects of imprisonment and the deterrent effects of various penal measures including capital punishment.

Bottoms, Anthony E. and Light, Roy, eds. *Problems of Long-Term Imprisonment*. Aldershot; Brookfield, Vt: Gower, 1987. (Cambridge studies in criminology; 58)
A valuable collection of 16 original essays examining theory, policy, management problems and ill-effects associated with long-term imprisonment.

British Journal of Criminology 22 (3, July, 1982). Special Issue on Dangerousness
Leading penologists assess the concept of dangerousness, including the scientific basis of and philosophical justifications for, preventive sentencing and protective punishment.

Burtch, Brian E. and Ericson, Richard V. *The Silent System: An Inquiry into Prisoners who Suicide and Annotated Bibliography*. Toronto: Centre of Criminology, University of Toronto, 1979. (Research report of the Centre of Criminology, University of Toronto, 1979)
This monograph synthesizes research on prisoner suicides and reports an empirical study of suicide in Canadian maximum-security penitentiaries.

Canada. Parliament. House of Commons. Subcommittee on the Penitentiary System in Canada. *Report to Parliament by the Sub-Committee on the Penitentiary System in Canada*. Ottawa: Ministry of Supply and Services, 1977. (Chair: Mark MacGuigan)
An official inquiry into the Canadian penitentiary system that revealed severe difficulties in organization and management, and serious problems regarding the inhumane treatment of prisoners.

Canadian Journal of Criminology 26 (4, October, 1984). Special Issue on Long-Term Incarceration
Canadian criminologists present analyses and opinion pieces regarding problems with imprisonment as a penal option, with particular reference to the negative effects of long-term imprisonment.

Canadian Sentencing Commission. *Sentencing Reform: A Canadian Approach: Report of the Canadian Sentencing Commission*. Ottawa: Canadian Govt. Publishing Centre, Supply and Services Canada, 1987. (Chairman: J.R. Omer Archambault)
A comprehensive overview of the history of punishment in Canada, contemporary issues and problems, and possibilities for reform through modification of the structure of sentences and control of judicial discretion.

Carlen, Patricia. *Women's Imprisonment: A Study in Social Control*. London; Boston: Routledge and Kegan Paul, 1983
The leading contemporary study of the particular problems and situations encountered by incarcerated women.

Chan, Janet B.L. and Ericson, Richard V. *Decarceration and the Economy of Penal Reform*. Toronto: Centre of Criminology, University of Toronto, 1981.(Research report of the Centre of Criminology, University of Toronto; 14)

An analysis of penal trends in Ontario focusing on how the expansion of penal sanctions other than imprisonment has affected rates of imprisonment and the functions of prisons.

Christie, Nils. *Limits to Pain*. Oxford: Martin Robertson, 1982

Argues that the resurgence of the justice model offers no advance over the rehabilitation model it seeks to displace, and that both models should be superseded by a commitment to minimizing the severity of punishment and maximizing citizens' participation in the administration of justice.

Chunn, Dorothy E. *From Punishment to Doing Good*. Toronto: University of Toronto Press (forthcoming)

The origins and impact of a different penal system regarding juveniles and family problems is examined in the Ontario context, showing how in the first half of the twentieth century this system became private and technocratic, with the legal rights of 'clients,' the participation of legal personnel, and input from the lay public, giving way to a 'welfare sanction.'

Cohen, Stanley. *Visions of Social Control: Crime, Punishment and Classification*. Cambridge; New York: Polity, 1985

The most comprehensive and best analysis of contemporary trends in penal ideologies, policies and practices, linking these trends to broader theories of social control.

Cohen, Stanley and Taylor, Laurie. *Psychological Survival: The Experience of Long-Term Imprisonment*. 2nd ed. Harmondsworth, Middx.: Penguin, 1981

An original empirical study of how prisoners facing long-term incarceration manage to cope with disrupted relationships, the fear of deterioration and other pains of imprisonment.

Culhane, Clare. *Still Barred from Prison: Social Injustice in Canada*. Montreal: Black Rose Books, 1985

A noted Canadian activist focuses on prison violence to further her critique of prisons and to advance the cause of abolition.

Cullen, Francis T. and Gilbert, Karen E. *Reaffirming Rehabilitation*. Cincinnati, OH: Anderson, 1982

Describes the evolution of the idea and practice of rehabilitation, the challenge to it posed by the justice model and the arguments in favour of maintaining rehabilitation as a central component of the penal system.

Dear, Michael J. and Wolch, Jennifer R. *Landscapes of Despair: From Institutionalization to Homelessness*. Princeton, N.J.: Princeton University Press, 1987

Analyzes the unintended consequences of policies of deinstitutionalization – especially regarding the mentally disabled – including homelessness, inadequate health and welfare provision, and neglect and recommends better community care planning and provision rather than a return to the heavy use of segregative institutions.

Desroches, Frederick J. 'Anomie: Two Theories of Prison Riots.' *Canadian Journal of Criminology* 25 (2, April, 1983): 173-90

Theorizes prison riots as resulting from a disjunction between the high expectations of inmates, officially fostered by the penal system, and the limited means available to achieve these expectations given the structure and conditions of imprisonment.

Dittenhoffer, Tony and Ericson, Richard V. 'The Victim/Offender Reconciliation Program: A Message to Correctional Reformers.' *University of Toronto Law Journal* 33 (1983): 314-47

An empirical study documenting that when penal reform ideas are translated into actual programs they are transformed in accordance with the organizational convenience and interests of those who operate the programs.

Downes, David. *Contrasts in Tolerance*. Oxford: Clarendon Press; New York: Oxford University Press, 1988

An excellent comparative study of contemporary penal policy in the Netherlands and in England and Wales as it relates to sentencing trends and levels of incarceration in the two jurisdictions.

Ekstedt, John W. and Griffiths, Curt T. *Corrections in Canada: Policy and Practice*. 2nd ed. Toronto: Butterworths, 1988

A good summary of the history of penal policy and practice in Canada, and of contemporary issues, trends and developments.

Ericson, Richard V. 'The State and Criminal Justice Reform.' In *State Control: Criminal Justice Politics in Canada*, pp. 21-37. Edited by Robert S. Ratner and John L. McMullan. Vancouver: University of British Columbia Press, 1987

A critical analysis of the role of the state in marshalling criminal justice reform, with examples specific to the penal system.

Ericson, Richard V., McMahon, Maeve W. and Evans, Donald G. 'Punishing for Profit: Reflections on the Revival of Privatization in Corrections.' *Canadian Journal of Criminology* 29 (4, October, 1987): 355-387

A critical analysis of the involvement of non-state agencies in the administration of penal sanctions, including theorizing on the implications of this development for our understanding of contemporary social control structures and processes.

Evans, Robin. *The Fabrication of Virtue*. Cambridge: Cambridge University Press, 1982
A fascinating study of the ideas and practices that formed English prison architecture in the late eighteenth and early nineteenth centuries, including 218 illustrations.

Foucault, Michel. *Discipline and Punish: The Birth of the Prison*. New York: Pantheon, 1977
A highly original, controversial and influential essay that addresses why the prison – rather than the spectacle of public executions or various non-carceral options – became the dominant mode of punishment in the nineteenth century, and how the prison continues to function as a manufactory for the production of docile and useful citizens.

Friedenberg, Edgar Z. 'The Punishment Industry in Canada.' *Canadian Journal of Sociology* 5 (3, Summer, 1980): 273-83
With reference to the MacGuigan (1977) report on the Canadian penitentiary system, a sharp critique of that system in terms of how it sustains itself and perpetuates various political and professional interests in spite of multiple signs of failure.

Garland, David. 'Foucault's *Discipline and Punish* : An Exposition and Critique.' *American Bar Foundation Research Journal* 4 (4, Fall,1986): 847-880
A lucid summary of Foucault's ideas, and a sustained and cogent critique of Foucault's thesis in light of what has occurred over the decade following the publication of his book in English.

Garland, David. *Punishment and Modern Society*. Oxford: Oxford University Press; Chicago, IL: University of Chicago Press, 1990
A very important synthesis of social and political theories of punishment, as well as a sophisticated treatment of the emergent cultural theories of punishment.

Garland, David. *Punishment and Welfare: A History of Penal Strategies*. Aldershot, Hants; Brookfield, VT: Gower, 1985
Inspired by Foucault, a superb critical analysis of late nineteenth and early twentieth century penal policies in Britain, focusing on how various forms of knowledge, including penology itself, helped to constitute penal strategies and practices.

Garland, David and Young, Peter, eds. *The Power to Punish*. London: Heinemann Educational Books; Atlantic Highlands, N.J.: Humanities Press, 1983
A first-rate collection of nine original articles by leading penologists, analyzing contemporary penal policies and practices from sociological perspectives.

Goffman, Erving. *Asylums*. New York: Doubleday, 1961
A brilliant, social psychological analysis of life in prisons, mental

hospitals and other total institutions with an emphasis on how the inmate is 'made' in terms of the social organization of the institution and what the inmate in turn makes out of institutional life.

Hay, Douglas, et al. *Albion's Fatal Tree: Crime and Society in Eighteenth Century England.* Harmondsworth, Middx.: Penguin, 1975
A collection of six original essays that examine selected types of crime and criminal events, how they were dealt with by the authorities, and how discretion by the authorities enhanced both their authority and the social order they wished to preserve.

Heath, James, ed. *Eighteenth Century Penal Theory.* London: Oxford University Press, 1963
An essay on eighteenth century penal theory, followed by extracts from the writings of twenty leading philosophers and penal reformers of the period.

Hogarth, John. *Sentencing as a Human Process.* Toronto: published by the University of Toronto Press in association with the Centre of Criminology, University of Toronto, 1971
A classic study in Canadian criminology, this book analyses variation in the sentencing practices of Ontario magistrates in terms of their personal philosophies, characteristics and proclivities.

Honderich, Ted. *Punishment: The Supposed Justifications.* new ed. Harmondsworth, Middx.: Penguin, 1976
A concise review of various philosophical justifications of punishment, and their social and political implications in terms of fundamental values including equality, liberty and freedom.

Ignatieff, Michael. *A Just Measure of Pain: The Penitentiary in the Industrial Revolution: 1750-1850.* London: Macmillan; New York: Pantheon, 1978
A major contribution to the revisionist history of punishment, this book examines the ideological origins of the penitentiary, early penitentiary practices and the continuing dialectic between ideology and practice in the politics of penal reform.

Ignatieff, Michael. 'State, Civil Society and Total Institutions.' In *Crime and Justice: An Annual Review of Research*, Vol. 3, pp. 153-92. Edited by Michael Tonry and Norval Morris. Chicago, IL: University of Chicago Press, 1981
This fine essay reviews the influential revisionist histories of punishment published in the 1970s, points out their flaws and limitations, and sketches a research agenda to overcome their shortcomings.

Irwin, John. *The Jail: Managing the Underclass in American Society.* Berkeley, CA: University of California Press, 1985
One of the few studies of the contemporary jail – inhabited largely by

those awaiting trial and those sentenced for minor violations or public
order offences – and how it functions to reproduce an 'underclass' at
the margins of society.

Jackson, Michael. *Prisoners of Isolation: Solitary Confinement in Canada*.
Toronto: University of Toronto Press, 1983
A lawyer and professor of law draws upon socio-legal research, legal
case materials and his own experiences defending prisoners against the
abuses of solitary confinement to provide a disturbing account of life in
the innermost region of the penitentiary.

Jacobs, James B. 'The Prisoners' Rights Movement and its Impacts, 1960-
80.' In *Crime and Justice: An Annual Review of Research*, Vol. 2, pp.
429-70. Edited by Norval Morris and Michael Tonry. Chicago, IL:
University of Chicago Press, 1980
A review of the political context of, and legal developments in, the
American prisoners' rights movement.

Jacobs, James B. *Stateville: The Penitentiary in Mass Society*. Chicago, IL:
University of Chicago Press, 1977. (Studies in crime and justice)
An important addition to the literature on the social organization of
prisons, incorporating contemporary issues and developments including
the increasing concern for the legal rights of prisoners.

Lerman, Paul. *Community Treatment and Social Control: A Critical
Analysis of Juvenile Correctional Policy*. Chicago, IL: University of
Chicago Press, 1975
A critical analysis of a famous experiment in community treatment,
focusing on the political processes involved in both the program itself
and its evaluation.

Lowman, John, Menzies, Robert J. and Palys, Ted S., eds. *Transcarcera-
tion: Essays in the Sociology of Social Control*. Aldershot, Hants;
Brookfield, VT: Gower, 1987. (Cambridge studies in criminology; 60)
A collection of 18 essays on contemporary trends in punishment, the
interchangeability of populations between prisons and other carceral
institutions and the growth of non-carceral penal sanctions that depend
on community-based mechanisms of surveillance.

Mandel, Michael. 'Democracy, Class and the National Parole Board.' In *The
Social Dimensions of Law*, pp.146-65. Edited by Neil Boyd. Scarborough, Ont: Prentice-Hall Canada, 1986
A critical essay on the arbitrary power invested in parole authorities,
and its implications of undemocratic practice and the reproduction of
inequality.

Mathiesen, Thomas. *The Defences of the Weak: A Sociological Study of a
Norwegian Correctional Institution*. London: Tavistock, 1965
An early critical study of the social organization of the prison that

provided the basis for Mathiesen's later highly influential work on penal reform.

Mathiesen, Thomas. *The Politics of Abolition*. London: Martin Robertson, 1974

An influential essay that analyzes ideological and practical limitations to social reform, including penal reform, and suggests ways of transcending these limitations.

McMahon, Maeve. *Changing Penal Trends: Imprisonment and Alternatives in Ontario, 1951-1984*. Toronto: University of Toronto Press (forthcoming)

A fine empirical examination of penal ideology and practice in Ontario over the past four decades, documenting a decrease in the use of imprisonment, and thereby challenging critical penologists who argue that decarceration policies have not had an impact on rates of imprisonment.

McNaughton-Smith, Peter. *Permission to be Slightly Free: A Study of the Granting, Refusing and Withdrawing of Parole in Canadian Penitentiaries*. Ottawa: Law Reform Commission of Canada, 1976

An insightful critical analysis of parole in Canada, highlighting the arbitrariness of official discretion and the predicament of the parolee.

Melossi, Dario. *The State of Social Control*. Cambridge: Polity, 1989

An analysis of law and punishment as they relate to theories of the state and social control.

Menzies, Ken. 'The Rapid Spread of Community Service Orders in Ontario.' *Canadian Journal of Criminology* 28 (2, April, 1986): 157-169

An analysis of the political processes which fostered the establishment and expansion of community service orders as a popular penal sanction of the past decade.

Menzies, Robert. *Survival of the Sanest: Psychiatric Order and Disorder in a Pre-Trial Forensic Clinic*. Toronto: University of Toronto Press, 1989

An excellent empirical study documenting the arbitrariness of official discretion regarding 'dangerous' persons who are detained for pre-trial psychiatric assessment, and the subsequent 'penal careers' of these persons as they are repeatedly cycled through prisons, mental hospitals, and welfare institutions.

Nuffield, Joan. *Parole Decision-Making in Canada: Research Towards Decision Guidelines*. Ottawa: Solicitor General Canada, 1982

An empirical study of parole decision-making in Canada and of factors associated with recidivism among parolees.

Richards, David A.J. 'Rights, Utility and Crime.' In *Crime and Justice: An Annual Review of Research*, Vol. 3, pp. 247-94. Edited by Michael

Tonry and Norval Morris. Chicago, IL: University of Chicago Press, 1981
A review of traditional justifications of punishment in the context of recent theorizing about rights.

Rothman, David J. *Conscience and Convenience: The Asylum and its Alternatives in Progressive America.* Boston, MA: Little, Brown, 1980
A comparative analysis of criminal justice, juvenile justice, and mental health control systems in America between 1900 and 1965, arguing that the humanitarian ideals of reformers were consistently translated into the organizational interests of those who operated these control systems, resulting in an expansion of official discretion and the entrenchment of bureaucratic and professional interests.

Rothman, David J. *The Discovery of the Asylum.* Boston, MA: Little, Brown, 1971
Among the influential revisionist histories of punishment, this book examines the ideological and political origins of segregative institutions in America.

Rothman, David J. 'Social Control: The Uses and Abuses of the Concept in the History of Incarceration.' *Rice University Studies* 67 (1981): 9-20
A fine critique of the much used and abused concept of social control in the study of punishment.

Rusche, Georg and Kirchheimer, Otto. *Punishment and Social Structure.* New York: Columbia University Press, 1939
A lasting contribution to the political economy of punishment, showing how changing social and economic conditions affect the way people think and act in relation to crime and punishment.

Rutherford, Andrew. *Prisons and the Process of Justice.* London: Heinemann, 1984
Argues that the contemporary expansion of the prison system in many Western countries is not inevitable, and can be checked through policies aimed at controlling decision-making throughout the criminal justice process.

Ryan, Mick and Ward, Tony. *Privatization and the Penal System: The American Experience and the Debate in Britain.* Milton Keynes: Open University Press, 1989
This book examines the role of various non-state organizations involved in penal policy and the administration of penal sanctions, raising questions about the role of the state and the blurring of traditional boundaries between the public and private spheres.

Scull, Andrew T. *Decarceration : Community Treatment and the Deviant: A Radical View.* 2nd ed. Cambridge: Polity, 1984

An analysis of American policies for decreasing the use of segregative institutions for criminal offenders and the mentally disabled, this work spawned research and debate internationally, and the second edition includes the author's critical reflections on the debate.

Scull, Andrew T. *Museums of Madness*. New York: St. Martins, 1979
An important contribution to revisionist histories of segregative institutions, this work analyzes the rise of the asylum and the social organization that constituted it in nineteenth century England.

Smandych, Russell. 'The Upper Canadian Experience with Pre-Segregative Controls.' Unpublished PHD thesis, University of Toronto, 1989
An excellent review and critique of how penologists use the concept of social control, and a study of how and why Upper Canadians managed social control without segregative institutions prior to the founding of the penitentiary at Kingston.

Spierenburg, Petrus C. *The Spectacle of Suffering*. Cambridge; New York: Cambridge University Press, 1984
A superb history of the development and decline of public executions in Europe, with important criticisms of, and refinements to, sociological theories of punishment and penal change.

Sykes, Gresham M. *The Society of Captives: A Study of a Maximum Security Prison*. Princeton, NJ: Princeton University Press, 1958
An early and lasting contribution to understanding the social organization of the prison.

Taylor, Brian B. *Le Corbusier: The City of Refuge, Paris 1929-33*. Chicago, IL: University of Chicago Press, 1987
A fascinating account of how an architect translated the Salvation Army's idea of a working and living environment for the rehabilitation of social outcasts into the City of Refuge Complex in Paris.

Verdun-Jones, Simon N. and Mitchell-Banks, Teresa. *The Fine as a Sentencing Option in Canada*. Ottawa: Dept of Justice Canada, Policy, Programs and Research Branch, 1988. (Research reports of the Canadian Sentencing Commission)
A review of issues and evidence concerning the use of the fine, a neglected topic in penology.

Von Hirsch, Andrew. *Doing Justice: The Choice of Punishments: Report of the Committee for the Study of Incarceration*. New York: Hill and Wang, 1976
An influential work advancing arguments in favour of the justice model in the context of the decline of the rehabilitative ideal.

Walker, Nigel. *Punishment, Danger and Stigma*. Oxford: Basil Blackwell, 1980

This book interrogates the retributive, reductive and denunciatory justifications of punishment with a fine blend of social, scientific and pragmatic arguments.

Waller, Irvin. *Men Released from Prison.* Toronto: University of Toronto Press in association with the Centre of Criminology, University of Toronto, 1974. (Canadian studies in criminology; 2)
An empirical investigation into what happens to ex-inmates of Canadian penitentiaries, comparing those released under parole supervision with those released outright.

Wilkins, Leslie T. *Evaluation of Penal Measures.* New York: Random House, 1969
A comprehensive review of concepts, methodologies, findings and policy implications of research on the effectiveness of penal sanctions.

Young, Peter. *Punishment, Money and Legal Order* (forthcoming).
A comprehensive sociological study of the fine as a penal sanction, the definitive work on the subject.

Zimring, Franklin E. and Hawkins, Gordon J. *Deterrence: The Legal Threat in Crime Control.* Chicago, IL: University of Chicago Press, 1973.
A lasting contribution to the study of deterrence, covering theory, research methods, research findings, and proposals for further research.

Law Reform and Policy

5

Politics and Crime: A Survey

Peter H. Solomon Jr.

Introduction

The study of crime and its control is hard to imagine without the inclusion of politics. In the modern state, governments define which acts are crimes and what punishments may be assigned to those who commit them. Political decisions also shape the institutions of criminal justice and determine the rules that govern their conduct. In France and Russia, jurists have long recognized the role of politics in criminal law and its administration, using the term 'criminal policy' (*la politique criminelle, uglovnaia politika*) to depict it. If the term 'criminal policy' sounds strange to the English speaking reader, it is because of the tradition among jurists in common law countries of downplaying the political origins of laws.

Nonetheless, from the 1960s serious study of politics and crime flourished in the United States, Canada and Great Britain. This new scholarship had roots in separate but reinforcing developments. First, a handful of pioneering sociologists, influenced by Marxian perspectives, turned away from the study of the causes and prevention of crime (criminology proper) to the investigation of the roots of the criminal law in the interests of social groups and classes (sociology of criminal law) (Chambliss, 1964; Gusfield, 1967). Second, following the lead of Sir Leon Radzinowicz, social and legal historians began inquiries about the history of the criminal law and its institutions (Hay, 1975; Radzinowicz, 1948–86; Thompson, 1975). Third, unusual features of political life within the United States attracted political scientists to the study of politics and crime. On the one hand, the political turmoil surrounding the anti-Vietnam War protests and the activities of black radicals called attention to political justice (Becker, 1971; Christenson, 1986). On the other hand, the prominence of law and order issues in the presidential election campaigns of 1964 and 1968 made studying politics in the administration of justice fashionable and assured political support for it (Cronin, 1981). Finally, members of a new generation of legal scholars in the United States rebelled against their seniors' denial of the political basis of law. Exponents of Critical Legal Scholarship, in the main of neo-Marxian inspiration, ran to the opposite extreme, arguing that the rule of law was little more than a myth to disguise the structure of power (Unger, 1976).

Now in the late 1980s, the study of politics and crime involves scholars in a variety of disciplines, ranging from political science to sociology, history and law.

This survey of literature on politics and crime stresses materials dealing with the United States, Canada and Great Britain, but also includes references relating to Western Europe and the USSR. I shall discuss four subject areas: (1) Political Crime, Policing and Justice; (2) Criminal Policy-Making and Development; (3) Criminology and Criminal Policy; and (4) Politics in the Administration of Justice.

Political Crime, Policing and Justice

In a sense, all crime is political. Public authorities decide which acts to designate as criminal, when those acts have been committed, and how to react to them. Yet, one can distinguish acts that authorities perceive to be threatening from those that merely contravene public order or morality. In the modern world, most regimes have made such a distinction, typically by stigmatizing some offences as political (such as treason) and using special laws (such as conspiracy), police forces and even tribunals. In addition to the core of political offences involving betrayal of allegiance, many regimes go further and treat as political crime various lesser challenges to their authority. Just which acts or kinds of speech particular rulers so treat varies with the country and the moment in its history. In short, the content of political criminality is elastic (Koistra, 1985).

The study of political crime and justice started with the experience of European countries, where jurists dealt more openly with the political dimensions of the law than their North American counterparts. Focusing on Germany and France in the twentieth century, Otto Kirchheimer, a German scholar transplanted to the United States, wrote a near definitive analysis of the uses of political trials in democratic and authoritarian states (Kirchheimer, 1961). More recently, Barton Ingraham completed a study of the laws relating to political crime and their administration in France, Germany and Great Britain from 1770 to 1970. Among his special concerns was explaining the decline of the liberal conception of political offender as hero, and the rise in the twentieth century of a preventive approach to political crime (Ingraham, 1979). In the same vein, an analysis of contemporary political policing stressed such preventive functions as the gathering of intelligence, control of information, neutralization of offenders, and intimidation of the general population (Turk, 1982, chap. 3).

In the wake of some events of the 1960s, American writers paid more attention to political trials than to political policing. Accounts of trials in the United States (e.g. Chicago Eight) against a background of trials in Germany, Ghana and the USSR, form the core of a collection edited by Theodore Becker (1971). A recent monograph by Ron Christenson combines detailed analysis of a different set of trials (including the SWAPO trial in South Africa, the trial of a bomber in Wisconsin, and the trial of militant Indians in Wounded Knee, South Dakota) with analysis of the types and functions of political trials. Christenson distinguishes political trials 'within the rule of law,' that is, fair contests, from mere 'partisan trials' that substitute political expediency for law (Christenson, 1986). While the distinction is important, even partisan trials may involve risks for authorities, if the challengers can use the courtroom to dramatize their cause (Kirchheimer, 1961).

The elasticity of what is defined as a political crime within particular countries makes an historical approach to the subject fruitful. In the history of the United States, for example, the treatment of Communists, and the use of the issue of loyalty by various social groups, offer a rich vein for the study of political policing and justice. On the one hand, the story includes the surveillance, persecution and prosecution of members of the Communist Party; and, with the receding of the Cold War and McCarthyism, the gradual shift of the Communist Party from number one political deviant to the status of politically marginal (Belknap, 1977; Caute, 1978). On the other hand, the issue of disloyalty associated with Bolshevism and Communism provided the symbols for two outbreaks of public hysteria, the Red Scare of 1919, and the era of purge known as McCarthyism (Caute, 1987; Murray, 1955). Since the victims in these outbreaks were, by and large, innocent of wrongdoing, one may describe them as instances of the manufacture of political deviance, a process characteristic of such tense times as war and its aftermath. Another instance of the manufacture of political deviance was the deportation and internment of Japanese-Americans during World War II (Irons, 1983). Canadian and American political history share some bêtes noires. The handling of the Winnipeg General Strike bore the marks of the American Red Scare (McNaught, 1975). Canadian politicians under the lead of Mackenzie King also deported Japanese-Canadians from the West Coast during World War II (Berger, 1981, chap. 4). Overall, though, the quiescent political tradition of Canada yielded a lower volume of political policing and prosecution than did that of the United States (McNaught, 1975). Political crime attracted the attention of Canadians most recently in the October Crisis of 1970. What bothered many observers was not the pursuit of the FLQ kidnappers but the seemingly unprovoked arrest of some 300 members of the Quebec intelligentsia. The story of this episode receives an unbiased recital in Haggart and Golden (1971). Raymond Breton analyzes the constellation of political forces that explain Trudeau's use of the War Measures Act (Breton, 1972).

Criminal Policy-Making and Development

Political scientists study policy-making for theoretical and practical reasons. The subject enables them to assess the relative importance of social groups and political actors. At the same time, it helps answer questions that all reformers need to confront. What obstacles get in the way of the adoption and implementation of changes in policies, and how can those obstacles be overcome?

Understanding the making and development of policies calls for familiarity with the phases of the policy process and the actors involved in it: the public, politicians and professionals. I have already discussed the phases of policy-making and their characteristics in another place (Solomon, 1981). Conventional wisdom suggests that, as a rule, the general public has but a slight impact on the development of criminal policy most of the time. The exception is issues that take on symbolic importance, such as the death penalty, or drugs and alcohol (Fairchild, 1981). Likewise, while issue-oriented interest groups from the public exercise influence in the playing out of some issues (Friedland, 1984, chaps. 3 and 4; Rock, 1986) the interest groups that consistently matter are those representing the professionals and officials in criminal justice (judges, police chiefs and bar associations). Especially active in the initiation and screening of proposals for change in criminal policy are the policy officials now prominent in most Western governments. These are civil servants who have no operational responsibilities, but who concern themselves with monitoring policies and advising politicians (Rock, 1986; Solomon, 1981). Working closely with policy officials, one often finds social scientists (criminologists or other experts bearing the mantle of scientific authority). See part three, Criminology and Criminal Policy, for further discussion of this matter.

The literature on the making and development of criminal policy consists mainly of case studies of changes in laws, institutions and programs.

One set of studies focuses on the criminal law itself, that is, instances of the criminalization or decriminalization of particular acts. The most serious crimes of violence and property have changed little in most Western countries, prompting two observers to describe them as a 'constant core of crime' (Radzinowicz and King, 1979). In contrast, victimless crimes, lesser breaches of order, and crimes relating to the economy, have changed frequently. The bulk of case studies of criminalization and decriminalization have focused on such acts as the use or abuse of alcohol and drugs, and on vagrancy (Boyd, 1984; Chambliss, 1964; Galliher, 1977; Gusfield, 1963; Scheerer, 1977). The few studies dealing with crimes relating to business and the economy (Carson, 1970; Carson, 1974; Levi, 1987, chap. 4) deserve successors.

A major theme in the literature on criminalization and decriminalization has been the way some issues acquire symbolic meaning that may influence resulting laws or policies more than any practical motives (Carson, 1974; Gusfield, 1967, 1981; Hay, 1975; Scheerer, 1977). Sometimes, decriminalization reflects changes neither in values nor meanings, but in such mundane administrative considerations as the manageability of court loads (Solomon, 1981).

Another set of case studies of policy-making focuses upon punishment. The emergence of imprisonment as the model form of punishment in the early nineteenth century forms the subject of monographs by David Rothman (1971) on the United States and Michael Ignatieff (1978) on England. This topic receives a different interpretation in the classic Marxian study of the history of punishment by Rusche and Kirchheimer (1939), which correlates major changes in punishment with shifts in the economy's demand for unskilled labour. The invention of probation and parole in the United States at the end of the nineteenth century, and their rapid adoption by most American states, receives definitive treatment in David Rothman's *Conscience and Convenience* (1980). This book warns that when criminal justice officials support a change for reasons of their own (convenience) that differs from those of reformers (conscience), the officials may distort the reforms in the cause of implementation. In short, beware of easy and strange alliances!

Finally, the politics of capital punishment has received considerable attention (Christoff, 1962; Jayewardene, 1972; Tuttle, 1961; Zimring, 1986). The best writing, though, has dealt not with the contemporary scene, but with England in the eighteenth and nineteenth centuries, where a long list of offences became subject to the death penalty and were subsequently removed from its domain. Explaining these changes has aroused sharp, but intellectually productive controversy, among social and legal historians (Hay, 1975; Langbein, 1983).

Other case studies in the development of policies relating to criminal justice have dealt with institutions and programs. Among the institutions of criminal justice that have changed most often in the twentieth century are those dealing with juvenile crime. The politics associated with the changes in the United States, from informal to formal juvenile court proceedings, and in England, from courts to social agencies, have received serious study (Bottoms, 1974; Lemert, 1970).

The largest and most expensive program ever mounted to improve law enforcement and crime prevention was the United States' 'War on Crime,' implemented from 1968 to 1978 by the Law Enforcement Assistance Administration. The story of this white elephant, and the lessons it suggests about fighting crime with money, deserve attention from politicians and reformers alike (Cronin, 1981; Feeley and Sarat, 1980). Perhaps the smallest program in criminal justice to receive full-length study was the victims initiative launched by the federal government of Canada in 1981. Paul Rock's study of this program offers deep insights into the world of policy officials in Ottawa, and how individual officials there go about promoting changes in policy.

Some of the case studies mentioned highlight the difficulty in introducing meaningful changes in criminal justice policy (Feeley and Sarat, 1980; Rothman, 1980). This message has led Richard Ericson and Patricia Baranek to a pessimistic fatalism about the possibilities for reform, a fatalism with which not all observers agree (Ericson and Baranek, 1985; Ratner, 1987, chaps. 2 and 3).

Criminology and Criminal Policy

Since the 1960s, when many governments established planning and research units for criminal justice, decisions in criminal policy often featured contributions from criminologists. Rarely, if ever, could these experts provide scientifically grounded solutions to policy problems, but criminologists could offer advice informed by research. As a rule, politicians treated this advice as just one kind of information, useful in not only reaching, but also in justifying decisions (Lindblom and Cohen, 1979; Merton, 1968). This approach disappointed some criminologists, who had hoped for a greater and more consistent impact on policy. They found it particularly frustrating when politicians failed to launch experimental research, disregarded advice, or used research merely to legitimate choices based on ideology (Hood, 1974; Solomon, 1983). In contrast, other scholars took a jaundiced view of the relevance of criminology for policy, warning criminologists not to sell politicians solutions based upon weakly grounded theories (Moynihan, 1969; Wilson, 1983).

The frustrations of scholars and politicians alike would diminish if they treated research in a different light. Instead of expecting solutions to problems, politicians should look to research for help in conceptualizing problems, and defining the agenda of policy-making. A growing number of scholars believe that the most fruitful and feasible use of social science research is enlightening policy-makers, not offering panaceas. (Lindblom and Cohen, 1979; Solomon, 1983; Weiss, 1978).

To perform either function, social scientists must communicate with politicians, overcoming the well-known gap between the languages of policy and research (Waller, 1979). This exercise may require policy analysis, argumentation aimed at relating the results of research to policy problems, and assessing their relative importance on the agenda of policy-making (Solomon, 1983). Policy analysis inevitably reflects the assumptions and biases of its authors, since policy choices themselves involve values. Policy analysis relating to criminal justice has featured a spectrum ranging from conservative (Wilson, 1983) to liberal perspectives (Morris and Hawkins, 1977).

Some of the most fruitful contributions to policy thinking use the lessons of history. Lawrence Friedman has demonstrated this in a review of American experience with discretion, in prosecution and sentencing, plea bargaining, and the handling of victimless crimes (Friedman, 1981).

Politics in the Administration of Criminal Justice

In all areas of policy, there is a gap between the measures adopted and enshrined in legislation, and the results achieved during implementation. At the minimum, implementation of policies reflects the interests of the officials conducting it. In criminal justice, the distance between policy and practice tends to be especially great because of the high degree of discretion vested in the hands of police, prosecutors, judges and penal officials. In some countries, this discretion finds support in the doctrines of judicial and police independence.

Governing the conduct of police officers has proven especially difficult, for even the chiefs may lack the information and resources needed to channel the discretion of their subordinates (Wilson, 1969). At the same time, the plethora of boards and commissions established in the United States and Canada to hold police accountable find it difficult to direct police chiefs about issues of policy (Goldstein, 1977, chap. 6). The chiefs often criticize rulings of boards as violations of their 'independence,' a value that gained prominence during campaigns to reduce corruption of the police (Sherman, 1978). While politicians and police commissions might have trouble directing their police, politics still affects the styles of policing in particular communities. In a classic study, James Q. Wilson demonstrates how policing in the United States varies with the type of local government, itself a reflection of local political culture (Wilson, 1969).

The importance of local traditions and values extends beyond policing into prosecution and sentencing. Two major studies have compared criminal justice practice in different American cities. In both instances, the authors attributed variations in plea negotiation and sentencing to differences in the legal and political cultures of the communities they studied (Eisenstein and Jacob, 1977; Levin, 1977). Prosecutors and judges may also share bureaucratic interests that override local variations. Research has shown that reforms of the courts (to improve efficiency or reduce plea negotiation) worked best when they offered incentives or benefits to the officials who had to implement them.(Feeley, 1983; Nimmer, 1978).

Another insight revealed by studies of reforms in the administration of criminal justice is that restricting discretion in one place may lead to the emergence of more discretion somewhere else. Thus, mandatory sentencing guidelines that reduce the discretion of judges tend to strengthen the hands of prosecutors engaged in plea negotiation. And where negotiation over sentencing was banned, the power to drop or lower charges (on the part of police or prosecutors) took on enhanced meaning (McCoy, 1984; Tonry, 1988).

Direct intervention by politicians in prosecution and sentencing have been rare in North America and England in the latter half of the twentieth century. In urban America, the rise of reform city governments run by professional managers helped to reduce the power of the political bosses, including their capacity to influence trials (Gardiner, 1970). In the USSR and other socialist bloc countries, however, political pressures, including interventions, have remained a characteristic of the administration of criminal justice (Solomon, 1987A; Solomon, 1987B).

Reading List

POLITICAL CRIME, POLICING AND JUSTICE

Balbus, Isaac D. *The Dialectics of Legal Repression; Black Rebels Before the American Criminal Courts*. New York: Russell Sage Foundation, 1973
Based on the experience of Los Angeles, Detroit and Chicago, this study argues that the nature and severity of sentences varies with local political structure and not with the magnitude of violence.

Becker, Theodore L., ed. *Political Trials*. Indianapolis and New York: Bobbs Merrill Co., 1971
Each of eleven chapters describes and analyzes a different political trial, including the trial of the Chicago Eight, the Sinyavsky-Daniel trial (in the USSR), the Spiegel affair (in Germany), and the Ghana treason trials.

Belknap, Michael R. *Cold War Political Justice: The Smith Act, the Communist Party and American Civil Liberties.* Westport, CT, and London: Greenwood Press, 1977. (Contributions in American History; no. 66)
The prosecution and trials of Communist Party leaders in the United States during the late 1940s and 1950s and the eventual constitutional review of the Smith Act by the United States Supreme Court.

Berger, Thomas R. *Fragile Freedoms: Human Rights and Dissent in Canada.* Toronto: Clarke, Irwin, 1981
Discusses such instances of political prosecution as the case of Louis Riel, the deportation of Japanese-Canadians during World War II, the handling of the Communist Party of Canada in the 1940s and 1950s, and the October Crisis in Quebec, 1970.

Breton, Raymond. 'The Socio-Political Dynamics of the October Events.' *Canadian Review of Sociology and Anthropology* 9 (1, February, 1972): 33–56
A keen analysis of the October Crisis in Quebec in 1970 attributing Trudeau's use of the War Measures Act to his appreciation of (and involvement in) conflicts within the French-Canadian intelligentsia.

Caute, David. *The Great Fear: The Anti-Communist Purge Under Truman and Eisenhower.* New York: Simon and Schuster, 1978
An encyclopedic study of the McCarthy era, including the activities of the House Un-American Activities Committee and the FBI, and the attacks on the Communist Party, the civil service, teachers and newspapermen, show business and the trade unions.

Christenson, Ron. *Political Trials: Gordian Knots in the Law.* New Brunswick, NJ: Transaction Books, 1986
After distinguishing 'partisan trials' from political trials operating within the rule of law, the author gives in-depth accounts of three political trials (the SWAPO trial in South Africa, the trial of the Wisconsin Bomber in 1973 and the Wounded Knee trial of 1974) and goes on to supply a jurisprudence of political trials.

Ford, Franklin L. *Political Murder: From Tyrannicide to Terrorism.* Cambridge, MA: Harvard University Press, 1985
An inquiry into the conditions that produce political murders and their consequences, based on the experience of antiquity, Europe from the Middle Ages and the modern world.

Haggart, Ron, and Golden Aubrey E. *Rumours of War.* new ed. Toronto: Lorimer, 1979
A lively, unbiased narrative of the October Crisis in Quebec, 1970.

Ingraham, Barton L. *Political Crime in Europe. A Comparative Study of France, Germany and England.* Berkeley, CA: University of California Press, 1979

After an initial presentation of a theory of political crime, the author analyzes the laws relating to political crime and their administration in three countries from 1770 to 1970.

Irons, Peter H. *Justice at War: The Story of the Japanese-American Internment Cases*. New York and Oxford: Oxford University Press, 1983
The story of *Korematsu* v. *US* and related cases, in which the United States Supreme Court approved the conviction of Japanese-Americans who refused to comply with orders to leave the prohibited West Coast.

Kirchheimer, Otto. *Political Justice; The Use of Legal Procedure for Political Ends*. Princeton, N.J.: Princeton University Press, 1961
This definitive study of the political trial and legal repression of political organizations considers political justice in a variety of democratic and authoritarian regimes.

Koistra, Paul G. 'What is Political Crime?' *Criminal Justice Abstracts* 17 (1, March, 1985): 100–15
Contrasts three different approaches to the definition of political crime, and then proposes a fourth approach that stresses the social dimension in the labelling process.

McNaught, Kenneth. 'Political Trials and the Canadian Political Tradition.' In *Courts and Trials: A Multidisciplinary Approach*, pp. 137–61. Edited by Martin L. Friedland. Toronto and Buffalo: University of Toronto Press, 1975
Reviews selected political trials (Louis Riel, Winnipeg General Strike, October, 1970 included) and argues that Canadian political tradition aligns courts with authorities in the defence of order.

Murray, Robert K. *The Red Scare: A Study in National Hysteria, 1919–1920*. Minneapolis, MN: University of Minnesota Press, 1955
An account of a year of labour strife in the United States and its sensationalist presentation in the press that culminated in raids by the FBI and the deportation of thousands of innocent alien workers.

Turk, Austin T. *Political Criminality: The Defiance and Defence of Authority*. Beverley Hills, CA: Sage Publications, 1982
A treatise analyzing the legal definitions of political crimes, political criminalization and political policing.

CRIMINAL POLICY-MAKING AND DEVELOPMENT

Bottoms, A.E. 'On the Decriminalization of English Juvenile Courts.' In *Crime, Criminology and Public Policy: Essays in Honour of Sir Leon Radzinowicz*, pp. 319–46. Edited by Roger Hood. London: Heinemann, 1974

Demonstrates how changes in the political configuration between 1965 and 1968 facilitated the shift of young offenders from the courts to the purview of social agencies.

Boyd, Neil. 'The Origins of Canadian Narcotics Legislation: The Process of Criminalization in Historical Context.' *Dalhousie Law Journal* 8 (1, January, 1984): 102–36

An insightful reinterpretation of the political and social conflicts that made the non-medical use of narcotics a criminal offence in Canada.

Carson, W.G. 'The Conventionalization of Early Factory Crime.' *International Journal of the Sociology of Law* 7 (1979): 37–60

An attempt to explain the low rate of criminal prosecution of managers and owners of textile mills in nineteenth-century Britain for violations of child labour laws.

Carson, W.G. 'Symbolic and Instrumental Dimensions of Early Factory Legislation: A Case Study in the Social Origins of the Criminal Law.' In *Crime, Criminology and Public Policy: Essays in Honour of Sir Leon Radzinowicz*, pp. 107–38. Edited by Roger Hood. London: Heinemann, 1974

Demonstrates how an issue that begins as instrumental may acquire a symbolic dimension.

Chambliss, William J. 'A Sociological Analysis of the Law of Vagrancy.' *Social Problems* 12 (1, Summer, 1964): pp. 67–77

An interpretation of the emergence of vagrancy laws in England in the fourteenth through eighteenth centuries, highlighting the law's role in increasing the supply of cheap unskilled labour to landowners.

Christoff, James B. *Capital Punishment in British Politics. The British Movement to Abolish the Death Penalty 1945–57.* London: Allen and Unwin, 1962

Interest groups and parliamentary politics, stopping short of the eventual abolition of capital punishment.

Cronin, Thomas E., Cronin, Tania Z., and Milakovich, Michael E. *US v. Crime in the Streets.* Bloomington, Indiana: Indiana University Press, 1981

How law and order became an issue in the national politics of the United States in the 1960s, the politics that resulted in the War on Crime, and the struggles of the Law Enforcement Assistance Administration.

Ericson, Richard V. and Baranek, Patricia M. 'Criminal Law Reform and Two Realities of the Criminal Process.' In *Perspectives in Criminal Law: Essays in Honour of John LlJ. Edwards*, pp. 255–76. Edited by Anthony N. Doob and Edward L. Greenspan. Aurora, Ont: Canada Law Book, 1985

Argues that as a rule, attempts to reform the criminal law prove futile, because the law serves its enforcers as a resource more than a constraint. For a rebuttal, see the essay by Peter H. Russell, 'The Political Theory of Contrology,' *ibid*, pp. 277–93.

Fairchild, Erika S. 'Interest Groups in the Criminal Justice Process.' *Journal of Criminal Justice* 9 (1981): 181–94

A review of recent research relating to criminal justice policies in various states of the United States, and spelling out a series of tentative generalizations.

Feeley, Malcolm and Sarat, Austin. *The Policy Dilemma: Federal Crime Policy and the Law Enforcement Assistance Administration, 1968–1978*. Minneapolis, MN: University of Minnesota Press, 1980

Argues on the basis of American experience that merely providing money and a call for innovation does not reduce the amount or severity of crime.

Friedland, Martin L. *The Case of Valentine Shortis: A True Story of Crime and Politics in Canada*. Toronto and Buffalo: University of Toronto Press, 1986

A readable and entertaining reconstruction of an extraordinary murder case from Quebec in 1895, which gives rich insights into the intersection of criminal justice with provincial and federal politics.

Friedland, Martin L. *A Century of Criminal Justice: Perspectives on the Development of Canadian Law*. Toronto, Ont: Carswell Legal Publications, 1984

A collection of essays dealing with pressure groups and the development of the criminal law in Canada, the politics of gun control in Canada and the United States, and the relationship between criminal and constitutional law in Canada.

Galliher, John F., McCartney, James L. and Baum, Barbara E. 'Nebraska's Marijuana Law: A Case of Unexpected Legislative Innovation.' In *Criminology: Power, Crime and Criminal Law*, pp. 70–86. Edited by John F. Galliher and James L. McCartney. Homewood, IL: Dorsey Press, 1977

How a conservative Republican government decriminalized the use of marijuana.

Gusfield, Joseph R. *The Culture of Public Problems: Drinking-Driving and the Symbolic Order*. Chicago and London: University of Chicago Press, 1981

Explores the development of public attitudes toward social problems, including fictions and myths, and the use of the law to confirm and dramatize those attitudes.

Gusfield, Joseph R. 'Moral Passage: The Symbolic Process in Public Designations of Deviance.' *Social Problems* 15 (2, Fall, 1967): 175–88
The first full exposition of the distinction between symbolic and instrumental issues in politics.

Gusfield, Joseph R. *Symbolic Crusade: Status Politics and the American Temperance Movement.* Urbana, IL: University of Illinois Press, 1963
Classic study of the political conflicts that produced Prohibition in the United States.

Hall, Stuart, et al. *Policing the Crisis: Mugging, the State and Law and Order.* London: Macmillan, 1978
Examines the roots of a 'moral panic' and a law enforcement campaign, paying particular attention to the role of the media and the orchestration of public opinion.

Hay, Douglas. 'Property, Authority and the Criminal Law.' In *Albion's Fatal Tree: Crime and Society in Eighteenth-Century England*, pp. 17–63. Edited by Douglas Hay, et al. New York: Pantheon, 1975
Brilliant Marxist interpretation of the politics underlying establishment and persistence of the capital code in eighteenth and early nineteenth-century Britain.

Ignatieff, Michael. *A Just Measure of Pain: The Penitentiary in the Industrial Revolution, 1750–1850.* New York: Pantheon Books, 1978
On the rise of the penitentiary as the dominant mode of punishment in England.

Ignatieff, Michael. 'State, Civil Society and Total Institutions: A Critique of Recent Social Histories of Punishment.' In *Social Control and the State: Historical and Comparative Essays*, pp. 75–105. Edited by Stanley Cohen and Andrew Scull. Oxford: Robertson, 1983. (Reprinted from *Crime and Justice: An Annual Review of Research*. Edited by Michael Tonry and Norval Morris. Chicago and London: University of Chicago Press, 1981)
A critical review of Rothman, *Discovery of the Asylum*, Foucault, *Discipline and Punishment* and Ignatieff's own *A Just Measure of Pain*, in which the author lays out a new perspective on the rise of penitentiaries.

Jayewardene, C.H.S. 'The Canadian Movement Against the Death Penalty.' *Canadian Journal of Criminology and Corrections* 14 (4, 1972): 366–90
A study in interest group politics.

Langbein, John. 'Albion's Fatal Flaws.' *Past and Present* 98 (February, 1983): 96–120
Rebuttal of Douglas Hay's interpretation of the persistence of the capital code in eighteenth-century and early nineteenth-century Britain.

Lemert, Edwin. *Social Action and Legal Change: Revolution within the Juvenile Court*. Chicago, IL: Aldine, 1970
The political history of the shift from paternalism to an emphasis on the procedural rights in the juvenile courts of California.

Levi, Michael. *Regulating Fraud, White-Collar Crime and the Criminal Process*. London and New York: Tavistock, 1987
This magisterial study deals with the development of law and policy toward commercial fraud, as well as with enforcement. The author combines original research on Great Britain with a fresh perspective on American experience.

Miller, Walter B. 'Ideology and Criminal Justice Policy: Some Current Issues.' *Journal of Criminal Law, Criminology and Police Science* 64 (2, 1973): 141–62
Analyzes the different perspectives on issues in the politics of criminal justice on the part of police chiefs, judges and academic criminologists.

Radzinowicz, Leon (Sir) and King, Joan. *The Growth of Crime: The International Experience*. Harmondsworth, Middx: Penguin, 1979
This authoritative overview of crime and law enforcement practices includes a chapter on continuity and change in the definition of criminal conduct.

Radzinowicz, Leon (Sir). *A History of English Criminal Law and its Administration from 1750*. London: Stevens, 1948–1986. 5 vols
The first volume deals with the movement to reform English criminal law in the eighteenth and early nineteenth century; the middle volumes with the establishment and operation of the police; and the final volume with the development of punishments and penal policy. At all times, the author (and his co-author for the fifth volume, Roger Hood) pay heed to the politics that surrounded the changes in law, policing and punishment described.

Ratner, Robert S. and McMullan, John L, eds. *State Control: Criminal Justice Politics in Canada*. Vancouver: University of British Columbia Press, 1987
This exercise in radical criminology explores such issues as the possibility of genuine reform in criminal justice, the meaning of the 'relative autonomy of the state' for criminology, justice, and the theory of the state.

Rock, Paul E. *A View from the Shadows: The Ministry of the Solicitor General of Canada and the Making of the Justice for Victims of Crime Initiative*. Oxford: Clarendon Press; New York: Oxford University Press, 1986
A detailed ethnographic study of a policy initiative, providing special insights into the world of policy officials inside the Canadian federal government.

Rothman, David J. *Conscience and Convenience: The Asylum and its Alternatives in Progressive America.* Boston: Little Brown, 1980
Major study of the origins and distortion of such progressive reforms as parole, probation and the juvenile court.

Rothman, David. *The Discovery of the Asylum: Social Order and Disorder in the New Republic.* Boston: Little Brown, 1971
Seminal study of the transition to institutional confinement (in penitentiaries, asylums and almshouses) as the primary way of dealing with criminals, mentally ill and the poor.

Rusche, Georg and Kirchheimer, Otto. *Punishment and Social Structure.* New York: Columbia University Press, 1939
Original, Marxist history of punishment, correlating major turning points, in the favoured sanctions in countries of Western Europe, with changes in the market for unskilled labour.

Scheerer, Sebastien. 'The New Dutch and German Drug Laws: Social and Political Conditions for Criminalization and Decriminalization.' *Law and Society Review* 12 (4, 1977/1978): 585–606
An inquiry into the reasons why in the late 1960s Germany passed more repressive laws against drug use, while Holland introduced partial decriminalization.

Small, Shirley. 'Canadian Narcotics Legislation, 1908–1923: A Conflict in Model Interpretation.' In *Law and Social Control in Canada*, pp. 28–42. Edited by William K. Greenaway and Stephen L. Brickey. Scarborough, Ont: Prentice Hall, 1978
The first serious attempt to understand the politics of the criminalization of the use of narcotics in Canada.

Solomon, Peter H., Jr. 'Criminalization and Decriminalization in Soviet Criminal Policy.' *Law and Society Review* 16 (1, 1981): 9–43
Attributes the shift of common petty offenses from the courts to administrative proceedings and comrades courts to the overload of cases in Soviet courts.

Solomon, Peter H., Jr. 'The Policy Process in Canadian Criminal Justice: A Perspective and Research Agenda.' *Canadian Journal of Criminology* 23 (1, 1981): 5–25
An attempt to define basic concepts and issues in the study of the policy-making process in criminal justice, with special reference to the Canadian scene.

Solomon, Peter H., Jr. *Soviet Criminologists and Criminal Policy: Specialists in Policy-Making.* New York: Columbia University Press and London: Macmillan, 1978
A study of the expansion and institutionalization of the participation of criminologists in the formation of Soviet criminal policy.

Solomon, Peter H., Jr. 'Soviet Penal Policy, 1917–1934: A Reinterpretation.' *Slavic Review* 39 (2, 1980): 195–217
Argues that the turn away from a progressive penal policy in 1929, and the expansion of labour camps, stemmed mainly from demands for convict labour.

Taylor, Ian. 'The Law and Order Issue in the British General Election and the Canadian Federal Election of 1979: Crime, Populism and the State.' *Canadian Journal of Sociology* 5 (3, Summer 1980): 285–311
Contrasts Britain, where the law and order issue played a major part in both electoral success of the Conservative Party and the development of a populist strand in its ideology, with Canada where the issue had less significance.

Thompson, Edward P. *Whigs and Hunters: The Origin of the Black Act.* London: Allen Lane, 1975
An in-depth analysis of the political basis of an eighteenth-century English law, illustrating the employment of law as 'an instrument and ideology in the service of the ruling class.'

Tuttle, Elizabeth Ann Orman. *The Crusade Against Capital Punishment in Great Britain.* London: Stevens; and Chicago: Quadrangle, 1961
An account of the movement against the death penalty in England from the early nineteenth century to 1957, and its partial victory.

Unger, Robert M. *Law in Modern Society: Toward a Criticism of Social Theory.* New York: Free Press, 1976
A broad historical and comparative study of the types of law and the basis of the ideal of 'rule of law' in liberal, capitalist societies.

Zimring, Franklin E., and Hawkins, Gordon. *Capital Punishment and the American Agenda.* Cambridge, Camb; New York: Cambridge University Press, 1986
The authors use the modern history of the death penalty in Western Europe and the former Commonwealth countries as a foil for understanding why the trend in the United States toward abolition was reversed.

CRIMINOLOGY AND CRIMINAL POLICY

Friedman, Lawrence. 'History, Social Policy and Criminal Justice.' In *Social History and Social Policy*, pp. 203–25. Edited by David Rothman and Stanton Wheeler. New York: Academic Press, 1981
Using research on the history of discretion and plea bargaining, the author demonstrates the lessons of history for current policies in criminal justice.

Hood, Roger. 'Criminology and Penal Change: A Case Study of the Nature and Impact of Some Recent Advice to Governments.' In *Crime, Criminology and Public Policy: Essays in Honour of Sir Leon Radzinowicz*, pp. 395–417. Edited by Roger Hood. London: Heinemann, 1974
Analyzes the failure of British politicians in the late 1960s and early 1970s to make proper use of criminological research and the advice of criminologists.

Hood, Roger. 'Some Reflections on the Role of Criminology in Public Policy.' *Criminal Law Review* (August, 1987): 527–38
Politicians should take criminological research more seriously, but criminologists should not oversell the implications of their findings, and should seek to avoid dependence on state resources that could shape the agenda of research.

Lindblom, Charles E. and Cohen, David K. *Usable Knowledge: Social Science and Social Problem Solving*. New Haven: Yale University Press, 1979
Intelligent, realistic analysis of the relationship of social science to other kinds of knowledge, and the role of both in the policy-making process.

Merton, Robert K. 'The Role of the Intellectual in Public Bureaucracy.' In *Social Theory and Social Structure* enl. ed., pp. 261–78. New York: Free Press, 1968
Original and insightful exposition of the constraints that experts may encounter working in or for agencies of government.

Morris, Norval and Hawkins, Gordon. *Letter to the President on Crime Control*. Chicago and London: University of Chicago Press, 1977
A concise argument from a liberal point of view, grounded in research, about what changes are needed in criminal policy.

Moynihan, Daniel Patrick. *Maximum Feasible Misunderstanding: Community Action in the War on Poverty*. New York: Free Press, 1969.
On the inappropriate use of a criminological theory (the opportunity theory of Cloward and Ohlin) to buttress a controversial and probably unsuccessful experiment for reducing crime (the Community Action Programs).

Reich, Robert B. 'Solving Social Crises by Commissions.' *Yale Review of Law and Social Action* 3 (3, 1973): 254–71
Distinguishes American 'crisis commissions' designed to reassure the public in times of trouble, from British royal commissions established to elaborate responses to problems.

Solomon, Peter H., Jr. *Criminal Justice Policy, from Research to Reform*. Toronto: Butterworths, 1983
Analyzes the implications of research on criminal justice in a county of

Ontario for such policy issues as styles of policing, plea bargaining and court delay.

Waller, Irvin. 'Organizing Research to Improve Criminal Justice Policy: A Perspective from Canada.' *Journal of Research in Crime and Delinquency* 16 (2, July, 1979): 196–217
Based upon his experience as a researcher inside government, the author offers suggestions for improving the working relationship between researchers and politicians.

Weiss, Carol. 'Research for Policy's Sake.' *Policy Studies Review Annual* 2 (1978): 67–81
Social research can more easily help decision-makers conceptualize problems and reassess their significance than provide effective solutions.

Wilson, James Q. *Thinking About Crime.* rev. ed. New York: Basic Books, 1983
This major conservative exercise in policy analysis includes chapters on the reasons for the rise in crime in the mid-twentieth century, on the rational response to this problem, and on the appropriate role for criminologists in the policy process.

POLITICS IN THE ADMINISTRATION OF CRIMINAL JUSTICE

Eisenstein, James and Jacob, Herbert. *Felony Justice: An Organizational Analysis of Criminal Courts.* Boston, MA: Little, Brown, 1977
Shows how differences in the patterns of courtroom working relations produce variations in plea negotiation and sentencing in three American cities.

Feeley, Malcolm M. *Court Reform on Trial: Why Simple Solutions Fail.* New York: Basic Books, 1983
On the basis of his assessment of a series of innovative programs in bail reform, pretrial diversion, sentencing and speedy trials, the author generalizes about such impediments to change as limited imagination, implementation and the routinization of reforms.

Gardiner, John A. *The Politics of Corruption; Organized Crime in an American City.* New York: Russell Sage Foundation, 1970
Chapters deal with the reasons for the non-enforcement of the criminal law against racketeers, and with the problem of corruption in law enforcement itself.

Goldstein, Herman B. *Policing a Free Society.* Cambridge, MA: Ballinger, 1977
Includes chapters on the direction of police agencies through local politics, the accountability of the police and police corruption.

Heinz, Anne, Jacob, Herbert and Lineberry, Robert L. *Crime in City Politics*. New York and London: Longman, 1983
A study of crime and politics in the American cities of Newark, Philadelphia, Minneapolis, Phoenix and San Jose, focusing on the period from World War II to 1980.

Levin, Martin A. *Urban Politics and the Criminal Courts*. Chicago: University of Chicago Press, 1977
Contrasts patterns of sentencing in Minneapolis and Pittsburgh, and concludes that the differences reflect the styles of the two cities.

McCoy, Candace. 'Determinate Sentencing, Plea Bargaining Bans, and Hydraulic Discretion in California.' *Justice System Journal* (Winter, 1984): 256–75
How restrictions on discretion in one part of the criminal justice system produce more discretion in other places.

Nimmer, Raymond T. *The Nature of System Change: Reform Impact in the Criminal Courts*. Chicago, IL: American Bar Foundation, 1978
Analyzes a series of experiments in the courts to improve efficiency (e.g. speedy trial statutes, calendar reform, omnibus hearings) and argues that success depends upon influencing the incentives of the major actors involved.

Reiner, Robert. *The Politics of the Police*. Brighton, Sussex: Wheatsheaf Books, 1985
Deals with the rise and fall of police legitimacy (in England 1856–1981), media presentations of policing, and the accountability of the police.

Scheingold, Stuart A. *The Politics of Law and Order: Street Crime and Public Policy*. New York and London: Longman, 1984
Relates evidence about public attitudes toward law and order to patterns of policing and judicial behaviour, stressing the importance of political culture as the crucial link.

Sherman, Lawrence W. *Scandal and Reform: Controlling Police Corruption*. Berkeley, CA: University of California Press, 1978
On the basis of case studies, this book explores the positive effects of scandals, and the ingredients of successful reorganization of police forces to reduce corruption.

Solomon, Peter H., Jr. 'The Case of the Vanishing Acquittal: Informal Norms and the Practice of Soviet Criminal Justice.' *Soviet Studies* 39 (4, October, 1987A): 531–55
How the system of assessing the work of procurators and judges led to a decline in acquittals and the substitution of alternative ways of solving weak cases.

Solomon, Peter H., Jr. 'Soviet Politicians and Criminal Prosecutions.'

Urbana, IL: Soviet Interview Project, University of Illinois. (Working Paper No. 33 ,1987B)

Patterns and rationale for interference by Soviet party bosses in the prosecution and trials of ordinary criminal cases.

'Special Issue on Plea Bargaining.' *Law and Society Review* 13 (2, Winter, 1979)

A large anthology dealing with the history of plea bargaining, its equivalents in European countries, efforts to limit or ban the practice, variations in different jurisdictions in the United States, and the philosophical implications of the practice.

Tonry, Michael. 'Structuring Sentencing.' In *Crime and Justice: An Annual Review of Research* 10 (1988): 267–337. (University of Chicago Press)

A major review of research on United States states' experience with determinate sentencing laws, revealing conditions under which particular measures relating to sentencing and plea bargaining prove effective.

Wilson, James Q. *Varieties of Police Behavior: The Management of Law and Order in Eight Communities.* Cambridge, MA: Harvard University Press, 1969

Demonstrates how different styles of policing in the United States relate to patterns of city politics and local political culture.

6

Narcotics: A Case Study in Criminal Law Creation

Chester N. Mitchell

Introduction

Canada's drug legislation embodies certain key factual assumptions. These assumptions are implied in the coverage and penalty structure of the *Narcotic Control Act* and the *Food and Drug Act*, the two major federal statutes criminalizing the sale and possession of drugs (MacFarlane, 1986; Solomon, 1988). The premises are also explicitly stated in government publications justifying these drug statutes and their regulations (Health and Welfare, 1988). The four central assumptions are as follows:

1. Some drugs (cannabis, cocaine, heroin) are extremely dangerous and crime-causing because of their inherent chemical properties whereas other drugs (alcohol, tobacco, coffee) are much less dangerous or not dangerous at all.
2. The *Opium Act* of 1908, the *Opium and Narcotic Control Act* of 1920 and the two modern statutes were enacted in response to these inherent chemical dangers (Health and Welfare, 1988, p. 16).
3. Granting statutory drug control authority to law enforcement agents and to physicians promotes public safety by ensuring that legally available drugs are 'safe and effective and are being used wisely'. (Health and Welfare, 1988, p. 9).
4. Canada's drug statutes reflect public concern and voter demand expressed through free and democratic elections.

Like scientific theories, these four legislative assumptions are open to experimental test. When tested, all these assumptions proved to be false. Yet though false, these premises continue to justify narcotic prohibitions and medical restrictions in Canada, the United States and elsewhere. This chapter reviews the experimental tests and examines the lawmaking process that permits legislators to enact statutes that either ignore or defy the known facts. While what follows concentrates on drug issues, the legislative process involved applies to the creation of any crime.

Testing the Dangerousness of Illicit or Restricted Drugs

That certain drugs are considered extremely dangerous is evident from the penalties set out in the *Narcotic Control Act*. Upon indictment, offenders who possess, cultivate or 'prescription shop' face a maximum penalty of seven years imprisonment and those who traffick, import or possess for trafficking purposes face a maximum of life imprisonment. Drug offence penalty scales match the penalties for sexual assault, robbery, manslaughter and attempted murder. Parliament erected this penalty scale and implicitly compared drug trafficking to serious crimes rather than to highway offences or public nuisances, on the basis of anecdotal claims. These claims, often borrowed from U.S. drug agents, held that opium, cocaine or marijuana use routinely led to uncontrolled violence, murder, rape and insanity (Murphy, 1922). Meanwhile, other statutes inflicted mild restrictions on alcohol and tobacco users and left caffeine users unpenalized.

The historical record, pharmacological evidence and sociological/psychological research all refute the thesis that illicit drugs are especially dangerous. Prior to 1908, cocaine, marijuana and opiate users were not penalized. Despite widespread use, these drugs were not regarded as grave social menaces (Rublowsky, 1974; Teff, 1975). Indeed, social reformers of that earlier period often claimed that alcohol and tobacco were more dangerous (Courtwright, 1982). Furthermore, in different cultures and periods, a wide variety of substances have faced prohibition, including coffee, tea, alcohol, and tobacco, while drugs now forbidden in Canada, like marijuana, have been revered as useful and benign (Brecher, 1972; Smart, 1983). Unlike theft or assault, which in some form are universally defined as crime, there is no historical consensus on drug dangers. Pharmacologists, who study the effects of drugs on humans and other animals, possess no well-established ranking of drugs based on inherent dangers. Those rankings so far produced by scientists do not match the law; for example, marijuana is usually ranked as safer than alcohol (Green, 1988). No good evidence supports Parliament's premise that 'narcotics' are especially addictive, health threatening or criminogenic (Bakalar and Grinspoon, 1984; Goldberg and Meyers, 1980; Goode, 1984; Szasz, 1974). In accurately assessing drug dangers, the choice of chemical is only one factor. Dose, method of use, frequency and duration of use, purity, age of user, and other objective factors must also be considered. The *Narcotic Control Act* ignores these factors.

Sociologists and psychologists, who study how humans interact with drugs, report that drug chemistry is less important than the human factor. Drug effects vary markedly according to user's objectives, expectations and social context (Zinberg, 1984). People at different times use the same drug for medicinal, religious, recreational or ceremonial purposes (Szasz, 1974). Any drug can be used wisely and any drug can be abused (Weil and Rosen, 1983). However, attitudes about drugs lack generality because through historical circumstance and the vagaries of fashion, specific drugs and methods of ingestion are closely associated with different groups of people. Drugs used by foreigners, ethnic minorities, criminals and dissidents are normally regarded with suspicion, if not hatred, whereas drugs used by successful captains of industry, moral majorities and legislators are safe and familiar (Satinder, 1980). Proscriptions against certain drugs, like food or clothing taboos, arise from inter-group competition and hegemonic domination unrelated to objectives of public health or safety (Lidz and Walker, 1980). Through cultural fixation and taboo, smoking marijuana becomes wrong, like eating non-kosher meat is wrong, because both challenge the authority and integrity of the group elders and lawmakers (McGinley, 1981).

Prohibition is also thought necessary to combat the crime-generating effects of certain drugs which either compel 'addicts' to finance habits by acquisitive crime or induce in users uncontrolled rage and aggression. The capacity of drugs, including alcohol, to induce violence is not well supported by research (Mitchell, 1988). Crime-drug connections do exist but mostly because certain classes of criminals adopt drugs like heroin as part of their anti-establishment life style (Wisotsky, 1986). Tattoos are connected to crime in the same non-causal fashion. Finally, police estimates of the theft, robbery and burglary attributable to illicit drug users turn out to be gross exaggerations (Kaplan, 1983).

Testing the Objectives of Drug Legislation

According to official pronouncements since 1908, drug statutes were enacted in the public interest to protect people from the inherent dangerousness of the drugs Parliament defined as 'narcotics'. Since the scientific evidence refutes the initial claim about special, severe drug dangers, it logically follows that Parliament either mistakenly acted out of ignorance or created drug laws for reasons other than public health and safety.

The ignorance hypothesis finds some support from U.S. studies indicating that those state legislators prohibiting marijuana use in the 1920s conducted no empirical studies and referred to no scientific evidence (Bonnie and Whitebread, 1970). Canadian Members of Parliament also knew little to nothing about marijuana when they classified it as a narcotic. But this ignorance was more wilful than innocent since legislators in both Canada and the U.S. ignored accurate evidence, which found marijuana to be relatively harmless, and relied instead on lurid, unfounded anecdotes from police, clergy and anti-drug crusaders (Bonnie and Whitebread, 1970, p. 1021–47).

A more plausible explanation of why legislators relied on the most distorted, least reliable evidence is that it suited their purposes. What were those purposes? Legal historians report that North American narcotics laws arose partly in response to anti-Chinese and anti-Mexican sentiment on the west coast (Boyd, 1984; Morgan, 1981). Opiate laws were tied in with international affairs between Britain, China and the U.S. (Musto, 1973). They were also connected in Canada with business competition between patent medicine producers, pharmacists and physicians (Murray, 1988). Labour conflict and anti-socialist objectives played a role as well (Comack, 1985). It was as Deputy-Minister of Labour that McKenzie King steered Canada's first opiate law through Parliament. This law exempted pharmaceutical opiates, which more people consumed, because it was only intended to affect Chinese immigrants (Boyd, 1984). In the 1930s, federal narcotic controls expanded to include marijuana in the U.S. in order for ex-Prohibition agents (after 1933) to survive in a Narcotics Bureau running out of opiate users to police (Bonnie and Whitebread, 1970). Historical research finds little evidence to support the claim that narcotics controls were intended to promote public health or safety.

The Purported Necessity of Police and Medical Controls

A third assumption underlying prohibition is that police action can prevent drug abuse, protect youth from drug 'exposure' and stop importation of illicit production. The available evidence is not very supportive of this third premise. Prohibition publicizes obscure drugs, shifts users to more potent forms of a drug and increases the risks of drug use (Brecher, 1972; Ray, 1978). Prohibiting popular drugs generates an extensive black market that encourages youth participation and invites violence (Hamowy, 1987; Inciardi, 1986). By adapting rapidly to enforcement tactics, black marketeers increased drug supplies and reduced prices over the last decade (Wisotsky, 1986). Efforts to reduce drug supplies 'at the source' in Third World countries prove futile and counterproductive (McNicoll, 1983; Mitchell, 1989). Finally, drug prohibition is the prime corrupter of enforcement agents and the main justification for official attacks on civil rights and political freedoms (Epstein, 1977; Helmer, 1975; Trebach, 1987). Drug prohibitions may succeed in the short-term against limited targets but, historically, there is no record of a successful legal eradication of a mass market drug (Smart, 1983).

The *Food and Drug Act* grants monopoly drug control authority to medical license holders (mostly physicians) on the assumption that prescription-only regulations are necessary to protect the public from adverse drug reactions and improper use. While the public's overuse of vitamins, antacids and other over-the-counter substances is well documented, the evidence indicates that the compulsory intervention of a prescribing physician does not improve matters (Mitchell, 1986a). Misuse and overuse still occur despite prescription-only availability. The apparent ineffectiveness of prescription control is understandable, however, if the law was enacted to increase the pay, power and prestige of organized medicine (Hamowy, 1984). If that objective, rather than public protection, was the statute's actual purpose, then the law was well-designed and succeeded admirably (Mitchell, 1986a).

The Alleged Popular Demand for Drug Laws

According to the fourth premise, Canada's drug statutes constitute Parliament's response to pre-existing public concerns about drugs. Most voters apparently do support drug prohibition now; in the 1988 elections all major party leaders in Canada and the U.S. promised to 'crackdown' on illicit drug activities (Bertrand, 1989). Current support, however, does not prove that public demand existed when opiates were restricted in 1908, when cocaine was banned in 1911, and marijuana in 1923, or when mandatory prescription was created in 1940. Since voter support may have followed these legislative initiatives, it is necessary to examine the historical record to see what came first.

The available evidence suggests the primary demand for drug prohibition in Canada came from a few vocal reformers, and from politicians, police, journalists, some Chinese and the federal drug bureaucracy (Boyd, 1984; Solomon and Green, 1988). One catalyst for the first *Opium Act* in 1908 was anti-Chinese racism, not concern for drugs. Having sparked an enforcement problem for Customs and police by banning non-medical opiates, Parliament passed the *Opium and Drug Act* in 1911 to give police and courts more power following the recommendations of a Royal Commission. Despite the 1908 and 1911 laws, drug crusaders in 1920 still felt the first step needed in the fight against drugs 'was to arouse the apathetic public' (Solomon and Green, 1988, p. 96). *Macleans* magazine, starting in 1920, published the first popular coverage of narcotics issues. Unfortunately, these articles were racist, sensationalist and inaccurate diatribes against black or Chinese 'pushers' who enslaved white youth and lusted after white women (Murphy, 1922).

Since most people lacked first-hand knowledge about narcotics, popular opinion naturally tended to follow the lead set by police, magistrates, drug crusaders and other 'authorities'. The RCMP and the federal Narcotic Division of the Department of Health, created in 1920, were the primary directors of the six legislative revisions culminating in the *Opium and Narcotic Drug Act* of 1929 (Solomon and Green, 1988). When the Minister of Health was asked whether any demand from the public existed for the new harsh provisions of the *Opium and Narcotic Drug Act*, he indirectly admitted there was no public demand (Boyd, 1984).

With the *Proprietary or Patent Medicine Act* also enacted in 1908, there was some public concern about the contents, safety and marketing of home remedies, but the main lobbyists for the Act were pharmacists and physicians (Murray, 1988). When the Act was amended in 1940 to create a new category of prescription-only drugs, almost the only people interested in the statute were physicians, pharmacists and pharmaceutical producers (Mitchell, 1986b).

Both Canada and the U.S. from the 1870s on witnessed a vigorous, continual public debate about the alleged evils of alcohol, saloons and the alcohol industry lobby. Despite the passage of many state, provincial and federal laws concerning alcohol, including some based on direct referendum, it is not always clear whether a majority of voters favoured alcohol prohibition. (Bonnie and Whitebread, 1970). In contrast to alcohol-related laws, early narcotics legislation was 'promulgated largely in a vacuum' where the law itself generated new public opinion (Bonnie and Whitebread, 1970, p. 981). With specific reference to the first state legislatures to prohibit marijuana use or distribution in the 1920s, the same authors conclude from their analysis of newspaper accounts and legislative debates that there was 'no evidence of public concern for, or understanding of, marijuana, even in those states that banned it along with the opiates and cocaine' (Bonnie and Whitebread, 1970, p. 1011).

Given the circumstances prior to 1908, it is not surprising that broad voter demand for drug prohibition did not exist. Many people consumed products like Coca-Cola and Vin Mariana that contained cocaine, alcohol or opiates, but since these nostrums did not identify ingredients, few consumers understood what they were taking. Even fewer had any direct experience with marijuana, hashish or opium 'dens'. Furthermore, drug habits prior to 1908 were mostly viewed as a medical problem unrelated to crime or immorality (Courtwright, 1982; Morgan, 1981). Only after the campaign against smoking opium linked 'drugs' with hated minorities, non-Christian practices and un-Canadian loyalties did citizens learn to support vicious anti-narcotics laws.

That voter support mostly followed rather than led the drug laws is a common feature of much legislation. A close study of most regulatory legislation, including income tax statutes, tariffs, marketing boards, professional monopolies and industrial controls will reveal that such laws are created in the face of public apathy, ignorance or even resistance (Downs, 1957; Olson, 1982; Trebilcock, 1975). Studies of legislative choice in representative democracies, like Canada, indicate that voters exercise little control over elected politicians who primarily respond to small but organized lobbyists such as producers, professions (police, physicians, lawyers) and bureaucrats (Buchanan, 1975). Drug legislation appears to be a standard example since most voters knew little or nothing about the drugs affected nor did they enjoy an opportunity to choose between alternative methods of regulation.

Evidence and Law Making

Dramatic cases occasionally arise where convicted persons, like Donald Marshall, Jr., are pardoned or acquitted when someone discovers that evidence relied on at trial was false. Such cases sometimes prompt extensive investigation into the criminal law system because unwarranted convictions based on improper evidence are widely perceived to challenge the integrity of the system. While this view is admirable, it is also seriously incomplete because at the system's most important stage – the creation of criminal offences – legislatures routinely employ false, discredited or incomplete evidence. Indeed, evidence is only critically evaluated at one of the criminal law system's three stages. It is this disregard for evidence that permits laws like the *Narcotic Control Act* and other vice offences to be created and sustained.

Under paragraphs s.3(2)(a) and (b) of the *Narcotic Control Act*, anyone possessing a marijuana cigarette can be sentenced to seven years imprisonment. This legal outcome is based on three steps: Parliament enacts the law, judge and jury find the accused guilty, and judge imposes the maximum penalty available. Preparing for trial, police spend many hours validating the necessary evidence. The prosecutor, defence lawyer, judge and jury at trial consider and weigh the evidence at length. Formal trials often take weeks. If the accused raises a technical defence, such as medical necessity, then the court may hear days of testimony from medical experts on the necessity of marijuana for glaucoma sufferers (Trebach, 1987).

In contrast, once the accused is convicted, the concern for evidence rapidly fades. Judges frequently impose a sentence in order to rehabilitate or deter the offender or deter other potential offenders without good evidence that such a sentence will have the desired impact.

The contrast between the rights of the accused and the convicted, while problematic, is overshadowed by the even greater contrast between evidentiary protections at trial and in the legislature. Apart from potential court supervision under the *Canadian Charter of Rights and Freedoms*, Parliament is under no legal obligation to consider relevant evidence before passing a law. As a result, law breakers can be carefully tried with great deliberation under ill-considered laws. Or put another way, Parliament criminally condemned all users of heroin, cocaine, and marijuana without any trial or even any hearing (Satinder, 1980). In 1908, the first anti-opiate bill moved through the House of Commons without discussion (Solomon and Green, 1988). The 1911 bill, prompted largely by police anecdotes and demands, excluded tobacco from the schedule of narcotics because Mackenzie King simply declared it was not a drug, or at least nor a habit-forming drug (Boyd, 1984).

In the following decades, legislators justified their law-making efforts by reference to anecdotes, newspaper articles, police reports and other hearsay evidence that would not be admitted for consideration in the most mundane criminal trial (Bellis, 1981). No legislature undertook any empirical or scientific study of drug effects before enacting drug prohibitions (Bonnie and Whitebread, 1970). Those studies on marijuana or opium that were available in the 1920s or 1930s were largely ignored. Opium-smoking Chinese immigrants and poor marijuana-using labourers were not given their 'day in the legislature' before their centuries-old drug practices were outlawed. Some opposition to narcotics laws arose from physicians and from the youth counterculture in the 1960s. The Canadian Medical Association in 1969 judged marijuana laws more deleterious than marijuana use. As a result, legislators finally responded with studies and commissions (King, 1972).

Government reports, like the Canadian Commission of Inquiry into the Non-Medical Use of Drugs, *Final Report*, 1973 challenged many legislative assumptions because unlike Parliament, the Commission examined the evidence. The Le Dain Commission spent $3.5 million, hired four hundred researchers and consultants to survey the literature, held scientific symposia and listened to 12,000 people at public hearings conducted across Canada. The Le Dain Report had almost no impact on Parliament (Giffen and Lambert, 1988). Likewise, the U.S. Shafer Commission in 1972 was ignored when it concluded that marijuana use did not constitute a danger to public safety (Julien, 1981). The same fate befell the 1968 Wooton Sub-Committee Report in Britain (which found no harmful effects from 'moderate' marijuana use), The Royal Commission of 1972 in South Australia and the earlier La Guardia Report in 1944, written by the New York Academy of Medicine. All were ignored by legislators though not by judges who, after 1970, substantially reduced penalties for marijuana possession.

Parliament is under no legal obligation to accept or even take notice of evidence presented by its own commissioned inquiries. Since evidence does not count, there is no obvious legal barrier to prevent Parliament from criminalizing the sale or possession of punk rock music, lipstick, bicycles or water skis. Prior to 1989 in Czechoslovakia, rock musicians were imprisoned for their musical choice. Such lack of legislative standards is usually thought of as the hallmark of fascist, totalitarian governments.

The different role evidence plays in court and in the legislature follows the different powers and functions of these two bodies. Courts adjudicate, they resolve disputes between contending parties who naturally desire to draw the court's attention to certain evidence. Since disputes are personal and concrete, and since the evidence is brought out in a public forum, most people can readily understand the proceedings. In jury trials, twelve ordinary citizens act as the fact finders. Parliament does not adjudicate, thus it need not gather evidence or pay attention to contending arguments. Instead, the legislature is primarily a brokerage where political support (money, votes, party position) is exchanged for favourable laws and regulations (Buchanan, 1975).

Parliament passed the first anti-opiate law to please certain groups who, in exchange, gave money, votes and other benefits to members of the governing party like Mackenzie King (Boyd, 1984). Unlike public trials, political brokering is private, complex and abstract. Since facts are not at issue, little relevant evidence is produced during Parliamentary debates. Marijuana was added to the list of prohibited drugs in 1923 with a statement by the Minister of Health that 'There is a new drug in the schedule' (Boyd, 1984). No discussion occurred in the Commons. As a result, most voters cannot observe or understand the lawmaking process. Without adequate information to judge proposed laws, voters are either indifferent or accept Parliamentary pronouncements on faith. The narcotics laws fit this pattern.

Political brokering depends on the capacity to deliver party approval, campaign support and votes. If attacking opiate users in 1908 produced such benefits then the law was good regardless of whether opiate use actually threatened society (Bellis, 1981; Schroeder, 1980). Indeed, the law could be 'good' for those making it, even if the statute threatened society more than did the few thousand Oriental opium smokers. This description of criminal law creation hardly accords with the orthodox view of Parliament as a well-informed, public-spirited body, but it does explain legislators' disinterest in the evidence about drugs, and about other 'vices', such as prostitution, pornography, crime comics and gambling (Woodiwiss, 1988).

Parliament, with few exceptions, is supreme. Government, with control of the House of Commons, can pass almost any law or regulation subject to political rather than legal constraints. In practice, this means that unlike Donald Marshall, Jr., the tens of thousands of Canadians with criminal records under the *Narcotic Control Act* cannot repudiate their guilty verdict by demonstrating that the legislative assumptions about use of heroin, cocaine, mescaline, LSD or marijuana are false. The Marshall case scandalizes ordinary observers because they can readily understand how certain police officers and prosecutors manipulated evidence to suit their own purposes. In contrast, most people are not scandalized by the much greater injustice done by politicians through narcotics prohibition and other vice offences because people do not recognize that legislators manipulated or ignored the evidence. The scandal is invisible because the popularly available evidence about drugs is thoroughly warped by the law itself, which controls what police, prosecutors and judges 'know' about drugs and who, in turn, are quoted by an uncritical media that prefers opinion and sensationalism to independent investigation (Cloyd, 1982; Wisotsky, 1986).

Much of the political manipulation of evidence is carried out by law enforcement agents and bureaucrats (Manning, 1980). For three decades after 1937, the U.S. Federal Bureau of Narcotics monopolized the distribution of information on marijuana and was thus able to ignore or discredit the soundest studies (Himmelstein, 1983). This process permits politicians to blame the disasters caused by their drug prohibition on the users and sellers of illicit drugs (Szasz, 1974). Additional bad policy feeds the problem and thus escalates the demand for more bad policy. These legislative vicious circles are difficult to break (Bakalar and Grinspoon, 1984; Fort, 1969; King, 1972).

Legal remedies are limited because Parliament cannot be challenged directly and because judges mostly defer to Parliamentary supremacy by accepting legislative directives at face value. Thus judges will hear evidence in a drug trial about police procedures, prosecutorial jurisdiction, accused identification, alibi, insanity and numerous other matters, but they will rarely listen to evidence challenging Parliamentary actions. A U.S. illustration of this judicial deference occurred in *Yun Quong* (1911) when the Supreme Court of California, in upholding a conviction for possession of opium, said:

> The validity of legislation which would be necessary or proper under a given state of facts does not depend upon the actual existence of the supposed facts. It is enough if the lawmaking body may rationally believe such facts to be established.

Canadian judges in *Venegratsky* (1928), *Sung Lung* (1923) and *Lore Yip* (1928) also accepted without evidence or question Parliament's assertion that narcotics were an evil threatening public order, safety and morals (Boyd, 1984). Basic questioning of statutory premises is left to formal commissions and political debate, neither of which are powerful reform tools.

Illicit drug producers do not lobby for repeal of prohibition because they benefit from the law or because, as outlaws, they cannot form the sort of trade organizations needed for successful lobbying. Illicit drug users do not form an effective voting block for reform either, because they are unorganized, non-uniform in their views and apathetic about the law (Erickson, 1980).

The most effective method of altering this political law-creating process is to more closely govern the governors by passing a constitutional rule compelling legislators to demonstrate with reliable evidence the necessity of any new criminal offence. As in criminal trials, the onus should rest with legislators to prove beyond a reasonable doubt that a proposed law is based on factually accurate premises. The most elaborate protections at trial are relatively worthless if the law itself is unjust and ill-founded.

Reading List

Bakalar, James B. and Grinspoon, Lester. *Drug Control in a Free Society*. London: Cambridge University Press, 1984
A well-reasoned discussion of drug policy, varieties of drug control and questions of risk and liberty related to drug use in sports, recreation and medicine.

Bellis, David J. *Heroin and Politicians: The Failure of Public Policy to Control Addiction in America*. Westport, CT: Greenwood Press, 1981
With reference to both underworld and upperworld interest groups, Bellis explains why U.S. governments initiated anti-narcotic legislation and why neither repression nor rehabilitation constitute effective response to heroin use.

Bertrand, Marie-Andree. 'Resurgence du mouvement antiprohibitionniste.' *Criminologie* 22 (1, 1989): 121–33
Describes the emergence of a new, international movement against drug prohibition and reviews the antiprohibitionist arguments and strategies.

Blackwell, Judith C. and Erickson, Patricia G. *Illicit Drugs in Canada: A Risky Business*. Scarborough, Ont: Nelson, 1988
The twenty-five chapters cover the effects and use of illicit drugs, the history of Canadian drug legislation, theoretical perspectives on the 'drug problem', drug offences in the criminal law system and policy initiatives, applications and alternatives. The most complete and comprehensive book on all aspects of illicit drug issues in Canada.

Bonnie, Richard J. and Whitebread, Charles H. 'The Forbidden Fruit and the Tree of Knowledge: An Inquiry into the Legal History of American Marijuana Prohibition.' *Virginia Law Review* 56 (6, October, 1970): 971–1203

The most comprehensive review of marijuana prohibition laws and court interpretations at the state and federal levels in the United States.

Boyd, Neil. 'The Origins of Canadian Narcotics Legislation: The Process of Criminalization in Historical Context.' *Dalhousie Law Journal* 8 (1, January, 1984): 102–36

An empirical examination of the genesis of narcotics laws that attributes these laws to a complex social conflict process affected both by material conditions and new concepts.

Brecher, Edward M. *Licit and Illicit Drugs.* The Consumers Union Report on Narcotics, Stimulants and Depressants. Boston, MA: Little, Brown, 1972

A famous book with a well-deserved reputation for presenting a treasure of information on drug use, drug laws and drug control efforts.

Buchanan, James M. *The Limits of Liberty: Between Anarchy and Leviathan.* Chicago, IL: University of Chicago Press, 1975

The Nobel Laureate in economics argues that legislators operate in an exchange system where, barring constitutional limits on political action, market demand determines legal outcomes.

Canada. Commission of Inquiry into the Non-Medical Use of Drugs. *Cannabis*, 1972; *Final Report*, 1973. Ottawa: Information Canada

Known popularly as the Le Dain Commission, the inquiry was conducted by five commissioners from law, criminology, political science, psychiatry and social work. At the cost of $3.5 million, the Commission generally recommended moving away from criminal controls over drug use. Still a useful literature and policy review.

Canada. Health Protection Branch, Department of National Health and Welfare. *Health Protection and Drug Laws*, 1988

This brief pamphlet of sixty pages describes the coverage and administration of the *Food and Drugs Act* and the *Narcotic Control Act* but also attempts to explain, without reference to substantial evidence, why such laws exist.

Cloyd, Jerald W. *Drugs and Information Control: The Role of Men and Manipulation in the Control of Drug Trafficking.* Westport, CT: Greenwood, 1982

Focuses on the role of information control in formulating drug laws, in enforcing those laws and in manipulating popular ideas about drugs, specifically the triumph of antidrug opinion by joining drugs with class and racial hostilities.

Comack, A. Elizabeth. 'The Origins of Canadian Drug Legislation: Labelling Versus Class Analysis.' In *The New Criminologies in Canada: Crime, State and Control*, pp. 65–86. Edited by Thomas Fleming. Toronto: Oxford University Press, 1985

In place of the conflict model, this paper offers a Marxist explanation of the narcotics laws whereby an essentially class conflict in western Canada was re-packaged and managed as a racist, moralist and foreign interventionist problem.

Courtwright, David T. *Dark Paradise: Opiate Addiction in America Before 1940*. Cambridge: Harvard University Press, 1982
Charts the transformation of opiate use from a medically-sanctioned treatment to an underworld, black market practice emphasizing intravenous use for euphoric objectives and attributes this change to the anti-opiate laws.

Downs, Anthony. *An Economic Theory of Democracy*. New York: Harper and Row, 1957
An early study provides evidence of how bureaucrats and politicians actually behave to refute the orthodox view of government as a well-informed, altruistic agency devoted to the public interest.

'Drogues et criminalites'. Drug symposium. *Criminologie* 22 (1, 1989): whole issue
The seven chapters include coverage of such topics as impaired driving laws and Bill C-51, international aspects of the war on drugs, models of distribution of formerly illicit drugs, women and heroin use, drug treatment at Donnacona Penitentiary and the emergence of an anti-prohibitionist movement.

Epstein, Edward J. *Agency of Fear: Opiates and Political Power in America*. New York: Putnams, 1977
Describes the formation and operation of the U.S. Drug Enforcement Agency in the early 1970s and attributes the growth of the D.E.A. to the Nixon Administration's plan to use drugs as an excuse to broaden federal policing power outside the F.B.I. and the C.I.A.

Erickson, Patricia G. *Cannabis Criminals : The Social Effects of Punishment on Drug Users*. Toronto: Addiction Research Foundation, 1980
An empirical inquiry into the costs and benefits of criminalizing cannabis users, the first to document the impact of criminal sanctions on cannabis offenders, concludes that criminal law control is a high-cost, low-benefit policy.

Erickson, Patricia G., Adlaf, Edward M., Murray, Glenn F., Smart, Reginald G. *The Steel Drug: Cocaine in Perspective*. Lexington, MA: Lexington Books, 1987
A thorough survey of cocaine's history, pharmacology, legal status and contemporary use in Canada and the United States.

Fort, Joel. *The Pleasure Seekers: The Drug Crisis, Youth and Society*. Indianapolis, IL: Bobbs-Merrill, 1969
An early advocate of removing all criminal controls from drug use and

in place of a selective prohibition, dealing with all drug use as a sociological, public health matter.

Giffen, P. James and Lambert, Sylvia. 'What Happened on the Way to Law Reform?' In *Illicit Drugs in Canada: A Risky Business*, pp. 345–69 Edited by Judith C. Blackwell and Patricia G. Erickson. Scarborough, Ont: Nelson Canada, 1988.

Charts the false starts and general legislative inaction in Parliament since the Le Dain Commission's *Final Report* in 1973; a case study in law reform inertia.

Goldberg, P. and Meyers, E.J. 'The Influence of Public Attitudes and Understanding on Drug Education and Prevention', pp. 126–52. Drug Abuse Council. *The Facts About Drug Abuse*. New York; Free Press, 1980

Of six chapters, four are written by Goldberg or Meyers. The article cited chronicles the propagandistic nature of most drug 'education' which, along with the law, thwarts attempts to change popular misconceptions about drugs.

Goode, Erich. *Drugs in American Society*. New York: Alfred A. Knopf, 1984

Offers a broad, critical survey of how drugs are defined, used, regulated and transformed into legal and social 'problems'.

Green, Melvyn. 'Towards Rational Drug Scheduling.' In *Illicit Drugs in Canada: A Risky Business*, pp. 186–208. Edited by Judith C. Blackwell and Patricia G. Erickson. Scarborough, Ont: Nelson Canada, 1988

After finding that no country's statutory drug classification is founded on a scientific appraisal of hazards, this paper examines different appraisal methods for rationally assessing the relative dangers of drug use.

Hamowy, Ronald. *Canadian Medicine: A Study in Restricted Entry*. Vancouver: Fraser Institute, 1984

The author, a University of Alberta history professor, describes the development of medical licensing from the beginning of British North America to the 1920s and concludes that despite claims about acting in the public interest, legislators and the medical profession acted almost purely in their own self-interest, usually to the detriment of the public.

Hamowy, Ronald, ed. *Dealing with Drugs: Consequences of Government Control*. Lexington, MA: Lexington Books, 1987

The nine chapters by leading researchers such as Grinspoon, Musto, Trebach, Szasz and Zinberg, discuss the social, economic and political effects of narcotics prohibition as well as the recent medical research concerning illicit substances.

Helmer, John. *Drugs and Minority Oppression*. New York: Seabury Press, 1975

Attributes the rise of U.S. drug laws to labour conflict, competition, repression of popular unrest and the oppression of Orientals, blacks and Mexicans and demonstrates that social class, not personal psychology, is the more important influence in one's choice of drug.

Himmelstein, Jerome L. *The Strange Career of Marihuana: Politics and Ideology of Drug Control in America.* Westport, CT: Greenwood Press 1983

Assesses four competing theories about why the U.S. Federal Bureau of Narcotics led the movement to criminalize marijuana in 1934.

Inciardi, James A. *The War on Drugs: Heroin, Cocaine, Crime and Public Policy.* Palo Alto, CA: Mayfield, 1986

One of the few scholarly attempts to justify current methods of drug control through criminal sanctions, foreign intervention and border patrol.

Julien, Robert M. *A Primer of Drug Action.* 3rd ed. San Francisco, CA: W.H. Freeman, 1981

An excellent, readable text on the pharmacology of recreational and psychoactive drugs including alcohol, central nervous stimulants, opiates, tranquilizers, marijuana and the hallucinogens. Recommended because of its fairly unbiased analysis.

Kaplan, John. *The Hardest Drug: Heroin and Public Policy.* Chicago, IL: University of Chicago Press, 1983

Reviews the development of heroin use as a social-legal problem and compares the costs and benefits of heroin prohibition with more liberal regulations.

King, Rufus. *The Drug Hang-Up: America's Fifty-Year Folly.* New York: W.W. Norton, 1972

A critical survey of narcotics laws and policies in the U.S. since 1914 with emphasis on constitutional rights and the politics of drug legislation.

Lidz, Charles W. and Walker, Andrew L. *Heroin, Deviance and Morality.* Beverly Hills, CA: Sage, 1980

A sociological analysis of moral crises with special attention paid to the creation of drug deviants and to the key transformation of drug activity from mundane to extraordinary allowing the identification between ordinary citizens and opiate users to be broken.

MacFarlane, Bruce A. *Drug Offences in Canada.* 2nd ed. Aurora, Ont: Canada Law Book, 1986

Used by prosecutors and defence lawyers when dealing with drug offences, this long, detailed treatise covers judicial interpretations of Canada's drug statutes.

Manning, Peter K. *The Narcs' Game: Organizational and Informational Limits on Drug Law Enforcement.* Cambridge, MA: MIT Press, 1980

Traces the creation of larger, better-funded agencies to control illicit drugs and describes the beliefs, values and organizational incentives shaping police work in the narcotics field.

McGinley, G.P.J. 'An Inquiry into the Nature of the State and its Relation to the Criminal Law.' *Osgoode Hall Law Journal* 19 (2, 1981): 267–300

A useful overview of criminal law creation based on historical and contemporary evidence and on a theory of the state's interest in and manipulation of the criminal law.

McNicholl, Andre. *Drug Trafficking: A North-South Perspective.* Ottawa: North-South Institute, 1983

Combines a survey of drug use and drug production in Third World countries, like Jamaica and Columbia, with an argument that the U.S.-dominated international police campaign against certain drugs makes matters worse in both North America and abroad.

Mitchell, Chester N. 'Le crime organise et la guerre aux stupefiants: crise et reforme.' *Criminologie* 22 (1, 1989): 41–65

Traces the evolution of the international, U.S.-led 'war against drugs', examines the impact of that war in North America and abroad, and speculates on the potential for legal reform emerging from the present crisis.

Mitchell, Chester N. 'Deregulating Mandatory Medical Prescription.' *American Journal of Law and Medicine* 12 (12, 1986b): 207–39

An empirically based study of the politics and impact of laws requiring consumers to obtain physician approval for the purchase, possession and use of certain drugs, concluding that such laws do not serve the public interest.

Mitchell, Chester N. 'The Intoxicated Offender: Refuting the Legal and Medical Myths.' *International Journal of Law and Psychiatry* 11 (1988): 77–103

This paper contrasts the empirical data on the drug-violence/crime connection with the legal assumptions underlying narcotics prohibition and the intoxication doctrine.

Mitchell, Chester N. 'A Justice-Based Argument for the Uniform Regulation of Psychoactive Drugs.' *McGill Law Journal* 31 (2, 1986a): 212–63

Argues on the basis of the scientific evidence that drug users should possess basic rights of legal protection, that discriminatory drug laws meet high standards of proof and that methods of drug control be subject to full democratic selection constrained by constitutional equality rights similar to those affecting freedom of religion, speech and assembly.

Morgan, H. Wayne. *Drugs in America: A Social History, 1800–1920* Syracuse, NY: Syracuse University Press, 1981

Morgan analyses the formative years during which problematic drug use was first characterized by physicians as disease, like alcoholism or cocainism, and prohibitionist movements developed as formal organizations and political parties.

Murphy, Emily F. *The Black Candle*. rep. Toronto: Thomas Allen, 1922, 1973

In the first Canadian book on narcotics, based partly on her *Macleans* magazine series, an Alberta magistrate, Murphy warned about the great dangers posed by certain 'evil' drugs pushed by demented, degenerate Chinamen, blacks and other undesirables. Widely read in the 1920s.

Murray, Glenn F. 'The Road to Regulation: Patent Medicines in Canada in Historical Perspective.' In *Illicit Drugs in Canada: A Risky Business*, pp. 72–87. Edited by Judith C. Blackwell and Patricia G. Erickson. Scarborough, Ont: Nelson Canada, 1988

Discusses how 'patent medicine' was defined as a social problem in Canada and analyses the origins of the *Proprietary or Patent Medicine Act* of 1908.

Musto, David F. *The American Disease: Origins of Narcotic Control*. New Haven, CT: Yale University Press, 1973

The standard reference work on the history of U.S. narcotics laws.

Olson, Mancur. *The Rise and Decline of Nations*. New Haven, CT: Yale University Press, 1982

An economic theory of political dynamics concludes from a wide survey of the evidence that given stable social conditions and sufficient time, every government criminalizes and regulates more and more social, personal and business activity in discriminatory fashion, except if legislators are thwarted by constitutional limits.

Ray, Oakley S. *Drugs, Society and Human Behaviour*. 3rd ed. St. Louis, MO: C.V. Mosby, 1983

The leading university-level textbook on all aspects of illicit drugs.

Richards, David A.J. *Sex, Drugs, Death and the Law: An Essay on Human Rights and Overcriminalization*. Totowa, NJ: Rowman and Littlefield, 1982

Argues on the basis of human rights that so-called 'victimless crimes' should merely be regulated, not prohibited.

Rublowsky, John. *The Stoned Age: A History of Drugs in America*. New York: Putnam, 1974

A lively, readable and unbiased account of alcohol, tobacco, marijuana and opiate use, folklore, politics, history and sociology in the New World.

Satinder, K. Paul. *Drug Use: Criminal, Sick or Cultural?* Roslyn Heights, NY: Libra Publishers, 1980

A Canadian psychologist usefully examines drug laws and policies and speculates about why legislators ignore or disregard scientific evidence on drug issues.

Schroeder, Richard C. *The Politics of Drugs: An American Dilemma.* Washington, DC: Congressional Quarterly Press, 1980
An insider's assessment and criticism of federal narcotics control strategies in the United States with a detailed consideration of whether marijuana use and distribution should be legalized.

Smart, Reginald G. *Forbidden Highs: The Nature, Treatment and Prevention of Illicit Drug Abuse.* Toronto: Addiction Research Foundation, 1983
In four sections, Smart addresses the historical background of drug use in Canada, the nature and extent of current drug use, efforts at control and prevention and future directions for illicit drug use in Canada.

Solomon, Robert R. and Green, Melvyn. 'The First Century: The History of Non-Medical Opiate Use and Control Policies in Canada, 1870–1970.' In *Illicit Drugs in Canada: A Risky Business*, pp. 88–116. Edited by Judith C. Blackwell and Patricia G. Erickson. Scarborough, Ont: Nelson, 1988
A detailed, well-documented analysis showing that actual effects of opiate drugs on users were the least significant factor in shaping narcotic control policy in Canada.

Szasz, Thomas S. *Ceremonial Chemistry: The Ritual Persecution of Drugs, Addicts and Pushers.* Garden City, NY: Anchor Press, 1974
The classic and still leading statement against the 'chemical fallacy', which blames religious, moral and political difficulties on the alleged pharmacological properties of supposedly 'bad' drugs.

Teff, Harvey. *Drugs, Society and the Law.* Farnborough, Hants: Saxon House; Lexington, MA: Lexington Books, 1975
Using primarily British law and drug data, Teff attempts to unravel the 'conventional misperceptions' about the drug problem and calls for an entirely new legal framework and a radically revised understanding of drug taking.

Trebach, Arnold S. *The Great Drug War And Radical Proposals That Could Make America Safe Again.* New York: Macmillan, 1987
A personal, readable account of the American anti-drug crusade, its follies and victims, by a leading strategist in the campaign against drug repression.

Trebilcock, Michael J. 'Winners and Losers in the Modern Regulatory System: Must the Consumer Always Lose?' *Osgoode Hall Law Journal* 13 (3, December, 1975): 619–47

Using various examples, it is argued that in most cases of modern regulation the law does not actually benefit consumers despite political declarations of legislating in the public interest.

Weil, Andrew and Rosen, Winifred. *Chocolate to Morphine: Understanding Mind-Active Drugs*. Boston, MA: Houghton Mifflin, 1983
An illustrated compendium of accurate, unbiased drug information written for young adults and adolescents that argues any drug can be used successfully, no matter how bad its reputation, while any drug can be abused, no matter how accepted it is.

Wisotsky, Steven. *Breaking the Impasse in the War on Drugs*. New York: Greenwood Press, 1986
Examines in detail the domestic and international impact of anti-narcotic law enforcement and argues that current drug laws are pathological and counter-productive.

Woodiwiss, Michael. *Crime, Crusades and Corruption: Prohibitions in the United States, 1900–1987*. London: Pinter, 1988
British historian Woodiwiss provides a detailed account from primary materials about the passage and administration of modern vice laws and illustrates with a number of case studies why such prohibitions have had such disastrous effects.

Zinberg, Norman E. *Drug, Set and Setting: The Basis for Controlled Intoxicant Use*. New Haven, CT: Yale University Press, 1984
Considered heretical by advocates of the disease model of addiction or alcoholism, this book presents evidence indicating that the permanent, out-of-control opiate addict is a myth.

7

The Charter and
the Criminal Process

Kent Roach

Since the enactment of the *Canadian Charter of Rights and Freedoms* in 1982 much has been written about its effect on the criminal justice system. The bulk of this scholarship has been by lawyers, who have devoted their considerable energies to tracing and guiding the path of the courts through the maze of legal issues presented by the new constitutional rights of those who are suspected, accused or convicted of crimes. More broadly focused, interdisciplinary scholarship in this new field is only starting to place the Charter in its context. Over the next decade we can expect to see an increasing diversity in Charter scholarship with more research being directed to the political and policy implications of the Charter's role in the criminal justice system. Social scientists have only begun the difficult task of undertaking empirical work to measure the effects of the Charter on the administration of criminal justice. The next decade will also undoubtedly see continued development of leftist and feminist critiques of the Charter's ability to structure and dominate discourse about criminal justice, as well as the burgeoning of both academic and popular work which is critical of the restraints that the Charter places, or is perceived to place, on the control of crime. For the present and with a few notable exceptions, readers in this area must satisfy themselves with literature about what the courts have done and should do in administering the legal rights contained in the Charter.

The Scope of the Charter

The Charter applies as part of the supreme law of Canada to the activities of Canadian legislatures and governments across a wide range of activities, but it is of particular importance to those interested in the study of crime. This is true both as a quantitative and qualitative matter. The Charter sets out fundamental freedoms such as freedom of expression; democratic rights such as the right to vote; mobility rights such as the right to pursue the gaining of a livelihood in any province; rights guaranteeing every individual equal protection of the law without discrimination and various minority language rights. It is, however, the Charter's legal rights (ss.7–14), designed to protect those subject to criminal investigations or charged with crimes, that play the most important role in the day-to-day administration of justice.

The broadest of the legal rights is found in s.7 which provides that everyone has the right to life, liberty and security of the person and the right not to be deprived thereof except in accordance with the principles of fundamental justice. In order to give content to this broad provision, the Supreme Court of Canada has suggested that principles of fundamental justice will be found in the 'basic tenets of the justice system' (*British Columbia Motor Vehicle Reference*, 1985). Building on this premise, courts are beginning to hold that s.7 requires the prosecutor to prove that the accused had some form of wrongful intention when he or she committed a criminal act, at least when the sanction for conviction is imprisonment and a special stigma (*Vaillancourt*, 1987). This is not to suggest that only traditional values fall under s.7. For example, it has been argued that s.7 prohibits excessively vague criminal sanctions, the discriminatory use of prosecutorial discretion and the denial of counsel to those who cannot afford to pay for legal representation. Only recently the Supreme Court of Canada reversed a Court of Appeal decision which held that *Criminal Code* provisions allowing the fingerprinting of those charged with serious offences violated s.7 by' threatening their mental integrity and reputation without adequate safeguards (Laskin, 1989).

The rest of the legal rights in the Charter are set out in a somewhat more specific form and pertain either to investigative methods, the conduct of the trial or the punishment of the convicted offender. The police are prohibited from using unreasonable searches and seizures (s.8) and arbitrary detentions (s.9) in the investigation of crime. The taking of statements from suspects is in part regulated by requirements that a person be informed of the reasons for an arrest or detention and of the right to retain and instruct counsel without delay (s.10). An accused standing trial has among other rights: rights to be tried within a reasonable time; not to be compelled to be witness at that trial; to be presumed innocent until proven guilty according to law in a fair and public hearing by an independent and impartial tribunal; to be tried by a jury if he or she faces five years imprisonment or more; to have the assistance of an interpreter; and when finally acquitted or convicted, not to be tried for the same offence again (ss.11–14). After conviction, the punishment and treatment received in penal institutions must not be cruel or unusual (s.12).

The actual content of the above rights depends on how broadly judges interpret them and much legal scholarship is devoted to this question (Atrens, 1989; Beaudoin and Ratushny, 1989; Gibson, 1986; Hogg, 1985; Manning, 1983; McDonald, 1989; Paciocco, 1987; Stuart, 1987; Whitley, 1989). Compliance with these rights is another matter. It will depend on the extent to which Charter violations are brought to the attention of courts and the choices judges make in the enforcement of Charter rights through the selection of remedies (s.24). Moreover, compliance will also depend on the inclination and ability of the administrators of criminal justice to respect Charter rights.

It appears as if those faced with criminal charges are prepared to make extensive use of their Charter rights. In the year and a half after the enactment of the Charter, Martin L. Friedland found a ten-fold increase in the number of reported criminal decisions on the Charter as opposed to the comparable period after the *Canadian Bill of Rights* was enacted in 1960 (Friedland, 1984). The extensive early use of the Charter in criminal litigation can in part be attributed to the fact that, unlike the *Canadian Bill of Rights*, the Charter applies to the law enforcement activities of provincial and municipal as well as federal authorities and was entrenched as part of the nation's constitutional law. The quantitative importance of the Charter in the criminal justice system has by all accounts persisted. In a study of 1,991 reported Charter cases decided across Canada between 1982 and 1985, political scientists Ted Morton and Michael Withey found that 90 per cent of the Charter arguments presented to courts were based on the legal rights (Morton and Withey, 1987). Likewise, in his study of 800 Ontario Charter cases in Ontario, Patrick Monahan found 85 per cent dealt with the legal rights provisions (Monahan, 1987).

The quantitative dominance of criminal justice matters in Charter litigation is even more striking when it is considered that many of the cases involving other rights also involve criminal justice. For example, various *Criminal Code* provisions prohibiting the wilful promotion of hate propaganda and communication for the purpose of prostitution have been challenged as infringing freedom of expression. Statutory provisions which disqualify inmates from voting have been challenged as infringements of the democratic rights. Numerous challenges based on the equality rights provisions have been raised by young offenders and others who claim they do not receive equal protection or benefit from the criminal law (Laskin, 1989).

As a qualitative matter it is important to distinguish those Charter challenges which are directed at the conduct of law enforcement officials and those which challenge criminal and quasi-criminal laws enacted by legislatures. If a law is found to infringe a Charter right, it is open for the state to prove under s.1 of the Charter that the infringement is a reasonable limit prescribed by law and demonstrably justified in a free and democratic society. For example, in a series of recent cases, the Supreme Court of Canada held that random spot checks and roadside breathalyser procedures set out in a provincial highway traffic act and the *Criminal Code* violated the rights of the motorists stopped not to be arbitrarily detained and to retain and instruct counsel without delay once detained. The Court then went on to decide that these infringements were justified under s.1 in order to deter drunk driving (*Hufsky*, 1988; *Thomsen*, 1988). Criminal laws can be upheld in the interests of important social objectives even though they may also infringe the rights of those suspected or accused of crimes.

The situation is very different, however, when law enforcement officials in the exercise of their own discretion violate Charter rights, as for example when a police officer denies a detainee the right to retain and instruct counsel without delay or when a trial is not conducted in a reasonable time. In most cases the courts have held that such discretionary activity is not prescribed by law and as such cannot be justified under s.1. Once the court concludes that a right has been violated, it will determine an appropriate and just remedy for the violation under the remedies section of the Charter. The remedies available can include the outright dismissal of the case or the exclusion of relevant evidence from the criminal trial (Gibson, 1986; Roach 1986, 1987).

Morton and Withey found that roughly two-thirds of the Charter cases they examined challenged the conduct of law enforcement officials with one half of these cases involving the conduct of the police. Monahan's study reflected similar results with a higher success rate in those cases which challenged the behaviour of officials as opposed to legislators and the highest success rates for claims of violations by the police of the search and seizure provisions of s.8 and the right to counsel provisions of s.10(b) (Monahan, 1987). These studies seem to support the prediction of political scientist Peter Russell that the Charter would be used to supervise the behaviour of the street-level bureaucrats who are charged with keeping order. As Russell (1982) stated:

> Judges who may be disinclined to second-guess decisions of elected legislators may feel much less restrained in assessing the reasonableness of actions or inactions of bureaucrats, policemen, or security agents that are not clearly mandated by law. In applying the requirements of a constitutional charter in this context, instead of vetoing elected legislators, the judiciary is more likely to be compensating for the weaknesses of legislative bodies in our system of parliamentary government in monitoring and sanctioning the activities of the executive.

It is important to emphasize that the role of the Charter in the control of police discretion is not perfect. Not all police misconduct will amount to a Charter violation. A person who has suffered from police misconduct is unlikely to raise a Charter claim if not brought into court on criminal charges. Even when charged, the person may enter a plea of guilty especially if charges are reduced by the prosecutor in an effort to avoid judicial scrutiny of the alleged Charter violation. Even when the issue gets to court, the police have resources of credibility and broad legal powers on their side. Even if the accused can convince the court that a Charter violation occurred, the remedies ordered may be inadequate to influence police behaviour. Despite these serious limitations as a control mechanism, Charter cases provide students of criminology with some insights into the exercise of discretion by law enforcement officials in all stages of the criminal process.

The Charter in Context: Politics and History

The Charter is no longer a toddler but it remains difficult to write the biography of an eight year old. Yet it is important to try to understand why, at this point in our history, it has emerged as the precocious child of criminal justice occupying so much attention. Preliminary accounts have stressed one or more of three basic life stories.

The most prevalent in early accounts was the story of progressive continuity. On first examination, many of the rights in the Charter (especially the legal rights) looked familiar to lawyers and the Charter was often portrayed as an important yet incremental stage in legal development (Friedland, 1984; Salhany, 1986). The legal rights governing criminal investigations were built by and large on existing legal doctrines concerning the admissibility of statements, the law of arrest and the law of search and seizure. Familiar concepts of bail and habeas corpus to protect the liberty of the individual were given constitutional status. The institution of the jury and the traditional burden of proof on the prosecutor were also enshrined. Evidence is not automatically excluded if obtained in violation of constitutional rights as in the United States but, following the experience of other Commonwealth jurisdictions, only excluded if the judge concludes after balancing all the factors that its admission would bring the administration of justice into disrepute. The Charter provides only a gradual erosion of Parliamentary sovereignty, given the ability of governments to justify violations of Charter rights under s.1 or to override the legal rights under s.33. The story of progressive continuity presents an optimistic picture of the functioning of the Canadian criminal process with the Charter offering moderate improvements.

Another of the Charter's life stories has stressed its place in a cycle of political conflict and change. The drafting of the Charter foreshadowed the political conflict that pervades its administration. Original drafts of the Charter were heavily influenced by provincial governments who were concerned with preserving their law enforcement powers. For example, there were no guarantees against 'unreasonable' searches, 'unreasonable' denials of bail or 'arbitrary' detentions, but rather only against those that were not 'in accordance with procedures, established by law.' Likewise, there was no provision for remedies, but rather a guarantee for governments that Charter rights would *not* affect the admissibility of evidence (McWhinney, 1982; Roach, 1987). During the arduous process of gaining consent for patriation, pressure groups representing civil libertarians and the criminal defence bar were able to beef up the legal rights and enforcement provisions much to the chagrin of the provincial governments and police organizations who would have to abide by them. The broader guarantees transferred power from elected representatives, prosecutors and the police to judges, defence counsel and the accused. With this transfer, the conflict between due process and crime control values in the political arena became visible in the judicial process. A recent quantitative study of Supreme Court decision-making has revealed a marked discrepancy between the receptiveness of individual judges to Charter claims (Petter and Monahan, 1988). Judges are more openly disagreeing on the priority of the values to be advanced, with some seeing individualistic due process values as a trump over the collective interest in crime control, while others are more reluctant to allow Charter rights to take precedence over crime control by excluding evidence or staying proceedings (Roach, 1986).

The present ascendance of a Charter-inspired rights ethic reflects larger patterns in politics, including an increasing reliance on the assertion of rights to resolve social conflicts (Williams, 1985). Officially recognized discretion and the pursuit of the public interest has become suspect throughout society and the Charter represents only a part of this larger change. Like all political movements, this one will in time produce its own reaction. For example, the Warren Court's civil libertarian decisions of the 1960s were followed by the ascendancy of new concerns in America about crime control and the war against drugs. Not surprisingly, Nixon and Reagan appointees to the federal judiciary presided over a move away from the rights of suspects (Arenella, 1983; Baker, 1983). In the story of political conflict, the Charter is primarily part of symbolic public discourse (Russell, 1983, 1985) and as such its meanings will change with the times.

The Charter's third life story contains elements of continuity and symbolism, but is characterized by a much darker vision stressing the continued repression of both the perpetrators and victims of crime. Critics have stressed the unequal access to the justice promised by the Charter (Boyd et al., 1987; Ericson, 1983; Marshall, 1988) and the fact that, even in the criminal context, some Charter victories applauded by civil libertarians have been won by large corporations in their efforts to avoid government regulation (*Hunter*, 1984; Monahan, 1987). When accused individuals assert Charter claims through state legal aid schemes (Mossman, 1985), their descriptions of what happened must overcome a credibility gap caused by their social and economic disadvantage. Even if the rights in the Charter could be vindicated, their vision of due process is questioned in that it legitimizes the imposition of the criminal sanction without regard to the underlying social problems which produce crime and the criminal law. The legalization of criminal justice politics can take penal and social reform proposals off the agenda of politicians happy to avoid them, or engender a politics which is reactive to a symbolic discourse revolving around the new procedural rights. At a practical level, the Charter's civil libertarian restraints on crime control are liable to have a disproportionate effect on women, minorities and the poor who are often victimized by crime (Kairys, 1982; Mandel, 1989). In the story of repressive continuity, the Charter functions as a legitimizing distraction of procedural justices in the larger and fundamentally unjust legal, political, economic and social order.

The Charter and the Criminal Process

Even given the prevalence of doctrinal examination of judicial decisions, the Charter has had some positive effects on criminal law scholarship. The range of Charter issues has encouraged legal scholars to examine the criminal law, not only as a set of doctrines concerning the imposition of criminal liability by trial and appellate judges, but as a more or less interconnected process involving the investigation of crime by the police, the processing of the accused through the pre-trial and trial stages of the criminal justice system and the ultimate disposition of the offender. The Charter has brought some of the work of law enforcement officials into the glare of legal scrutiny and criticism. Thus, the Charter provides an opportunity to understand how the law in the books is translated to the law of the streets, station houses, courthouses and prisons. Although most criminologists would contest that the criminal process view still takes too narrow a focus on crime in society, it remains broader than that traditionally taken by legal scholars.

The criminal process approach owes much to the work of Herbert Packer who set out contrasting crime control and due process models of the criminal process (Packer, 1968). In the crime control model, criminal justice was an assembly line which stressed the ability of the police and the prosecutor to screen out those who had not committed crimes. The factual guilt of the accused was stressed and most cases ended quietly in a guilty plea. In contrast, the due process model was an obstacle course in which the defence counsel and judge played crucial roles in determining whether there had been compliance with all legal requirements before a conviction could be registered. Writing in the 1960s, Packer saw America moving from the empirical reality of the crime control assembly line to the due process obstacle course. He could point to the rulings of the Warren Court which had increased access to counsel and set down rules for search and seizure and custodial interrogation, rigorously enforced by the exclusion of evidence in their breach (Baker, 1983). More generally, Packer could point to an increasing scepticism about the use of the criminal sanction and a determination that, at the very least, the disadvantaged caught in the criminal process be accorded equal justice. The due process model lost much of its relevance in an American criminal justice system increasingly preoccupied with feverish battles against crime (Arenella, 1983; Whitebread and Slobogin, 1986). Has the enactment of the Charter given due process a new northern home?

The short answer is that Canada has embraced some aspects of the due process model while eschewing many others. The right to counsel has become the preeminent legal right which is rigorously enforced by the exclusionary sanction. Interrogation law has developed along lines remarkably similar to the American *Miranda* doctrine with its emphasis on prophylactic standards against unfair self-incrimination (Paciocco, 1987, 1988). Rights against entrapment or unreasonably delayed trials have been protected by sacrificing convictions through stays of proceedings (Laskin, 1989) and the Supreme Court has expressed its preference for the prior judicial authorization of searches (*Hunter*, 1984).

On the other hand, Canadian courts have adhered to the traditional crime control model in their unwillingness to exclude relevant and reliable real evidence of crimes (Delisle, 1987; Elman, 1987, 1988) and in their sensitivity to the practical constraints placed on the police in the investigation of crime over a broad range of subjects such as searches incident to arrest and the authorization of electronic surveillance (Laskin, 1989). The continued prevalence of guilty pleas and enthusiasm for the use of the criminal sanction suggest that, despite the addition of new elements of due process, the empirical reality of the criminal process still largely conforms to the crime control model.

The Charter has shed some light on the practices of the police when they investigate crime. An important caveat is that judicial adjudication of pre-trial conduct may be unable to reveal an accurate account of what happens on the streets and in the station-houses (Ericson and Baranek, 1982). In his landmark study on the practices of American police, sociologist Jerome Skolnick pointed out the process through which the standards for a legal arrest can be neutralized in police practice: (Skolnick, 1975)

> ... as one district attorney expressed it, 'the policeman fabricates probable cause.' By saying this, he did not mean to assert that the policeman is a liar, but rather that he finds it necessary to construct an *ex post facto* description of the preceding events so that these conform to legal arrest requirements, whether in fact the events actually did so or not at the time of the arrest. Thus, the policeman respects the necessity for 'complying' with the arrest laws. His 'compliance,' however, may take the form of *post hoc* manipulation of the facts rather than before-the-fact behaviour.

Recent Canadian research has confirmed that the police possess social, organizational and legal resources which enable them to deviate from legal rules designed to constrain them (Shearing, 1981). With these caveats in mind, students of criminology should examine Charter cases for an understanding of the formal requirements the Charter places on the administrators of criminal justice.

The Charter raises interesting issues involving police practices in questioning suspects and taking confessions. The questioning of suspects is one of the more important forms of criminal investigation and it is an area in which a suspect can be coerced into self-incrimination (Ericson and Baranek, 1982). Prior to the Charter when the prosecutor sought to introduce a confession as evidence in a criminal trial, he or she bore the burden of proving that the confession was voluntary (Mewett, 1988; Salhany, 1986). Section 10 of the Charter now provides everyone who is arrested or detained with the right to be informed promptly of the reasons and of the right to retain and instruct counsel without delay. If these rights are not complied with, then the evidence that is obtained may be excluded from the criminal trial if the court determines under s.24(2) that its admission will bring the administration of justice into disrepute. Appellate courts have taken a dim view of failures of the police to honour these rights. In one of its first Charter cases, the Supreme Court excluded the relevant evidence of a breathalyser certificate which would have been evidence of guilt of a drunk driving offence because the accused was not informed of his right to retain and instruct counsel before he provided the incriminating sample of his breath (*Therens*, 1985). In other cases, the Supreme Court embarked on the type of intensive judicial supervision of custodial interrogations undertaken in America by suggesting that once a detained person asks to speak to a lawyer, then all questioning should cease (Paciocco, 1987, 1988). The importance of these rulings depends in large part on the remedies which are ordered. In a recent case the Supreme Court decided that although a suspect's right to counsel was denied when he was not allowed to phone his lawyer from his house while it was searched, the drugs subsequently discovered should not be excluded (*Strachan*, 1988). We do not know how effective the Charter is in regulating police questioning of suspects as opposed to other alternatives such as prohibiting the use of all confessions in trials or requiring the video-taping of interrogations (Friedland, 1989; Grant, 1987; Ratushny, 1979).

The Charter regulates search and seizure practices but it is an open question whether its controls are effective. In an early Charter case, the Supreme Court stated that, wherever feasible, prior judicial authorization in the form of a search warrant was required in order to prevent unjustified searches (*Hunter*, 1984). In ordinary cases this means that a judicial official, usually a justice of the peace, must conclude that reasonable and probable grounds have been established on oath that there is evidence of an offence in the place to be searched. Following in the wake of this ruling, courts have struck down some statutory provisions authorizing warrantless searches and have held some, but not all, warrantless searches to be unconstitutional (Laskin, 1989). How much of a safeguard is this new constitutional warrant requirement? Search warrants are issued by lower judicial officers in closed proceedings without hearing from the person to be searched (Mewett, 1988). The independence of justices of the peace has been challenged in several provinces and concerns still linger on whether they enjoy sufficient independence from the provincial governments which employ them to screen search warrant applications rigorously (Russell, 1987). The Law Reform Commission of Canada conducted an important pre-Charter study of search warrant practices in seven Canadian cities and found that in a large number of cases the search warrants issued did not meet the standards of legality set out in the *Criminal Code* (Law Reform Commission of Canada, 1983). Similar studies need to be conducted to determine if matters have improved since the introduction of the Charter. This is especially important because once the police have obtained a warrant, courts are reluctant to exclude evidence seized pursuant to it even if the warrant is subsequently found to be defective (*Strachan*, 1988; Whitebread, 1986).

As for the actual criminal trial, the most important new Charter rights are those which give the accused the right to a trial in a reasonable time and those which protect the presumption of innocence. Determining the reasonable time limits for trials inevitably requires judges to assess the adequacy of the institutional resources accorded to the criminal justice system and to balance the prejudice the accused suffers from delay against the inherent time limitations of prosecutions and appeals and the state's interests in prosecution (Laskin, 1989). Unfortunately it is not known in what way prosecutors, judges and governments have responded to the threat of judicial termination of proceedings which have not been prosecuted in a reasonable time.

The courts have generally been quite active in striking down statutes which take the burden of proof off the Crown to prove to the trier of fact that the accused has committed all the elements of the criminal offence charged. For example, a provision in the *Narcotics Control Act* which required a person found to possess narcotics to prove that he or she did not have the drugs for the purpose of trafficking was struck down in one landmark case (*Oakes*, 1986). Not enough is known, however, about the effect such presumptions have on judges or juries or if striking them down has made a difference. Some preliminary evidence suggests that the *Oakes* ruling has not reduced the frequency or success of trafficking charges (Mandel, 1989). Despite legal instructions to the contrary, those who appear in court charged with a criminal offence may be presumed by lawyers, judges and juries to be guilty. When dealing with the presumption of innocence as a matter of law, courts have at times deferred to important legislative and social interests. For example, the Supreme Court has upheld provisions that require a person charged with a weapons offence to prove proper registration of a firearm, and courts have deferred to the interest in prosecuting drunk driving by upholding presumptions that those in the driver's seat were going to drive and that the results of a breathalyser test indicate the accused's blood alcohol concentration at the time of driving (Laskin, 1989).

The Charter has the potential not only to affect criminal investigations and trials but also the ultimate disposition of offenders. So far, however, Charter litigation has not attained widespread reform in sentencing practices or prison conditions. In its recent decisions striking down a mandatory minimum sentence of seven years imprisonment for importing narcotics and upholding the indeterminate imprisonment of dangerous offenders until they prove to a parole board that they are no longer a social danger, the Supreme Court has incorporated the traditional multiple purposes of sentencing in their constitutional jurisprudence (Roach, 1989). This means that while it is unconstitutional to impose a harsh sentence for deterrent purposes regardless of individual circumstances, the much criticized indeterminate imprisonment of dangerous offenders in the interests of social protection and preventing them from committing crimes in the future has received the constitutional seal of approval. Critics argue that this Charter jurisprudence only serves to legitimatize the discretion that sentencing judges and parole authorities wield (Mandel, 1989). Charter litigation has succeeded in protecting procedural rights in prison disciplinary and transfer proceedings, but not in reforming prison conditions, as courts have upheld conditions such as double bunking and solitary confinement and have absolved prison officials of responsibility for prison violence (Laskin, 1982–).

As this overview reflects, Charter issues arise throughout the criminal process and despite the considerable energy devoted to due process challenges, little is known about the actual effects the Charter has had on the criminal law and its enforcement.

The Charter and Comparative Law

The Charter, drawn eclectically from the American *Bill of Rights* and various international documents such as the International Covenant on Civil and Political Rights and the European Convention for the Protection of Human Rights and Fundamental Freedoms, has the potential to stimulate comparative law scholarship (Friedland, 1984). By and large, however, comparative work has centred on the American experience (MacDougall, 1985) with judges making increasing reference to American cases when deciding Charter issues (Friedland, 1984).

Reliance on American sources has burdens as well as benefits. The Americans obviously have valuable experience with constitutional criminal procedure and Canadians would be foolish to ignore this huge body of law, commentary and research. At the same time, reliance on American authority carries much ideological baggage. Scholars celebrate (Monahan, 1987) or decry (Fiss, 1988; Friedenberg, 1984) perceived differences between the two cultures. A lack of Canadian enthusiasm for protecting individual rights and using judicial power to control the police can be taken as a sign of a distinctive Canadian identity or mere legal and cultural backwardness (Roach, 1986).

Whatever the merits of the cultural debate, there seems to be little practical danger of Canadian courts simplistically importing American ideas. For example, when interpreting the principles of fundamental justice, the Supreme Court rejected an American dichotomy between procedural and substantive justice and embarked on a uniquely Canadian task of constitutionalizing the requirement of blameworthy intent (Archibald, 1988; Grant, 1988). The ability of Canadian courts to justify violations of rights under s.1 and of Canadian governments to override rights under s.33 are unique features of the Charter. Canadian courts have rejected American approaches which exclude evidence to deter police misconduct and have built their own jurisprudence based on determining when the admission of evidence would bring the administration of justice into disrepute (*Collins*, 1987; Gibson, 1986). In doing so, however, they have often ignored the helpful experience of other Commonwealth jurisdictions who have taken a similar path (Dawson, 1982) and have perhaps underestimated the incentives their decisions present to the police (Friedland, 1989). The Charter is and will remain uniquely Canadian but Canadians can still learn much from the comparative experience of other countries.

The Charter and the Social Sciences

Many of the most interesting issues the Charter raises for students of criminology need to be explored by increased social science research designed to evaluate its effects on society. At a practical level, courts have been attracted to the relevance of social science research in Charter litigation. Although they have rejected the use of public opinion polls to determine when admission of evidence would bring the administration of justice into disrepute (*Collins*, 1987; Gibson, 1986), they have deferred to social science evidence demonstrating the importance of random spot checks and roadside breath testing to the deterrence of drunk driving (*Hufsky*, 1988; *Thomsen*, 1988; Vingilis and Vingilis, 1983). If governments intend to justify criminal laws that infringe Charter rights under s.1 of the Charter, they will often have to produce social science evidence to demonstrate the importance of their objectives and the lack of feasible alternatives.

It is important to understand the impact of the Charter on the administrators of criminal justice. To take only one example, it is remarkable how little is known about the controversial use of exclusion of evidence as a remedy for a constitutional violation. Morton and Withey examined 450 cases in which the accused claimed that evidence seized through a Charter violation should be excluded from criminal proceedings because its use would bring the administration of justice into disrepute. In 39 per cent of these cases the evidence was excluded, most often for violations of the right to counsel or unreasonable searches and seizures (Morton and Withey, 1987). Since that time, the Supreme Court has suggested that the threshold is higher for the exclusion of real evidence that existed irrespective of the constitutional violation (e.g. drugs) than for evidence that was produced through self-incrimination and a Charter violation (e.g. confessions, breath samples) (*Collins*, 1987). This distinction between types of evidence has been criticized as inappropriate and based on thinly disguised crime control values (Delisle, 1987; Elman, 1987, 1988). From the time of its ruling in *Collins* to the end of cases reported in 1988, the Supreme Court refused to exclude real evidence in six out of six cases while excluding self-emanating evidence produced through the Charter violation in three out of five cases. We do not know what the effect of the *Collins* ruling has been on the practices of the lower courts or the police, but we should.

Evidence in the United States suggests that despite popular perceptions, a remarkably low percentage of convictions are lost because of the exclusion of unconstitutionally obtained evidence (Nardulli, 1983). Is this because the police and prosecutors are abandoning charges because of possible constitutional violations or because they can find other evidence? Has police behaviour changed as a result of exclusion of evidence? These questions require further social science research which would improve our knowledge of the interactions between the courts and the police. Such knowledge is vital in assessing the impact of the Charter on the criminal process.

At the larger societal level, it is important to understand what effect the Charter has had on the attitudes of different sectors of the public toward crime. Has the Charter, for example, contributed to a process in which some elite groups hold due process values in high esteem, while the ordinary person is much more sceptical about the value of judicial rulings which appear to allow criminals to go free? (McClosky and Brill, 1983) If the public were better informed of the facts would they be more sympathetic to the actions of the courts as they appear to be in the case of sentencing? (Doob, 1985) The larger issues of the Charter's impact on our social and political attitudes are only beginning to be explored and require further empirical and theoretical work in the social sciences.

The Charter and its Critics

Some commentators argue that the impact of the Charter on the phenomena of crime in society has been negligible because of its symbolic orientation or even negative because of its regressive dimensions. At the symbolic level of public discourse, the legal rights of the Charter can be seen as a means to shift public attention from fundamental problems which produce crime. The imposition of the criminal sanction is legitimized by requiring compliance with a narrow form of procedural justice. The same disadvantaged people can be thrown in jail as before the Charter, but the public can be satisfied that they had a 'fair' trial. For example, Michael Mandel emphasizes how the standards set out in the Charter legitimize the imposition of the criminal sanction upon the disadvantaged. He writes that the promise of procedural justice held out to the accused by the Charter (Mandel, 1989)

> ... is a democratization of a purely formal sort. Procedural rights entail no actual shift in the balance of social power...Criminal procedure is required to treat accused persons as if they were equal to each other and everyone else; but in fact nothing else about them changes. Neither their class, nor the social locale, nor the historical determinants of their crimes. Does the

presence of a lawyer change whether a crime was committed, the nature of it, the accused's criminal record or employment status? Does it change the unemployment rate or any of the other determinants of crimes and sentences, who commits them, and who gets them? Does it change the double standard for corporate crime and street crime? Does it change poverty or unemployment? Does it stop crime itself? A fair procedure changes neither the political nature nor the political context of criminal law. Due process puts a big blindfold on Justice but it does not put her sword in the hands of those without social power.

In the American context, David Rudovsky similarly stresses the legitimizing role of constitutional rights in the criminal process. He writes: (Kairys, 1982)

> The most significant social impact of the constitutional principles of due process and equal protection is not their effect on crime, which is minimal or nonexistent, or even the basic fairness they can and do provide in some circumstances. Rather, it is the appearance of fairness they lend the criminal justice system, as well as their legitimation of a class- and race-biased judicial process.

In the British context, Doreen McBarnet has suggested that, contrary to Packer's theory, due process and crime control values are mutually supportive. The rhetoric of due process sustains the illusion that the criminal justice system is stacked in favour of the accused; in reality, the system functions smoothly as a crime control vehicle with the vast majority of accused pleading guilty or being convicted. For these critics, the Charter only legitimizes the imposition of the criminal sanction because 'due process is *for* crime control' (McBarnet, 1981).

The Charter can also be seen as fundamentally flawed because it is a liberal civil libertarian document operating in the modern bureaucratic conditions of late capitalism. The government is portrayed by the Charter as the problem whereas it must, for these critics, be part of the solution to the social determinants of crime such as poverty, racism, sexism or the economic and political forces which lead to the extensive use of the criminal sanction against the disadvantaged. By offering only protections against the state, the Charter can be used in a regressive fashion by the powerful. For example, it can be used to thwart the successful deterrence and prosecution of corporate crime (Petter and Monahan, 1988).

Even within the context of the procedural rights of the Charter, the disadvantaged suffer from simply not being believed by those in control. Important areas in law enforcement such as prosecutorial and sentencing discretion are not adequately controlled by the standards of equal justice held out by the Charter (Boyd et al., 1987; Marshall, 1988). The many gaps in the Charter's application provide ample room for the continued repression of the disadvantaged in the criminal justice system. Even when accused people are accorded the benefits of Charter rights, critics do not always find the results socially desirable. The problem of crime falls disproportionately on the disadvantaged – the poor, minorities and women – and to the extent the Charter does actually restrain crime control it may only contribute to the victimization of these segments of the population.

Feminists have approached the Charter from a number of perspectives. The Charter holds out prospects of reform of some of the criminal laws and practices which do not provide women with the Charter's promise of equal protection and benefit of the law and contribute to their subordination. The Charter can be used to achieve selective law reform, in particular the (temporary) decriminalization of abortion. The Charter may also help improve the treatment that the female offender receives (Boyle et al, 1985).

On the other hand, to the extent that the Charter privileges abstract legal reasoning without regard to consequences and gives the judges who employ this type of reasoning more power, the Charter presents a serious threat to women across a broad range of topics. For example, the Charter can be used to protect pornography (MacKinnon, 1987; Weiler and Eliot, 1986) and to constitutionalize requirements for the proof of the accused's wrongful intention. This latter use of the Charter presents an obstacle to attempts to have the victim's or a reasonable person's perspective count in determining criminal liability for crimes of violence (Pickard, 1980). Similarly, attempts to reform the criminal trial process to make it more sensitive to the victim's position are vulnerable to Charter challenges based on abstract and a priori reasoning about the primacy of the accused's right to a full defence (Sheehy, 1989). These Charter obstacles are especially formidable because they create a battle which pits the accused's 'constitutional rights' against 'public policy' or the 'interests' of women.

Conclusion

The Charter can be criticized as rhetoric designed to legitimate the imposition of the criminal sanction while maintaining an unjust society. Its symbolic conflict between crime control and due process values threatens to dominate public discourse about criminal justice to the exclusion of more fundamental political, economic and social problems which produce crime and the criminal law. For those willing to take a liberal, reformist perspective the Charter has both potential and dangers. It can be used selectively to reveal inequities in the system and to obtain some court-mandated law reform. The danger even within the reformist framework is that the Charter will be seen as a panacea rendering criminal justice reform the exclusive domain of litigation in courts while ignoring legislative and administrative avenues for reform (Friedland, 1989; Grant, 1987; Law Reform Commission, 1983, 1985; Lewis, 1986; Ratushny, 1979). Students of criminology should not to be mesmerized by the glamour and the promise of the Charter; at best, it should be seen as an important instrument among many for achieving some reforms and as a possible obstacle to others.

Reading List

Archibald, Bruce P. 'The Constitutionalization of the General Part of Criminal Law.' *Canadian Bar Review* 67 (3, 1988): 403–54
An analysis of the possible effect of the Charter on the fundamental principles of criminal liability with special attention to the mental element of wrongful intention and the legal defences open to those accused of crime.

Arenella, Peter. 'Rethinking the Functions of Criminal Procedure: The Warren and Burger Courts' Competing Ideologies.' *Georgetown Law Journal* 72 (2 December 1983): 185–48
A survey of the differences between the Warren and Burger courts' approach to criminal procedure. Builds on Packer's distinction between the crime control and due process models of criminal procedure.

Atrens, Jerome. *The Charter and Criminal Procedure: The Application of Sections 7 and 11*. Toronto: Butterworths, 1989
A legal text which examines judicial interpretations of the rights contained in sections 7 and 11 with special attention to the review of prosecutorial decisions.

Baker, Liva. *Miranda: Crime, Law and Politics*. New York: Antheneum, 1983
A fascinating and readable account of the *Miranda* case protecting the right to counsel in custodial interrogations and the case's many legal and political repercussions. A helpful guide to the political and social context that produced the Warren Court's due process revolution and subsequent judicial and political retrenchment.

Beaudoin, Gerald A., Ratushny, Ed and Tarnopolsky, Walter Surma, eds. *The Canadian Charter of Rights and Freedoms: A Commentary*. 2nd ed. Toronto: Carswell, 1989
A legal text written by various legal experts with detailed chapters on s.7 of the Charter, the protection of persons upon arrest or detention, the rights of the accused in criminal trials and the enforcement of Charter rights.

Belobaba, E.P. and Gertner, E., eds. *The Supreme Court Law Review.* Toronto: Butterworths. annual. Vol. 1, 1980–
An annual critical review of the Supreme Court's decision-making over the preceding year. Includes regular analysis of developments in constitutional law, criminal law, criminal procedure and evidence as well as essays on various matters involving the Supreme Court.

Borovoy, A. Alan. *When Freedoms Collide: The Case For Our Civil Liberties.* Toronto: Lester & Orpen Dennys, 1988
A provocative survey of the conflict of values in civil liberties issues. Chapters are devoted to the control of security intelligence agencies and the ambit of police powers.

Boyd, Neil, Lowman, John and Mosher, Clayton. 'Case Law and Drug Convictions: Testing the Rhetoric of Equality Rights.' *Criminal Law Quarterly* 29 (4, Sept 1987): 487–511
An article examining disparity in drug prosecutions and convictions along provincial, age and gender lines and on the basis of the drug used.

Boyle, Christine et al. *A Feminist Review of Criminal Law.* Ottawa: Minister of Supply and Services Canada, 1985
A comprehensive critique of criminal law and procedure from feminist perspectives with specific chapters on Charter issues affecting women.

Cohen, Stanley A. *Due Process of Law: The Canadian System of Criminal Justice.* Toronto: Carswell, 1977
A valuable pre-Charter account of important due process issues in the investigative and trial stages of the criminal process with special attention to the effect of the *Canadian Bill of Rights.*

Dawson, J.B. 'The Exclusion of Unlawfully Obtained Evidence: A Comparative Study.' *International and Comparative Law Quarterly* 31 (July, 1982): 513–49
A comparative study of the exclusion of evidence in British, American and Australian law.

Delisle, R.J. '*Collins*: An Unjustified Distinction.' *Criminal Reports* (3d) 56 (1987): 216–19
A critique of the Supreme Court's leading decision on the exclusion of evidence under s.24(2), with particular attention to the higher threshold for the exclusion of real evidence that exists irrespective of a Charter violation as compared to evidence produced through a Charter violation.

Doob, Anthony N. 'The Many Realities of Crime.' In *Perspectives in Criminal Law: Essays in Honour of John Ll.J.Edwards,* pp. 61–80

Edited by Anthony N. Doob and Edward L. Greenspan. Aurora, Ont: Canada Law Book, 1985.
An empirical account of public attitudes toward sentences which suggests that perceptions of excessive leniency may change when people are more fully informed of the facts of individual cases.

Edwards, J.Ll.J. 'The Attorney General and the Charter of Rights.' In *Charter Litigation*, pp. 45–68. Edited by Robert J. Sharpe. Toronto: Butterworths, 1987

Edwards, J.Ll.J. 'The Charter, Government and the Machinery of Justice.' *University of New Brunswick Law Journal* 36 (1987): 41–57
Accounts of the Charter's impact on the status and decision-making of Attorneys-General with particular emphasis on judicial review and the role of the Attorney General in supervising criminal prosecutions.

Elman, Bruce P. '*Collins* v. *The Queen*: Further Jurisprudence on Section 24(2) of the Charter.' *Alberta Law Review* 25 (3, 1987): 477–86

Elman, Bruce P. 'Returning to *Wray*: Some Recent Cases on Section 24 of the Charter.' *Alberta Law Review* 26 (3, 1988): 604–20
Critiques of Supreme Court and other appellate court decisions under s.24(2) of the Charter which are reluctant to exclude real evidence such as illegal drugs.

Ericson, Richard V. *The Constitution of Legal Inequality*. Ottawa: Carleton University Information Services, 1983
A published lecture which criticizes the Charter as built on legal fictions of formal and procedural equality which obscure the power and discretion that law enforcement agencies have in enforcing order. The ability of the Charter to legitimate the imposition of the criminal sanction and dominate the public culture of reform is also examined.

Ericson, Richard V. and Baranek, Patricia. *The Ordering of Justice: A Study of Accused Persons as Dependents in the Criminal Process*. Toronto: University of Toronto Press, 1982
A pre-Charter empirical account of the criminal process which stresses the power that the police and lawyers have over accused. Describes search and seizure, arrest and interrogation practices that would not be in accord with the Charter but yet might escape judicial review.

Fiss, O. 'Coda.' *University of Toronto Law Journal* 38 (1988): 229–44
An article which suggests that the Canadian legal system is deficient in achieving broad based reform needed for greater compliance with constitutional values.

Friedenberg, E.Z. 'Law, Liberty and Community Standards.' *Canadian Journal of Sociology* 9 (2, Spring 1984): 207–13
A short essay about Canadian political culture and the Charter which builds on the author's controversial earlier work. The author stresses and criticizes Canadians' deference to authority and their inability to support the civil liberties of the individual in the same way as Americans.

Friedland, Martin L. 'Criminal Justice and the Charter.' In *A Century of Criminal Justice*, pp. 205–31 by Martin L. Friedland. Toronto: Carswell, 1984
A comprehensive outline of the criminal justice issues raised under each of the legal rights and the relation of the Charter to the law prior to the enactment of the Charter.

Friedland, Martin L. 'Controlling the Administrators of Criminal Justice.' *Criminal Law Quarterly* 31 (3, June 1989): 280–317
A valuable survey of the different methods to achieve compliance with the law and especially the Charter. Materials are drawn from the law in several countries and social science research. A number of problem areas are examined including wiretapping, entrapment, search and seizure, right to counsel, bail, trial delay, double jeopardy and sentencing.

Gibson, R. Dale. *The Law of the Charter: General Principles.* Toronto: Carswell, 1986
A legal textbook outlining the principles of interpretation of the Charter with special attention to the remedies available for Charter violations.

Gold, Alan D. *Annual Review of Criminal Law.* Toronto: Carswell, 1982– annual
An annual review of important court decisions which includes long excerpts from the judgments. This series started with the enactment of the Charter, and the first half of each volume is devoted to Charter issues, divided both by section and topics. The volumes also include select bibliographies of recent articles.

Grant, Alan. 'Videotaping Police Questioning: A Canadian Experiment.' *Criminal Law Review* (June 1987): 375–83
Videotaping of police interrogations may be an effective means to control misconduct without reliance on the Charter. This article is a preliminary account of the experimental use of videotaping of interrogations and its effects on the police, suspects, defence counsel, prosecutors and judges.

Grant, Isabel. 'R. v. *Vaillancourt*: The Constitutionalization of Mens Rea.' *University of British Columbia Law Review* 22 (2, 1988): 369–90

An analysis of the most important and ambiguous Supreme Court case to date constitutionalizing the requirement for proof of blameworthy intent for essential elements of crimes.

Griffiths, C.T. and Verdun-Jones, S.N. *Canadian Criminal Justice*. Toronto: Butterworths, 1989

A valuable text dealing with all aspects of the criminal process written from a broad criminological perspective. Several chapters deal with Charter issues in the investigation of trial, the criminal trial and the disposition of offenders. A specific chapter on native peoples and the criminal law is also included.

Hogg, Peter W. *Constitutional Law of Canada*. 2nd ed. Toronto: Carswell, 1985

The most widely used legal text on Canadian constitutional law. Includes relatively short chapters on the legal rights and the courts' preliminary interpretation of these rights.

Jackson, Michael. 'Cruel and Unusual Treatment or Punishment?' *University of British Columbia Law Review* (Charter ed) (1982): 189–212

A preliminary survey of the issues raised by the prohibition against cruel and unusual punishment in the Charter.

Kairys, David, ed. *The Politics of Law: A Progressive Critique*. New York: Pantheon Books, 1982

An important collection of essays by critical legal studies scholars. Excellent preliminary essays on legal reasoning with three essays on the role of law in the criminal justice system.

LaFave, Wayne R. and Israel, Jerold H. *Criminal Procedure*. St. Paul, MN: West, 1985

A widely-used text designed for American law students is an abridgement of the original 1984 three volume work. Deals comprehensively with American case law, especially constitutional jurisprudence, in both the investigation of crime and the criminal trial process. Yearly supplements are provided to update the materials.

Laskin, John B. et al. *The Canadian Charter of Rights Annotated*. Aurora, Ont: Canada Law Book, 1989. 1982– 4 vols (looseleaf)

An annotated monthly service providing brief descriptions of reported decisions under each section of the Charter. The service also provides the legislative history of each section and an excellent bibliography of legal scholarship arranged around each section of the Charter. The quickest and most accessible means to research Charter case law.

Law Reform Commission of Canada. *Police Powers: Search and Seizure in Criminal Law Enforcement*. Ottawa: Law Reform Commission of Canada, 1983. (Working paper 30)

A detailed study of the law of search of seizure including an empirical study of the legality of search warrants in seven Canadian cities. Includes proposals for statutory reform.

Law Reform Commission of Canada. *Arrest*. Ottawa: Law Reform Commission of Canada, 1985. (Working Paper 41)
A study of the present law of arrest with proposals for statutory reform.

Lewis, Clare E., Linden, Sidney B. and Keene, Judith. 'Public Complaints Against Police in Metropolitan Toronto – The History and Operation of the Office of the Public Complaints Commissioner.' *Criminal Law Quarterly* 29 (1 December 1986): 115–44
An account of the development of the innovative Toronto system of combining internal police and external civilian review of complaints against the police.

Macdougall, Donald V. 'The Exclusionary Rule and Its Alternatives – Remedies for Constitutional Violations in Canada and the United States.' *Journal of Criminal Law and Criminology* 76 (3, Fall 1985): 608–65
A comparative analysis of American exclusionary doctrine and the preliminary experience in Canada, with attention to alternative remedies such as criminal prosecutions and civil actions.

MacKinnon, Catharine A. *Feminism Unmodified: Discourses on Life and Law*. Cambridge, MA: Harvard University Press, 1987
A collection of essays by an influential feminist thinker with special attention to the role of courts and a constitutional bill of rights in preventing attempts to regulate pornography.

Mandel, Michael. *The Charter of Rights and the Legalization of Politics in Canada*. Toronto: Wall & Thompson, 1989
An important and provocative book which is highly critical of the Charter's role in legalizing political issues and increasing the power of judges and the legal profession. Contains a detailed chapter on the role of the Charter in the criminal justice system.

Manning, Morris. *Rights, Freedoms and the Courts: A Practical Analysis of the Constitution Act, 1982*. Toronto: Emond-Montgomery, 1983
An early legal text on the Charter which makes extensive use of American and international decisions.

Marshall, Patricia. 'Sexual Assault, the Charter and Sentencing Reform.' *Criminal Reports* (3d) 63 (1988): 216–35
A valuable account of trial and sentencing decisions in unreported sexual assault cases which illustrates bias in favour of male defendants and against female victims.

McBarnet, Doreen J. *Conviction: Law, the State and Construction of Justice*. London: MacMillan, 1981

A socio-legal study of criminal cases in Scotland. Stress is placed on how legal rules allow the prosecution to obtain convictions routinely despite the rhetoric of due process values which favour the accused.

McClosky, Herbert and Brill, Alida. *Dimensions of Tolerance: What Americans Believe About Civil Liberties?* New York: Russell Sage Foundation, 1983
An empirical survey of Americans' attitudes toward civil liberties and courts' decisions. Includes samples of the views of the general public, political elites and legal elites.

McDonald, David C. *Legal Rights in the Canadian Charter of Rights and Freedoms.* 2nd ed. Toronto: Carswell, 1989
A legal text, written by a respected judge of the Alberta Court of Queens Bench, dealing with the interpretation of the various legal rights of the Charter. This text is particularly helpful in that it provides extensive excerpts from the leading decisions interpreting the legal rights.

McWhinney, Edward. *Canada and the Constitution 1979–1982: Patriation and the Charter of Rights.* Toronto: University of Toronto Press, 1982
An account of the political events which led to the enactment of the Charter. Includes helpful appendices of the various drafts of the Charter.

Mewett, Alan W. *An Introduction to the Criminal Process in Canada.* Toronto: Carswell, 1988
An excellent introduction to the legal and institutional framework of the criminal process in the post-Charter era. Contains a specific chapter on the Charter as well as chapters on search, seizure and surveillance, arrest and bail, interrogation and confessions, and illegally obtained evidence, all of which deal with the Charter. The book also deals with the criminal trial process including the jury, the proof of guilt, defences, punishment and appeals. The book is designed for those without a legal background.

Monahan, Patrick. *Politics and the Constitution: The Charter, Federalism and the Supreme Court of Canada.* Toronto: Carswell, 1987
A collection of essays examining the impact of the Charter and the political role of the Supreme Court. Contains an interesting empirical account of the dominance of legal rights in Charter litigation and suggests that this is related to the traditional values of these rights and the courts' expertise and legitimacy in the field of criminal justice. Also contains a defence of distinctive Canadian political culture which is sceptical of judicial review of democratically enacted policies.

Morgan, Donna C. 'Controlling Prosecutorial Powers – Judicial Review, Abuse of Process and Section 7 of the Charter.' *Criminal Law Quarterly* 29 (1, Dec 1986): 15–65
A survey of legal methods available to control prosecutorial misconduct before and after the Charter.

Morton, F.L. and Withey, M.J. 'Charting the Charter, 1982–5: A Statistical Analysis.' *Canadian Human Rights Yearbook* 4 (1987): 65–90
An important empirical study based on a large sample of reported cases. The authors admit that the sample may be biased (probably toward 'positive' results in which Charter violations are found) in that it deals only with those cases that the editors of commercial law reports think are important enough to publish.

Mossman, Mary Jane. 'The Charter and the Right to Legal Aid.' *Journal of Law and Social Policy* 1 (1985): 21–41
An article outlining Charter arguments for legal aid and a survey of the relevant American constitutional law.

Nardulli, Peter F. 'The Societal Cost of the Exclusionary Rule: An Empirical Assessment.' *American Bar Foundation Research Journal* (summer, no.3, 1983): 585–609
An empirical study of the application of the American exclusionary rule to suppress evidence, statements and identifications. The study suggests both a low rate of exclusionary applications relative to the total sample of cases and extremely low rates (less than one per cent) of loss of convictions because of the exclusion of evidence. The article also contains a helpful summary of other empirical studies concerning the effect of the exclusionary rule in the United States.

O'Connor, Fergus. 'The Impact of the Canadian Charter of Rights and Freedoms on Parole in Canada.' *Queen's Law Journal* 10 (2, Spring 1985): 336–91
A survey of the role of the Charter in the parole process with particular attention to the right to a fair hearing and the right to counsel.

Paciocco, David M. *Charter Principles and Proof in Criminal Cases.* Toronto: Carswell, 1987
A legal text dealing with the impact of the Charter on the law of evidence in criminal cases with special attention to the relevant American law and the right of accused persons to call evidence in their own defence.

Paciocco, David M. 'More on Miranda – Recent Developments under Subsection 10(b) of the Charter.' *Ottawa Law Review* 19 (3, 1987): 573–80

Paciocco, David M. 'The Development of Miranda-Like Doctrines under the Charter.' *Ottawa Law Review* 19 (1, 1987): 49–70
Two articles analyzing recent Supreme Court of Canada cases dealing with the right to counsel and comparing them to American law.

Packer, Herbert L. *The Limits of the Criminal Sanction*. Stanford, CA: Stanford University Press, 1968
A landmark book presenting contrasting due process and crime control models of the criminal process as well as examining ethical limits of punishment and the use of the criminal law.

Petter, Andrew J. and Monahan, Patrick J. 'Developments in Constitutional Law: The 1986–7 Term.' *Supreme Court Law Review* 10 (1988): 61–145
A critical account of the Supreme Court's performance in constitutional law matters with an interesting empirical account of a wide range (21–61 per cent) of acceptance rates of Charter claims by the different judges on the Court.

Pickard, Toni. 'Culpable Mistakes and Rape: Relating Mens Rea to the Crime.' *University of Toronto Law Journal* 30 (1980): 75–98; 415–420
A critique of a Supreme Court case holding that as long as an accused has a mistaken but honestly held belief in a victim's consent to sexual activity, it need not be reasonable or attempt to understand the victim's perspective.

Pink, Joel E. and Perrier, David. *From Crime to Punishment: An Introduction to the Criminal Law System*. Toronto: Carswell, 1988
A collection of 21 short essays dealing with many of the issues in the investigation and trial of criminal offences. Intended as a text for teaching criminal law and procedure to undergraduate students in criminology courses.

Ratushny, Edward. *Self-Incrimination in the Canadian Criminal Process*. Toronto: Carswell, 1979
A pre-Charter book dealing with a concept that has become very important under the Charter. Contains provocative proposals to reform interrogation practices by prohibiting the use at trial of statements to police officers and of having judicial officials conduct interrogations.

Roach, Kent. 'Constitutionalizing Disrepute: Exclusion of Evidence After *Therens*.' *University of Toronto Faculty of Law Review* 44 (2, Fall 1986): 209–56

Roach, Kent. 'Section 24(1) of the Charter: Strategy and Structure.' *Criminal Law Quarterly* 29 (2, 1987): 222–72
Two articles dealing with the remedial options courts have under s.24 of the Charter in responding to constitutional violations in the criminal process. Also includes a legislative history of the enact-

ment of s.24. Outlines four models of judicial decision-making (crime control, community standards, police regulation and rights protection) which could govern judicial selection of remedies.

Roach, Kent. '*Smith* and the Supreme Court: Implications for Sentencing Policy and Reform.' *Supreme Court Law Review* 11 (1989): 433–79
An article dealing with recent Supreme Court judgments concerning what punishment is cruel and unusual and suggesting the implications of this jurisprudence for sentencing policy and reform.

Russell, Peter H. 'The Effect of a Charter of Rights on the Policy-making Role of Canadian Courts.' *Canadian Public Administration* 25 (1, Spring 1982): 1–33
An account of the new policy-making role of the judiciary in administering various Charter rights which concludes that the novelty of judicial policymaking under the Charter is often exaggerated.

Russell, Peter H. 'The First Three Years in Charterland.' *Canadian Public Administration* 28 (1985): 367–96
A critical account of the first three years of Charter decisions with particular emphasis on the political implications of the courts' decisions.

Russell, Peter H. *The Judiciary in Canada: The Third Branch of Government.* Toronto: McGraw-Hill Ryerson, 1987
A political science text on the judiciary with an excellent introductory account of the nature of judicial power and the political, social and legal environment in which it is exercised. Subsequent chapters deal with judicial independence, the appointment of judges and the Supreme Court of Canada. A chapter is devoted to the lower criminal courts.

Russell, Peter H. 'The Political Purposes of the Canadian Charter of Rights and Freedoms.' *Canadian Bar Review* 61 (1983): 30–54
An account of the political origins of the Charter with special attention to its role in national unity and the implications of the selling of rights to the citizenry.

Ryan, H.R.S., 'The Impact of the Canadian Charter of Rights and Freedoms on the Canadian Correctional System.' *Canadian Human Rights Yearbook* 1 (1983): 99–165
An article surveying the possible effect of the various rights in the Charter on sentencing decisions and the decisions made by prison officials.

Salhany, Roger E. *The Origin of Rights.* Toronto: Carswell, 1986
A readable, historical account of the origin of Charter rights with some examination of contemporary issues and case law. The legal rights in the Charter are presented as an inevitable culmination in the development of the law.

Shearing, Clifford D., ed. *Organizational Police Deviance: Its Structure and Control*. Toronto: Butterworths, 1981
A collection of essays dealing with social, political, legal and organizational factors which contribute to police deviance from legal rules.

Sheehy, L. ' Canadian Judges and the Law of Rape: Should the Charter Insulate Bias.' *Ottawa Law Review* 21 (1, 1989)
A feminist critique of judicial decisions striking down *Criminal Code* restrictions on the evidence of a victim's past sexual history in sexual assault trials.

Skolnick, Jerome H. *Justice Without Trial: Law Enforcement in Democratic Society*. 2nd ed. New York: John Wiley, 1975
A landmark sociological study of police practices stressing the insular nature of police culture and the ability of the police to neutralize constitutional and legal rules.

Stuart, D. 'Four Springboards from the Supreme Court of Canada: *Hunter, Therens, Motor Vehicle Reference* and *Oakes*: Asserting Basic Values of our Criminal Justice System.' *Queen's Law Journal* 12 (2, 1987): 131–54
An examination of four of the Supreme Court's most important cases in criminal justice.

Vingilis, Evelyn and Vingilis, Violet. 'The Importance of Roadside Screening for Impaired Drivers in Canada.' *Canadian Journal of Criminology* 29 (1, 1987): 17–33
An empirical and legal account of the role of roadside screening in the deterrence of drunk driving.

Weiler, Joseph M. and Elliot, Robin M., eds. *Litigating the Values of a Nation: The Canadian Charter of Rights and Freedoms*. Toronto: Carswell, 1986
A collection of essays on the Charter. Part four contains three essays from different perspectives on the relation between freedom of expression as protected in the Charter and attempts to regulate pornography.

Whitebread, Charles H. and Slobogin, Christopher. *Criminal Procedure: An Analysis of Cases and Concepts*. 2nd ed. Mineola, NY: Foundation Press, 1986
The most accessible general text dealing with the range of procedural issues in the American criminal process. Special attention is given to search and seizure law under the Fourth Amendment. Each chapter has a helpful conclusion and bibliography of the leading articles for each topic.

Whitley, Stuart James. *Criminal Justice and the Constitution*. Calgary: Carswell Legal Publications (Western Division) 1989

A legal text dealing with constitutional issues in the administration of criminal justice. Includes chapters on the division of powers, fundamental freedoms, the legal rights, equality rights, multiculturalism and remedies.

Williams, Cynthia. 'The Changing Nature of Citizen Rights.' In *Constitutionalism, Citizenship and Society in Canada*, pp. 99–131. Alan Cairns and Cynthia Williams, research coordinators. Toronto: University of Toronto Press, 1985. (The Collected Research Studies: Royal Commission on the Economic Union and Development Prospects for Canada; Vol. 33)

An historical account of the development of a language of rights in the post World War II era in Canada.

Selected Supreme Court Cases on the Charter and the Criminal Process

The decisions of the Supreme Court of Canada are officially reported in *Canada Supreme Court Reports* [SCR] published by the Queen's Printer. The decisions are also published commercially in various law reports, such as *Canadian Criminal Cases* (CCC) published by Canada Law Book.

British Columbia Motor Vehicle Reference, 1985 [1985] 2 SCR 486; 23 CCC(3d) 289

A decision striking down legislation providing for imprisonment upon proof only of doing the prohibited act, in this case driving with a suspended license. The Court held that this provision could punish the morally innocent and was not justified because it could have been formulated to include a defence of due diligence.

Vaillancourt, 1987 [1987] 2 SCR 636; 39 CCC(3d) 118

A decision striking down legislation that provided for a murder conviction when death resulted during the commission of a serious criminal offence without any proof of either intent or foresight that the death would result. The plurality judgment suggested that because of its special stigma, a murder conviction required proof beyond a reasonable doubt of subjective foresight of death but that, in any event, the impugned provision did not guarantee even objective foresight of death in the eyes of the reasonable person as opposed to the particular accused.

Hunter, 1984 [1984] 2 SCR 145; 14 CCC(3d) 97

A decision striking down a provision in the *Combines Investigation Act* providing for searches without independent judicial authorization on the basis that there should be prior judicial authorizations for searches whenever feasible in order to protect privacy interests. The accused in this case was Southam Newspapers.

Oakes, 1986 [1986] 1 SCR 103; 24 CCC(3d) 321

A decision striking down a provision in the *Narcotics Control Act* which provided that once possession of narcotics was proven, the accused had to establish on a balance of probabilities that he or she did not have the drugs with the intent to traffic. The Court held that the presumption of innocence was a fundamental value of criminal justice and that the requirement for an accused to disprove an essential element of an offence violated the presumption and could allow a conviction despite a reasonable doubt. The presumption was not justified under s.1 because there was no rational connection between the proven fact (possession) and the presumed fact (intent to traffic).

Hufsky, 1988 [1988] 1 SCR 621; 40 CCC(3d) 398

A decision holding that the random stopping of motorists constitutes an arbitrary detention but is justified under s.1 of the Charter as a means to facilitate the detection of motor vehicle offences such as drunk driving offences.

Thomsen, 1988 [1988] 1 SCR 640; 40 CCC(3d) 411

A decision holding that compliance with a request under the *Criminal Code* to provide a road-side breath test infringes the right to retain and instruct counsel without delay, but is justified under s.1 of the Charter to facilitate the deterrence of drinking and driving.

Therens, 1985 [1985] 1 SCR 613; 18 CCC(3d) 481

Evidence of a breathalyser reading was excluded when the suspect was not informed of his right to counsel before providing the incriminating breath sample.

Collins, 1987 [1987] 1 SCR 265; 33 CCC(3d) 1

The most important Supreme Court case to date interpreting when evidence should be excluded under s.24(2) of the Charter. Factors which affect the fairness of the trial such as the production of incriminating evidence while the Charter is being violated generally require the exclusion of evidence. In other cases, the danger of judicial approval of police misconduct and the effect of excluding important evidence on the repute of the administration of justice should be balanced.

Strachan, 1988 [1988] 2 SCR 980; 46 CCC(3d) 479

A case holding that while the police deprived an arrestee of his right to call a lawyer, the admission of drugs subsequently discovered would not bring the administration of justice into disrepute.

8

Mental Disorder in the Criminal Justice System

C.D. Webster

Anglo-American law has long held that it is unfair to try in court a person who is not present mentally as well as physically (Quen, 1981). It has also enshrined the idea that it is unjust to punish a person who was insane at the time of committing a serious offence (Dickens, 1981). The criminal law is fashioned with the 'reasonable person' in mind. It is by allowing for unreason as exculpation that the criminal law can be applied fairly, or seemingly so, in the great preponderance of court cases. The exception of madness is not hard to defend in general principle. Yet it gives rise to intricate philosophical issues around free will and other matters (Bartol, 1983), to legal complexities (Martin, 1985), and to some very practical problems regarding the disposition of persons found to be 'insane' (Quinsey, 1981).

Definitional Issues

The determination of insanity in court is a legal matter. It is decided by judges and by juries. Yet the *Criminal Code* of Canada is not very precise in its definitions. Terms like 'state of natural imbecility' and 'disease of the mind' are considered arcane and outdated by contemporary psychiatric authorities. There is a wide mismatch between the pertinent legal and medical concepts and languages. The former relies on tradition and the application of like cases in seeking to establish a fairly enduring standard; the latter depends on scientific study and recognizes that criteria shift, sometimes rapidly, with the acquisition of new knowledge (Webster, 1984). On the one hand the law is mistrustful of evidence, including scientific 'fact'; on the other it recognizes the value, if only for the sake of form (Appelbaum, 1984), of adducing psychiatric and psychological opinion as it applies to the case under consideration. Forensic psychiatrists and psychologists are apt to see the law as being archaic when applied to issues involving mental disorder; they also see that their testimony can be distorted and nullified under the customary adversarial court procedures (Jeffery, 1964). The relationship between psychiatry and the law is therefore inherently fraught. Legal scholarship and court proceedings depend largely on inductive reasoning and dialectical discourse; psychiatric and psychological research and practice relies mainly on deductive argument and demonstrative reasoning (Rychlak, 1981).

So far, we have suggested that the law acts as 'gatekeeper.' The courts decide whether or not a person is fit to stand trial (Roesch, Webster and Eaves, 1984) or not guilty by reason by insanity (McGee, Atcheson and Orchard, 1981). If, as is explained in more detail below, the legal decision is one of insanity, then the individual will be passed to the mental health authorities for care and treatment. But insanity is by no means necessarily a permanent condition. Some new decision will likely later have to be made, in concert with mental health officials, as to release from hospital. It might even appear at this later time that the individual was improperly found by the courts to be not guilty by reason of insanity (NGRI) or not fit to stand trial (NFST) in the first place. If the court decides that the prisoner was sane at the time of the offence and to be guilty of it, he or she will likely be sent to a correctional institution for a fixed term. Yet on arrival at the prison or penitentiary, or at some later time, the person may appear decidedly mentally disordered. It may seem to the correctional officials and to the institution's mental health staff that the court erred, that the person should have been found NFST or NGRI. The general point is that it is hard, if not impossible, to define 'insanity' in a satisfactory way. It should also be clear that the attempts at definition have critical effects upon individuals before the courts; it is there decided whether they are to be prisoners or patients, bad or mad.

Why is it so difficult to define 'insanity'? We have already mentioned that the law is unable to take into account the full amount of knowledge available in contemporary psychiatry and psychology. The standard diagnostic guide, the American Psychiatric Association's *Diagnostic and Statistical Manual* (1987, DSM-III-R), lists some three hundred and fifty mental disorders (Harry, 1985; Menzies and Webster, 1989). How could a law be framed to take all of these into account? A second point, one already made, is that the APA changes its diagnostic schemes rather frequently. The first edition, DSM-I, appeared about forty years ago. Only seven years elapsed between DSM-III and DSM-III-R. A new DSM-IV is being prepared and will be published inside a few years. Can the court be expected to make adjustments acknowledging these changes, not just the ones which are minor in terms of detail but even some of those which are fundamental from a conceptual point of view? It must also be added as a third point that the

APA's scheme is by no means the only one in existence (e.g., the World Health Organization's *International Classification of Diseases*, 1977). As a fourth point it must be admitted that individual psychiatrists and psychologists, even if they follow the same diagnostic scheme, will not necessarily agree upon a diagnosis (Martin, 1985). A fifth point is that psychiatrists and psychologists often, sometimes without necessarily being aware of it, offer a diagnosis not so much because it best describes the state of a particular person before the court, but because it is particularly apt to secure one dispositional end rather than another. If the assessor describes the individual as having a primary diagnosis of, say, 'antisocial personality disorder,' there is an increased chance that the person will not be found NGRI. If the assessed person is said to be schizophrenic, then there is an increased likelihood that he or she will be considered insane and sent to a hospital. If the mental health witnesses are not in agreement, then the stage is set for a 'battle of the experts' (Dix, 1980). Under such circumstances, the availability of money to pay the experts may play a role in the eventual determination of the outcome one way or the other. A sixth consideration is the presence or absence of mental health facilities and the extent to which key psychiatrists and psychologists in those places convey expectations that certain classes of patients can be helped. If there exists a program in a hospital which purports to treat successfully, say, sexual deviants, then the courts may be enticed to allow this information some weight in settling the insanity issue. Strictly speaking, they should perhaps not do this. But it would not be hard to understand were they to allow such considerations to be influential. A seventh consideration has to do with public opinion. If the insanity defence is perceived by the public in high-profile cases (e.g., John W. Hinckley, Jr. in the USA, Andrew Leyshon-Hughes in Canada) as being 'soft,' the whole defence may be weakened, even eliminated for a period in some jurisdictions. It is therefore likely that unfavourable public response to an 'acquittal' on the grounds of insanity can affect a decision in the particular case. Even though there may be grounds for thinking a person 'insane' during the period of committing a series of, say, gruesome murders, the court may not be willing to entertain the insanity verdict. The Yorkshire Ripper is a case in point. It turned out that the insanity defence was rejected by the English court but that, once found guilty and imprisoned, his psychiatric condition was so evidently poor that he had to be transferred to a hospital.

Procedural Issues

To this point we have discussed the notion of 'insanity' in rather general terms. It is now necessary, at the risk of a slight amount of redundancy, to offer a little more detail about how insanity is judged in Canada and how the provincial mental health systems adapt to these judgments. It is important to note at the outset that it is the police who offer the greatest number of 'judgments' about insanity (Teplin, 1984). A certain proportion of persons apprehended daily by the police give rise to questions around mental stability or competence. Depending upon the importance and seriousness of the incident, the officer must make a decision as to whether to take the person into custody or to try to have him or her admitted to a psychiatric hospital. If the person is acting in a seemingly bizarre or peculiar fashion, the decision may be to take the person to the psychiatric hospital emergency room. There a physician can make a determination under the provincial *Mental Health Act* as to whether the person should be admitted on an involuntary basis. If the person is certified and the incident was not serious, the matter may end so far as the police officials are concerned. The person becomes a patient, at least for a matter of a few days. If the person is denied admission, the officer can then lay charges if this seems the best course of action. Whether or not the person is admitted to hospital depends in part on the way the provincial Act is written. Some provinces allow the physician broad scope to detain on the grounds that the person is mentally ill and dangerous, others are more restrictive. Of course, a good deal hinges upon the physician's assessment of the person, the availability of beds, the amount of family support available, and so on (Gerson and Bassuk, 1980). The law as it relates to civil certification is a complicated topic in itself (Wexler, 1981).

Opportunity for mental health involvement does not cease if the individual is turned away from the hospital or, because of the seriousness of the incident, charges are laid. The police may well indicate in the record something to the effect of 'nut case' or 'should see a shrink.' Influenced by this, or for other reasons, the Crown or the defence lawyer may induce the judge to ask for a medical opinion about fitness to stand trial. In such cases the prisoner is normally assessed by a psychiatrist in the jail or detention centre. If it is the physician's view that further investigation is needed the judge may order a 'Warrant of Remand' under the *Criminal Code*. This means that the person will be sent to a hospital for some 30 or 60 days as an in-patient. Whether the assessment is brief or protracted, a psychiatric report will be conveyed to the court. Although the *Code* does not stipulate what type of information these reports will contain, a subject of much debate and controversy (Law Reform Commission of Canada, 1976; Webster, Menzies and Jackson, 1982), there will normally be an opinion as to whether the prisoner is fit to stand trial. If considered fit by the court, the matter is at end so far as further immediate mental health involvement is concerned. If considered unfit, the court may be induced to concur with psychiatric opinion at a formal fitness hearing. Live testimony may be offered by opposing experts at this stage. Should the court deem the individual unfit, the prisoner becomes a patient. He or she is placed on a 'Warrant of the Lieutenant-Governor' (WLG) and will be ordered to a mental health facility. This means indefinite detention with the proviso that the patient's case be reviewed within six months by a Board specially constituted under the *Criminal Code*. The Board normally consists of a judge, or retired judge, two psychiatrists, a lawyer, and a lay person. These Boards, administered provincially under the federal *Code*, must review all cases at least annually following the first review. In making their determination they must consider whether or not the person has 'recovered' from mental illness and whether or not release 'is in the interest of the public' (i.e., whether or not the person poses a risk to the community in terms of possible future conduct dangerous to himself or herself or to the public). If and when the Board is satisfied that the person is now fit, the person is returned to Court. The Court may then proceed with the charges or, depending upon the circumstances, drop the case. It is evident that the mentally handicapped are at a relatively increased risk of being found unfit simply because they may lack the requisite intelligence to understand the nature of the charges against them, to give instructions to counsel, and to comprehend the penalties which could be applied against them. Such misapplication of the fitness provisions in Canada have been noted (Griffiths, Klein and Verdun-Jones, 1980; Jobson, 1969). The Lieutenant-Governors Boards of Review also administer not guilty by reason of insanity cases. In fact, the bulk of Canadian WLG patients, which number about one thousand in total, are NGRI cases (Webster, Phillips and Stermac, 1985).

It should be clear that the administration and care of WLG patients is an exacting and costly undertaking. The main aim, as has been said, is to prevent the full force of the law falling upon persons who are not fully able to protect themselves. There can be little doubt that the arrangement, one which has parallels in the United States and Britain, works well in many cases. Consider the case of a young man who, while in the grips of a schizophrenic episode, kills his child or parent. Although it is invariably difficult if not actually impossible to assess his state of mind at the time of the incident, it may nonetheless appear that he was indeed in a highly unusual psychological state. His condition may later remit quite quickly with or without medication, with or without specific treatments. The mental health workers, though of course never able to be absolutely confident that there may not be a recurrence, might consider him to be relatively unrisky. It would be possible to loosen the conditions of his Warrant and allow him to live in the community. With this step taken, it might later seem reasonable to vacate the Warrant in its entirety. The NGRI defence in such a case averts the need for lengthy and possibly detrimental imprisonment. It allows for rapid reintegration into society. The man recovers and society is not placed at great risk.

More problematic than the above is the example of a case where, in the patient's view, buttressed by legal counsel, recovery is complete yet the Board will neither recommend the loosening nor the vacating of the Warrant. Such a patient may argue that he or she is being detained longer in hospital under the Board than would have been the case with an ordinary guilty plea resulting in a penitentiary term. It may be hard to prove that there has been a recovery from mental illness if it was never clear that such a condition existed in the first place. This can occur particularly around a diagnosis such as 'antisocial personality disorder.' Some authorities would have it that disorders of this kind are not really psychiatric illness at all, that in fact it is a term which applies perfectly well to the bulk of people incarcerated in prisons and penitentiaries on grounds of offences related to violence, sexual misconduct, and the abuse of alcohol and drugs ('A Mental Health Profile,' 1990). How does a psychiatrist or psychologist help a person recover from a disorder which either does not exist at all, or if it does, is refractory to treatment (Hare, 1981)?

Mental Health Decision Making Issues

So far in this chapter, it has been pointed out that psychiatrists and psychologists play a vital role in the day-to-day work of the criminal courts. Foucault (1978) explains that initially mental health workers won acceptance from the courts because they were useful in being able to offer motivational theories. They helped the courts explain the bizarre or senseless conduct of certain defendants. The courts still have a hunger for this kind of information but, as well, they call upon mental health officials to help around routine fitness decisions. Some 600 brief evaluations are conducted annually in Toronto alone by the Metropolitan Toronto Forensic Service (METFORS) (Webster, Menzies and Jackson, 1982).

As noted above, the involvement of psychiatrists, nurses, social workers, and others in criminal justice matters can be of decided benefit to some prisoners and to society generally. Yet there has been a considerable amount of scholarship in recent years pointing to the unexpected and seemingly untoward consequences of such clinical endeavours (Menzies, 1989; Pfafflin, 1979; Pfohl, 1978; Schiffer, 1978, 1982). 'Dangerousness' is a key concept in clinical criminology. This is perhaps already apparent from what has been written so far. Psychiatrists and psychologists advise the courts, review boards, parole authorities, and correctional officials as a matter of routine. Whether or not they should in fact be offering such services, given the apparent inaccuracies in their predictions, is a matter of much heated debate (Faust and Ziskin, 1988). It is only in the past twenty years or so that researchers have come to the realization that clinicians tend greatly to over-predict the extent to which prisoners and patients will in fact behave violently in the future. Part of the difficulty is that experimental research would be extraordinarily difficult to conduct. No judge, no parole board, will release individuals at random to satisfy the canons of science. But, as it turns out, there have been important rulings in the United States which have led to releases of whole classes of purportedly dangerous patients (Steadman and Cocozza, 1974; Steadman and Keveles, 1972; Thornberry and Jacoby, 1979). At follow-up a few years later the finding from these kinds of studies has been that the clinicians had earlier been highly conservative in their opinions. This is not, of course, altogether surprising. Making a false positive error (i.e., the patient or prisoner is detained unnecessarily) is not the same as making a false negative error (i.e., the patient or prisoner presumed safe commits a violent act). In attempts to reduce false negatives, false positives increase of necessity. The finding that clinicians tend to make large numbers of false positive errors is well substantiated (e.g., Menzies, Webster and Sepejak, 1985a; Menzies, Webster and Sepejak, 1985b). There are many reasons why clinicians are apt to err in this direction (see Webster, Dickens and Addario, 1985). For present purposes it is perhaps only necessary to note that almost any behaviour which occurs at a low rate is hard to predict. As well, the reader should know that there exist no reliable and valid psychiatric and psychological tests for the prediction of violent conduct.

Some authors have concentrated their interest not so much on the prediction problem *per se* but have instead examined how clinicians form their opinions as to the dangerousness of persons under assessment. In what is perhaps the most useful single source of information on the topic, Monahan (1981) has argued that, too often, clinicians tend, in the course of doing fitness and other such evaluations, to 'launder' information. That is, they take 'facts' from police reports, social work summaries, hospital records, and the like, and weave them into a convincing case (Pollock, McBain and Webster, 1989). His point is that much of this information would not meet ordinary evidentiary standards. Pfohl (1979) has provided excerpts from transcripts drawn from conversations between psychiatrists, psychologists, and social workers. The clinicians studied by him were undertaking assessments of dangerousness for the courts. He argues that dangerousness is 'constructed' through the record, and through clinical discussion. The mental health workers have, in his view, a vested interest in appearing expert. Common sense opinions are dressed up to give the appearance of being scientifically backed. Menzies (1989) has recently concentrated his energies on showing how mental health workers may frequently do their patients a disservice by recording opinions, which at least in theory, ought to be irrelevant to the issues of central interest to the court. His work aims to show that clinicians do not frame their evaluations with scientific principles in mind, that rather they often respond to the not inconsiderable pressures applied by courts, colleagues and administrators.

We have so far pointed out that the prediction of dangerousness, so central to legal/medical matters, rests on an uncertain scientific base. It has also been made clear that opinion is nonetheless constantly being sought on these matters by police (e.g., the interest in 'profiling' killers and rapists) (Pinizzotto and Finkel, 1990), by courts, and by corrections. One particular aspect of 'dangerousness' as it applies to the criminal law is of particular interest to legal and psychiatric scholars. This has to do with the *Criminal Code* 'Dangerous Offender' provisions. These were last revised in 1977. Under the pertinent sections it is possible for an application to be made against an individual who has been convicted of a 'serious personal injury offence.' Such an offence must be punishable by at least ten years imprisonment. The case is heard by a judge sitting alone. The law requires that at least one psychiatrist testify for the prosecution and one for the defence. Psychologists and criminologists may also be qualified to offer opinion. Should a person be found to be a 'Dangerous Offender,' the court has the power to impose, as it most usually does, indefinite detention. This is a serious penalty because, although the individual would appear to receive a privilege in being able to ask for parole after three years, boards find it difficult to characterize someone as nondangerous who, three years previously, had been judged to be a menace (Jakimiec, Porporino, Addario and Webster, 1986). Despite the fact that the 'Dangerous Offender' provisions are used sparingly, though more in some provinces than in others, the effect of this law is actually very striking when plea-bargaining is taken into account. Not infrequently the Crown can induce a guilty plea on the index offence by raising the spectre of 'Dangerous Offender' proceedings. Our point is that the power of psychiatrists in these hearings is considerable. Their opinion carries great weight. It might indeed be possible to say that, the case proper already having been decided, mental health testimony is all that is of interest in these hearings. We are then led again to wonder about the extent to which the law ought to be reframed better to take account of the realities and limitations of clinical decision making. If mental health workers are so poor at predicting future dangerous behaviour, as the published research would suggest, is it fair to have a law and a set of procedures based on an assumption that reliable and accurate forecasting is possible?

Concluding Comment

The theory of criminal law rests on the notion that persons should be held responsible for their acts. Court proceedings allow for exploration of intent or motivation. Psychiatry and psychology as disciplines claim to possess knowledge about what causes conduct. As well, these professions have come to assume the leading role with respect to the care and treatment of the mentally ill. Clinicians have become more or less indispensable to the courts, not just in major cases but in routine matters. The accommodation between law and medicine is far from perfect. Yet the complicated issues raised by mental disorder and personal responsibility are such as continually to induce important developments in both disciplines. The law forces psychiatry to be precise in its claims and can even act as a spur to research. Certainly it obliges practitioners to try to explain their terms and findings in words which can be understood by lay persons. Psychiatry brings to the courtroom, a generally sceptical place, its recent offerings as well as its well established 'truths.' There is at least a possibility that new findings and outlooks from mental health officials can influence the fate of seriously disturbed and disabled persons.

Reading List

Applebaum, Paul S. 'The Supreme Court Looks at Psychiatry,' *American Journal of Psychiatry* 141 (7, July 1984): 827–35

Bartol, Curt R. *Psychology and American Law.* Belmont, Ca.: Wadsworth, 1983

Diagnostic and Statistical Manual of Mental Disorders: DSM-III-R. 3rd rev. ed. Washington, D.C.: American Psychiatric Association, 1987

Dickens, Bernard M. 'The Sense of Justice and Criminal Responsibility.' In *Mental Disorder and Criminal Responsibility*, pp. 33–61. Edited by Stephen J. Hucker, Christopher D. Webster and Mark H. Ben-Aron. Toronto: Butterworths, 1981

Dix, George E. 'Clinical Evaluation of the 'Dangerousness' of 'Normal' Criminal Defendants.' *Virginia Law Review* 66 (3, 1980):523–81

Faust, David and Ziskin, Jay. 'The Expert Witness in Psychology and Psychiatry.' *Science* 241 (1, July 1988): 31–5

Foucault, Michel. 'About the Concept of the 'Dangerous Individual' in Nineteenth-Century Legal Psychiatry.' *International Journal of Law and Psychiatry* 1 (1978): 1–18

Gerson, Samuel and Bassuk, Ellen. 'Psychiatric Emergencies: An Overview.' *American Journal of Psychiatry* 137 (1, January 1980): 1–11

Greenland, Cyril. 'Dangerousness, Mental Disorder and Politics.' In *Dangerousness: Probability and Prediction, Psychiatry and Public Policy*, pp. 25–40. Edited by Christopher D. Webster, Mark H. Ben-Aron and Stephen J. Hucker. New York: Cambridge University Press, 1985

Griffiths, Curt T., Klein, John F. and Verdun-Jones, Simon N. *Criminal Justice in Canada*. Toronto: Butterworths, 1980

Hare, Robert D. 'Psychopathy and Violence.' In *Violence and the Violent Individual*, pp. 53–74. Edited by J. Ray Hays, Thomm K. Roberts and Kenneth S. Solway. New York: SP Medical & Scientific Books, 1981

Harry, Bruce. 'Violence and Official Diagnostic Nomenclature.' *Bulletin of the American Academy of Psychiatry and the Law* 13 (4, 1985): 385–8

Jakimiec, J., Porporino, F., Addario, S. and Webster, C.D. 'Dangerous Offenders in Canada: 1977–1985.' *International Journal of Law and Psychiatry* 9 (4, 1986): 479–89

Jeffery, Ray. 'The Psychologist as an Expert Witness on the Issue of Insanity.' *American Psychologist* 19 (1964): 838–43

Jobson, K.B. 'Commitment and Release of the Mentally Ill Under Criminal Law.' *Criminal Law Quarterly* 11 (2, February 1969): 186–203

Law Reform Commission of Canada. *Mental Disorder in the Criminal Process*. Ottawa: Law Reform Commission, 1976

Martin, Barry A. 'The Reliability of Psychiatric Diagnosis.' In *Dangerousness: Probability and Prediction, Psychiatry and Public Policy*, pp. 65–86. Edited by Christopher D. Webster, Mark H. Ben-Aron and Stephen J. Hucker. New York: Cambridge University Press, 1985

Martin, G.A. 'Mental Disorder and Criminal Responsibility in Canadian Law.' In *Mental Disorder and Criminal Responsibility*, pp. 15–31. Edited by Stephen J. Hucker, Christopher D. Webster and Mark H. Ben-Aron. Toronto: Butterworths, 1981

'A Mental Health Profile of Federally Sentenced Offenders.' *Forum on Corrections Research* 2 (1, 1990): 7–8

McGee, R., Atcheson, J.D. and Orchard, B.C.L. 'Psychiatrists, Lawyers and the Adversary System.' In *Mental Disorder and Criminology Responsibility*, pp. 111–19. Edited by Stephen J. Hucker, Christopher D. Webster and Mark H. Ben-Aron. Toronto: Butterworths, 1981

Menzies, Robert J. *Survival of the Sanest: Order and Disorder in a Pretrial Psychiatric Clinic*. Toronto: University of Toronto Press, 1989

Menzies, Robert J. and Webster, Christopher D. 'Mental Disorder and Violent Crime.' In *Pathways to Criminal Violence*, pp. 109–36. Edited by Neil A. Weiner and Marvin E. Wolfgang. Beverly Hills, CA: Sage, 1989

Menzies, Robert J., Webster, Christopher D. and Sepejak, Diana S. 'The Dimensions of Dangerousness: Evaluating the Accuracy of Psychometric Predictions of Violence Among Forensic Patients.' *Law and Human Behavior* 9 (1, 1985a): 49–70

— 'Hitting the Forensic Sound Barrier: Predictions of Dangerousness in a Pretrial Psychiatric Clinic.' In *Dangerousness: Probability and Prediction, Psychiatry and Public Policy*, pp. 115–43. Edited by Christopher D. Webster, Mark H. Ben-Aron and Stephen J. Hucker. New York: Cambridge University Press, 1985b

Monahan, John. *Predicting Violent Behavior: An Assessment of Clinical Techniques*. Beverly Hills, CA: Sage, 1981

Pfafflin, Friedemann. 'The Contempt of Psychiatric Experts for Sexual Convicts: Evaluation of 936 Files from Sexual Offence Cases in the State of Hamburg, Germany.' *International Journal of Law and Psychiatry* 2 (4, 1979): 485–97

Pfohl, Stephen J. *Predicting Dangerousness: The Social Construction of Psychiatric Reality*. Lexington, MA: Lexington Books, 1978

— 'From Whom Will We Be Protected? Comparative Approaches to the Assessment of Dangerousness.' *International Journal of Law and Psychiatry* 2 (1, 1979): 55–78

Pinizzotto, Anthony J. and Finkel, Norman J. 'Criminal Personality Profiling: An Outcome and Process Study.' *Law and Human Behavior* 14 (3, 1990): 215–33

Pollock, Nathan L., McBain, Ian and Webster, Christopher D. 'Clinical Decision-Making and the Assessment of Dangerousness.' In *Clinical Approaches to Violence*, pp. 89–115. Edited by Kevin Howells and C.R. Hollin. Chichester: Wiley, 1989

Quen, Jacques M. 'Anglo-American Concepts of Criminal Responsibility: A Brief History.' In *Mental Disorder and Criminal Responsibility*, pp. 1–10. Edited by Stephen J. Hucker, Christopher D. Webster and Mark H. Ben-Aron. Toronto: Butterworths, 1981

Quinsey, Vernon L. 'The Long Term Management of the Mentally Abnormal Offender.' In *Mental Disorder and Criminal Responsibility*, pp. 137–55. Edited by Stephen J. Hucker, Christopher D. Webster and Mark H. Ben-Aron. Toronto: Butterworths, 1981

Roesch, Ronald, Webster, Christopher D. and Eaves, Derek. *The Fitness Interview Test: A Method for Examining Fitness to Stand Trial*. Toronto: Centre of Criminology, University of Toronto, 1984. (Research Reports; 17)

Rychlak, Joseph F. *Introduction to Personality and Psychotherapy.* 2nd ed. Boston, MA: Houghton Mifflin, 1981

Schiffer, Marc E. *Mental Disorder and the Criminal Trial Process.* Toronto: Butterworths, 1978

Schiffer, Marc E. *Psychiatry Behind Bars: A Legal Perspective.* Toronto: Butterworths, 1982

Steadman, Henry J. and Cocozza, Joseph J. *Careers of the Criminally Insane: Excessive Social Control of Deviance.* Lexington, MA: Lexington Books, 1974.

Steadman, Henry J. and Keveles, Gary. 'The Community Adjustment and Criminal Activity of the Baxstrom Patients: 1966–1970.' *American Journal of Psychiatry* 129 (3, Sept 1972): 304–10

Teplin, Linda A., ed. *Mental Health and Criminal Justice.* Beverly Hills, CA: Sage, 1984

Thornberry, Terrence P. and Jacoby, Joseph E. *The Criminally Insane: A Community Follow-up of Mentally Ill Offenders.* Chicago, IL: University of Chicago Press, 1979

Webster, Christopher D. 'On Gaining Acceptance: Why the Courts Accept Only Reluctantly Findings from Experimental and Social Psychology.' *International Journal of Law and Psychiatry* 7 (3/4, 1984): 407–14

Webster, Christopher D., Dickens, Bernard M. and Addario, Susan. *Constructing Dangerousness: Scientific, Legal and Policy Implications.* Toronto: Centre of Criminology, University of Toronto, 1985. (Research Report; 22)

Webster, Christopher D., Menzies, Robert J. and Jackson, Margaret A. *Clinical Assessment Before Trial: Legal Issues and Mental Disorder.* Toronto: Butterworths, 1982

Webster, Christopher D., Phillips, M.S. and Stermac, Lana. 'Persons Held on Warrants of the Lieutenant-Governor in Canada.' *Canada's Mental Health* 33 (3, Sept 1985): 28–32

Wexler, David B. *Mental Health Law: Major Issues.* New York: Plenum Press, 1981

World Health Organization. *The International Classification of Diseases. Clinical Modification. ICD.9.CM.* Ann Arbor, MI: U.S. National Center for Health Statistics, 1978. 3 vols

PART III

Social Hierarchies, Crime and Justice

9

Feminist Perspectives on Criminology

Mariana Valverde

Introduction

Over the past ten or twelve years, there has been a flood of feminist books and articles on topics in criminology, and in related fields such as social control, deviance, and the state. It is now no longer true that women's issues are being ignored, for there are whole shelves of works on women as victims of male violence, women offenders, and women police officers. The more extreme examples of sexism found in criminological theory have been thoroughly discredited – at least in the eyes of those who read feminist works.

Feminist views have been allowed into print, and into the classroom, but they have been immediately marginalized. Gender is not a central analytical category in mainstream criminology, which tends to include women only when discussing such topics as sexual deviance. Male blue-collar and white-collar crime continue to hold centre stage, while the criminalization of women's choice in abortion legislation, or the high rates of non-prosecution in rape cases, are treated as special interest topics instead of being part of the standard curriculum for courses at university level.

Even the left-wing 'new' criminologists, who one might think might be influenced by feminism, have shown little tendency to move. The important work *The New Criminology* (Taylor, Walton and Young, 1973) contains absolutely nothing about women. This is not a mere oversight which could easily be fixed by adding a paragraph or a chapter. Rather, their lucid discussion of the class basis of both classical and positivist criminological theory is internally flawed by a lack of analysis of the gender basis of both social contract theory (the ground of classical criminology) and the positivist social science of the late nineteenth century. Given the importance of these two approaches in criminology, it is important to examine them to see if they favour male experience and thought, a bias which feminists call 'masculinism.'

Social contract theory, which is the ultimate basis of liberal democracy and continues to ground legal and judicial practice, holds that the state, including the law, is supposed to respect the private sphere and leave it largely unregulated. Feminist political theorists note that this division was clearly envisioned by men, since for women the private sphere is more a workplace than a haven to pursue free self-expression and leisure. Feeling imprisoned in the realm of privacy, women in liberal democracies have historically fought for increased access to the public realms of waged work and politics, while also claiming more rights in the private sphere (for instance, custody rights over their children). After decades of agitation, women were granted formal citizenship and the right to enter into contracts, but given that the domestic realm was left largely untouched, women's ability to participate in the public world was, and remains, limited. Because of this mixed historical experience, there are now heated debates among feminist legal scholars regarding the usefulness of strategies pursuing equal rights for women (see section of the Reading List on Feminist Jurisprudence and Legal Theory).

The positivist social science of the late nineteenth century was based on a more organic, less individualist concept of society than liberal contract theory. It focused not on the individual and legal rights, but rather on measuring and preventing crime as a social problem. The sociology of deviance was born partly out of the claims to expertise about crime made by non-legal professionals (Nye, Robert. *Crime, Madness and Politics in Nineteenth-Century France*. Princeton, NJ: Princeton University Press, 1984) and partly out of the failure of the 'invisible hand' individualist model of classical political economy when confronted with the increasingly serious urban problems of crime, 'vice,' and pauperism (Abrams, 1968). That early positivist criminology produced many egregious views about women offenders is well known, but what is not well known is that the *approach* of the early positivists (minus their more blatantly sexist opinions) continues to be applied more to women offenders than to men. David Garland's fine history of English criminology, for instance, traces the emergence of therapeutic modes of treating offenders (as opposed to merely punishing them) and remarks on the growing medicalization of crime (Garland, 1985). He neglects, however, to point out that women (and children) were much more readily medicalized, and that some strategies later used for offenders generally, such as reformatories and indefinite sentences, were pioneered with women offenders (Freedman, 1981).

Perhaps more fundamentally, the new social sciences of the nineteenth century (the sociology of deviance, criminology and social work) all relied on a basic dichotomy between observer and observed, knowing subject and known object. The belief that offenders could/should not speak for themselves, but should rather be interpreted by experts to governmental and judicial authorities, was easily accepted partly because there was an important precedent. Women, or one half of humanity, have been regarded from Aristotle to Freud, as 'closer to nature,' as less than fully rational, as objects to be seduced or studied, but not as subjects in their own right (Lloyd, 1984; Sydie, 1987). This process, known among feminist thinkers as the objectification of women, has not been abandoned, despite a few women gaining access into institutions of scholarship in the last century. Reason was associated with masculinity, while women as a group were always regarded as subject to the sway of the irrational, whether the result was feats of intuition or hysterical fits. A few women might be granted honourary male status, especially if they refrained from having children, and did not show any active sexuality (women's sexuality, unlike that of men, is often seen as disqualifying them for public duty and rational thought). But these women in no way threaten gender subordination as a system.

The task of feminist social science is thus, as Alison Jaggar points out, echoing Dorothy Smith, to begin to think 'from the standpoint of women' (Jaggar, 1983, pp. 369–76; Smith, 1987). This phrase does not indicate, contrary to some feminist opinion, that anything that women happen to think is feminist knowledge, or that one can reconstruct social science from the untheorized experience of women. Rather, it means that any research project has to include a thorough examination for possible masculine bias, not only in hypotheses, but also in the most fundamental methodological assumptions. Since one of the methodological assumptions that has been definitively challenged is the construction of women as objects under the (male) philosopher's gaze, any theoretical framework and/or research design has to provide for the active empowerment of women and ordinary people. What feminist research is most definitely *not* doing is studying women the way biologists study ants.

Feminist political, social and legal thought seeks not so much to find a theory that will fit female offenders – whose situation cannot in any case be understood solely in terms of gender – but to challenge the organization of the basic social categories: family, civil society, the state, normality and deviance. A few comments under each of four headings relevant to criminology may give a preliminary sense of how this could be accomplished.

The Public vs the Domestic Realm

Feminist legal theorists point out that women's oppression is both enacted and disguised by being mediated through the public/private split that is a fundamental principle of the legal and political systems of liberal states (O'Donovan, 1985). Despite general agreement among feminist scholars of the importance of this insight, the issue has been muddled by the failure to distinguish the legal meaning of public vs. private (that is, the state vs. civil society) and the feminist meaning (which usually refers to the state *and* civil society, on the one hand, and the domestic realm on the other). Some work exists, however, which begins to clarify the various meanings of 'public' and 'private' and the multiple contradictions which have to be theorized; Fran Olsen's neglected book-length article is the best attempt thus far (Olsen, 1983). Feminist scholars have to acknowledge that the public/private split can on occasion be used to advantage by women (most notably in the use of privacy-rights arguments to decriminalize abortion). But in the long run, the perpetuation of this split, both in legal discourse and in social life, harms women by masking gender domination. The theoretical chapters of *Abortion and Woman's Choice* recognize that women have something to gain by claiming formal privacy rights along with men, but simultaneously challenge the privatization of reproduction and domesticity, (Petchesky, 1985).

Crime and Justice

Marxist criminology argues that class injustices are obscured by the criminal justice system's almost exclusive interest in individual criminals. In a similar vein, feminism calls attention to the prevalence of gender injustices. For instance, the absence of proper child care facilities is a gender injustice insofar as it prevents mothers from pursuing jobs and other public activities, even if this does not rate as a crime of negligence in the present legal system. Feminists also argue that pornography is a collective injustice, in that it creates or perpetuates male beliefs that women are sexual objects (Mackinnon, 1987). In fact, much of the suffering of women as a gender is not due to individual crimes by men (although the 'dark figure' of unreported male violence, especially in the home, is extremely significant) but rather to social structures.

Women's experiences of order and disorder, risk and fear, are not accurately captured by the concept of crime, despite repeated police attempts to claim that women are afraid to walk the streets at night because of crime. Many injustices to women take place in the domestic realm, which is generally exempt from surveillance. Other gender injustices take place in the area between public and private, for instance in social benefits, which often label single mothers, or other women living outside the patriarchal family, as abnormal. Even within the sphere of public crime, a very small percentage of violent crimes or major property offences are committed by women.

Therefore, the very category of criminal justice as an apparently separate sphere does not reflect the experiences of women. Family law and administrative law have more effect on women's lives as women, and it is perhaps significant that these areas do not have the glamorous status of criminal law.

Social Control

Hagan has argued that it is the exception for women to be regulated through criminal justice, and they are usually controlled through informal social control mechanisms, ranging from the family to the medical system's paternalistic treatment of women patients (Hagan, et al 1979). Despite the apparent truth of this statement, one has to examine the possible masculinist bias in the distinction between formal and informal social control. The hundreds of thousands of Canadian women who are regularly beaten by their husbands are not likely to say that their mates' violent habits constitute a merely 'informal' system of control. If the term 'social control' is to have any meaning at all, it has to include the everyday mechanisms by which men subordinate women. As Gayle Rubin has said, paraphrasing Marx's comment on how black people are turned into slaves, 'A woman is a woman. She only becomes a domestic, a wife, a chattel, a playboy bunny, a prostitute, or a human dictaphone, in certain relations. Torn from these relationships, she is no more the helpmate of man than gold in itself is money' (Rubin, 1975, p. 158). These social relationships ought to be included in any study of agencies of social control.

It may be possible that the term 'social control,' with its connotations of a monolithic society exerting control over individuals undifferentiated by gender, class or race, creates more problems than it solves. Linda Gordon argues, in her study of the history of family violence, that the left's tendency to see social agencies as agents of social control has obscured the ways in which women are sometimes able to manipulate the agencies to serve their clients' interests and help them against violent or economically irresponsible husbands (Gordon, 1988). Feminist theory's emphasis on seeing women and ordinary people generally as active agents makes the whole notion of social control problematic.

The State

Some of the most interesting work in feminist social and political thought concerns the state and its problematic relationship to the family, gender and sexuality. Some writers see the state as upholding the patriarchal family, for instance by declaring males as household heads, or by allowing tax credits to married men to support non-employed wives (MacIntosh, 1978). Others have drawn attention to the way in which women gained certain concessions from the state, such as custody rights and property rights, against the interests of husbands. This has generally been seen not as an unequivocal victory for women, but rather the transformation of 'familial' into 'social' or state patriarchy (Burstyn, 1983; Ursel, 1986). Shelley Gavigan's work on abortion law in Canada shows that husbands have indeed lost rights over reproductive decisions, but rights have accrued more to doctors than to women (Gavigan, 1986). Recently, issues such as reproductive technology have led feminists to ponder the apparently conflictive ways in which gender, motherhood, and fatherhood are being regulated. Carol Smart argues that British legal practice around reproductive technology is giving fathers increasing rights over reproduction and children (Smart, 1987). The debates on the state are very fruitful for feminist research and theory. They promise to help give feminist criminology a more solid theoretical grounding, since the question of crime and criminal law cannot be considered in isolation from the state.

Feminist criminology is not a distinct field with its own literature. As the reading list shows, anyone interested in investigating gender must cover a very wide spectrum of work, some of which is not criminological at all. This makes the task a difficult and arduous one. Criminology is already interdisciplinary, and transforming it through gender analysis will involve broadening the scope of research. In the long run, however, this broader perspective will allow us to gain a more thorough understanding of the social world around us.

In devising categories for the reading list, we could not rely on any established system, nor expect to cover all the relevant works. This somewhat arbitrary selection emphasizes theoretical works rather than empirical studies. Apart from the general works on women and crime listed in the section on Women and Crime, Feminist Criminology and the legal literature mentioned in the section on Feminist Jurisprudence and Legal Theory, we decided to cover only three of all the possible topics of interest: feminist analyses of violence, sexual and reproductive issues, and gender analyses of social control and the state. These three areas cover much of the relevant current feminist work, but clearly, they are not exhaustive.

The field of 'women and the law' is vast and rapidly expanding. The section of the reading list on Feminist Jurisprudence and Legal Theory omits technical legal literature, choosing only works, principally of a theoretical nature, which are both relatively accessible and influential.

Many of the issues of concern to women that overlap with criminological concerns are related either to sexuality and sexual regulation, or to reproduction. There is a vast literature on these issues, some of it scholarly, much of it from grassroots feminists, and some which combines the two approaches. In the section on Sexual and Reproductive Politics, a few significant recent titles are singled out in the areas of abortion, prostitution, pornography and censorship, reproductive technology, and sexual politics generally.

Few women come into direct contact with the criminal justice system. Most interact with the state through apparently benevolent systems (social security, education, health care) which, feminists argue, perpetuate women's oppression even when providing some material aid or service. The readings in the section on Women, Social Control and the State, are a sampling of the growing literature in this field, all of which is relevant in studying the social control of women through the state.

Reading List

Mary Jackson and Mariana Valverde

ARTICLE REFERENCES

Abrams, Philip. *The Origins of British Sociology,1834–1914; An Essay with Selected Papers*. Chicago, IL: University of Chicago Press, 1968
The development of a national school of sociology is described in a book which consists of an introductory historical analysis and selected readings from seminal works in the creation of British sociology.

Burstyn, Varda. 'Masculine Dominance and the State.' In *The Socialist Register*, pp. 45–89. London: Merlin Press, 1983
A critique of Marxist perspectives on the state from a feminist viewpoint, this article argues that masculine dominance is as integral to state formation as class rule.

Freedman, Estelle B. *Their Sisters' Keepers: Women's Prison Reform in America 1830–1930*. Ann Arbor, MI: University of Michigan Press, 1981
Emphasizes the ambiguous historical role of women philanthropists and social workers in the care and control of women offenders.

Garland, David. *Punishment and Welfare: A History of Penal Strategies*. Aldershot, Hants; Brookfield, VT: Gower, 1985
Garland's landmark book is a critical analysis of changes in the British penal system from late Victorian to modern times, showing the importance of the new reform movements of criminology, eugenics, social work and social security, and welfare state strategies operating in the penal system and in the wider social sphere.

Gordon, Linda. *Heroes of Their Own Lives: The Politics and History of Family Violence.* New York: Viking, 1988
An historical study of child welfare work in the United States, emphasizing that although mothers were often harassed and stigmatized by agencies, they could also manipulate social workers, and mobilize them against violent husbands. Gordon uses her evidence to question the usefulness of social control theory to understand women's experience.

Hagan, John, Simpson, John H. and Gillis, A.R. 'The Sexual Stratification of Social Control: A Gender-Based Perspective on Crime and Delinquency.' *British Journal of Sociology* 30 (1, March, 1979): 25–38
A questionnaire on delinquent behaviour given to high school students in a Toronto suburb upholds the assumption that formal and informal social controls are inversely related. Males have more access to the world of crime and delinquency and are more subject to formal controls (law and its application) than females, who are more subject to informal social controls (in the family).

Jaggar, Alison M. *Feminist Politics and Human Nature.* Totowa, NJ: Rowman and Allanheld; Sussex: Harvester, 1983
A basic introduction to the main currents in feminist political philosophy.

Lloyd, Genevieve. *The Man of Reason: Male and Female in Western Philosophy.* London: Methuen; Minneapolis: University of Minnesota Press, 1984
The claim that reason is 'male' is studied by Lloyd in the writings of philosophers from Augustine to Kant and she finds that philosophy has been deeply affected by the social organization of sexual difference, by the absence of women philosophers and male philosophers defining ideals of reason through exclusion of the female.

MacKinnon, Catherine A. *Feminism Unmodified: Discourses on Life and Law.* Cambridge, MA: Harvard University Press, 1987
A very influential collection of speeches by a leading American radical feminist, who argues that women's oppression is rooted in the objectification of women in sexuality, and that law is essentially concerned with maintaining this victimization of women. Pornography and violence against women are the main two substantial topics covered.

O'Donovan, Katherine. *Sexual Divisions in Law.* London: Weidenfeld and Nicholson, 1985
Women's oppression is organized primarily through the division between the public (regulated) sphere and the private (unregulated) sphere. An influential text which suffers from some conceptual

problems noted by Fran Olsen (see section on Feminist Jurisprudence and Legal Theory).

Petchesky, Rosalind P. *Abortion and Woman's Choice: The State, Sexuality, and Reproductive Freedom*. Boston, MA: Northeastern University Press, 1985, ©1984

This massive and thorough study is acknowledged as the key feminist text on both the regulation of abortion and feminist perspectives on reproductive politics. It emphasizes class and race factors in their interaction with gender.

Rubin, Gayle. 'The Traffic in Women: Notes on the 'Political Economy' of Sex.' In *Toward an Anthropology of Women*, pp. 157–210. Edited by Rayna R. Reiter. New York: Monthly Review Press, 1975

A feminist reading of texts, by Sigmund Freud and Claude Levi-Strauss, attempts to define elements of a sex/gender system which may explain women's oppression by men. It borrows concepts from psychoanalysis and anthropology, such as the kinship system, where women are exchanged as gifts in marriage, or as tribute by men who have rights over their female kin.

Smart, Carol. ' 'There is of Course the Distinction Dictated by Nature': Law and the Problem of Paternity.' In *Reproductive Technologies*, pp. 98–117. Edited by Michelle Stanworth. New Brunswick, NJ: Rutgers University Press, 1987

New reproductive technologies emerge at a time when fatherhood is being re-emphasized, and men's groups demand greater control over children. Some recent legal opinions show a reluctance to allow a woman alone to exercise parental rights, in circumstances such as a child born after artificial insemination by a donor. If the legal concept of paternity is extended, the power of the state to restrict autonomous motherhood will be increased.

Smith, Dorothy. *The Everyday World as Problematic: A Feminist Sociology*. Toronto: University of Toronto Press, 1987

Women's exclusion from men's intellectual, cultural and political world has led to an effort to create a feminist alternative to standard sociology, and to practical questions on how to conduct feminist research.

Sydie, Rosalind A. *Natural Women, Cultured Men: A Feminist Perspective on Sociological Theory*. Toronto: Methuen, 1987

A feminist discussion and critique of sociological theory examines some of the work of Durkheim, Weber, Marx and Engels, and Freud and their descendants in the field of sociobiology. Feminist social theory is also considered in this undergraduate text by an associate professor of sociology at the University of Alberta.

Taylor, Ian R., Walton, Paul and Young, Jock. *The New Criminology: For a Social Theory of Deviance*. London: Routledge and Kegan Paul, 1973
The first comprehensive critique of all European and American studies of crime and deviance. It stresses a critical understanding of the larger social theories upon which particular studies of crime and deviance must rest, including an account of criminology's relationship to the social sciences and the new conflict theories.

WOMEN AND CRIME, FEMINIST CRIMINOLOGY

Adelberg, Ellen and Currie, Claudia. *Too Few to Count: Canadian Women in Conflict with the Law*. Vancouver: Press Gang, 1987
The only Canadian book on this topic intended for a general audience has some valuable data and includes areas for further research. Except for an article by Karlene Faith on the portrayal of women prisoners in film and television, however, the analytical component is limited.

Adler, Freda. *The Incidence of Female Criminality in the Contemporary World*. New York: New York University Press, 1981
Notorious among feminists because of the claims that there is a rising wave of female crime and that this is due to the women's movement, Adler's book is based on international quantitative studies, but many other scholars have disputed her use of statistics.

Adler, Freda and Simon, Rita James. *The Criminology of Deviant Women*. Boston, MA: Houghton Mifflin, 1979
A collection of reprinted articles and excerpts from books on the topic of women offenders and the crimes they typically commit. Very descriptive, and does not discuss causes or treatment.

Box, Stephen. *Power, Crime and Mystification*. London, New York: Tavistock, 1983
One chapter on rape and another chapter on 'Powerlessness and Female Crime' are relevant for women. Gender is generally included in its analytical framework, and there is a useful review of the literature. Box, however, tends to portray women as victims.

Bowker, Lee H., ed. *Women and Crime in America*. New York: Macmillan, 1981
A reader reprints many significant articles which appeared in specialized journals. Each section has a preface summarizing the debates in the area.

Carlen, Pat, ed. *Criminal Women: Autobiographical Accounts*. Cambridge: Polity Press; New York: Basil Blackwell, 1985
A collection of first-person stories by women offenders, which does

much to shatter myths about women criminals and the criminal justice system.

Carlen, Pat and Worrall, Anne, eds. *Gender, Crime and Justice.* Milton Keynes: England; Philadelphia: Open University Press, 1987
This reader emphasizes the interaction between class and race on the one hand and gender on the other. It provides much detailed information on the treatment of women offenders and crime victims in the British courts. The discussions of rape and prostitution tend to portray women only in their role as powerless victims, a problem compounded in Carlen's introduction.

Chesney-Lind, Meda. 'Women and Crime: The Female Offender.' *Signs: Journal of Women in Culture and Society* 12 (1, 1986): 79–96
A very useful review-essay analyzing many of the works listed here, and giving an account of the development of feminist work within criminology.

Dobash, Russell P., Dobash, R. Emerson and Gutteridge, Sue. *The Imprisonment of Women.* Oxford, U.K., New York: Basil Blackwell, 1986
The key British study of the origins and development of women's prisons. Much of their analysis is applicable to other English-speaking countries such as Canada.

Freedman, Estelle B. *Their Sisters' Keepers: Women's Prison Reform in America, 1830–1930.* Ann Arbor: University of Michigan Press, 1981
Emphasizes the ambiguous historical role of women philanthropists and social workers in the 'care' and control of women offenders.

Heidensohn, Frances. *Women and Crime.* London: Macmillan Education, 1985
Using a social control perspective, this book shows how female offenders are seen through cultural prejudices, such as women's sexual nature. Contains a useful section outlining the feminist critique of traditional criminology.

Leonard, Eileen B. *Women, Crime and Society: A Critique of Theoretical Criminology.* New York: Longman, 1982
A review both of traditional theories of women's crime and of feminist perspectives. Useful to criminology students wanting a critical approach, but like most of the books listed here, it remains very much within the framework of criminology and only questions the gender bias of theories which might well be criticized on more general grounds.

Mann, Coramae Richey. *Female Crime and Delinquency.* University, AL: University of Alabama Press, 1984
Covers both the historical origins of current ideas about women offenders, and current debates in the literature. A narrowly American

focus presents United States case law as though it constituted sociological evidence. Gender bias is criticized within a traditional framework.

Messerschmidt, James W. *Capitalism, Patriarchy and Crime: Toward a Socialist Feminist Criminology.* Totowa, NJ: Rowman and Littlefield, 1986
Pitched at a rather high level of abstraction, this book does offer some useful insights, not present in most feminist works, on the relationship between class and gender.

Morris, Allison. *Women, Crime and Criminal Justice.* Oxford, UK; New York: Basil Blackwell, 1987
A review of most of the major studies (primarily but not exclusively British) of women in the criminal justice system. Very extensive bibliography.

Morris, Allison and Gelsthorpe, Loraine, eds. Women and Crime: Papers Presented to the Cropwood Round-Table Conference, December 1980. Cambridge: University of Cambridge, Institute of Criminology, 1981. (Cropwood Conference series; no.13)
Somewhat outdated conference proceedings give a good sense of which areas were or were not being researched by many of the best-known women in the field.

Naffine, Ngaire. *Female Crime: The Construction of Women in Criminology.* Sydney: Allen and Unwin, 1987
One chapter is devoted to each of the main frameworks used in the sociology of deviance (such as strain theory or labelling theory) examining the applicability of each framework to women and its possible gender bias. While the criticisms are insightful, Naffine's notion of a 'feminist criminology' suffers from internal contradictions.

Resources for Feminist Research. Special issue: Women and the Criminal Justice System 13 (4, December–January, 1985–86)
Containing a large number of very short articles, this is useful as a source of references, to gain a quick overview of feminist research in the field in the Canadian context. Many of the articles are policy oriented and take positions on current controversies.

Smart, Carol. *Women, Crime and Criminology: A Feminist Critique.* London; Boston: Routledge and Kegan Paul, 1976
The first major work to criticize criminology from a feminist perspective, Smart's book has stood the test of time in many ways. Its well-integrated, interdisciplinary approach contrasts favourably with that of authors who remain caught up in either legal or sociological frameworks.

Weisberg, D. Kelly. *Women and the Law: A Social Historical Perspective.* Cambridge, Mass: Schenkman, 1982. 2 vols (Volume one of this two-volume study is subtitled: Women and the Criminal Law)

A collection of articles, almost all historical, on women's crime and the social control of women through the criminal law, by leading scholars in history and criminology.

Weisheit, Ralph A. and Mahan, Sue. *Women, Crime and Criminal Justice.* Cincinnati, OH: Anderson, 1988

A review of the literature (primarily in sociology) on criminality also contains a description of the treatment of women in the American justice system. A useful section on women as agents of social control is included. The book advocates a greater integration of women into slightly altered current structures.

FEMINIST JURISPRUDENCE AND LEGAL THEORY

Atkins, Susan and Hoggett, Brenda M. *Women and the Law.* Oxford: Basil Blackwell, 1984

A general survey of gender discrimination in British law and in court practices. Oriented toward law reform, it is divided into three sections: work, the home and the state.

Canadian Journal of Women and the Law. Ottawa: National Association of Women and the Law, 1985– (Suite 400, 1 Nicholas St., Ottawa, Ontario, K1N 7B7)

This journal is a key resource for Canadian scholars in both law and feminist theory. Volume 2, 1987 was a special issue on reproductive technology.

Edwards, Susan S.M. *Female Sexuality and the Law: A Study of Constructs of Female Sexuality.* Oxford: Martin Robertson, 1981

A study of the social control of women through the court system, this book focuses mainly on rape.

Edwards, Susan S.M., ed. *Gender, Sex and the Law.* London: Dover, NH: Croom Helm, 1985

A collection of articles on a wide variety of topics about sexuality.

Feminist Discourse, Moral Values and the Law: A Conversation.' *Buffalo Law Review* 34 (1, 1985): 11–87

A discussion of feminist analyses of law between Ellen Dubois, Mary Dunlap, Carol Gilligan, Catherine MacKinnon and Carie Menkel-Meadow.

Freedman, Lisa. *Women and the Law in Canada: A Bibliography 1975–1982.* Toronto: Osgoode Women's Caucus, 1983. (Available at the University of Toronto, Faculty of Law Library)

Despite its limited accessibility, this is still a useful source, though many of the items listed in it are, in turn, not widely available.

Gelsthorpe, Loraine. 'Towards a Skeptical Look at Sexism.' *International Journal of the Sociology of Law* 14 (2, May, 1986): 125–52

A critical look at the uses and abuses of the concept of 'sexism' in the feminist criminological literature.

International Journal of the Sociology of Law 14 (3/4, 1986) Special issue: Feminist Perspectives on Law

A double issue presents a series of papers from the European Critical Legal Studies Conference held in London in April 1986. The papers provide 'feminist critiques of existing formulations and interpretations of law.'

MacKinnon, Catharine A. *Feminism Unmodified: Discourses on Life and Law*. Cambridge, MA: Harvard University Press, 1987

A very influential collection of speeches by a leading American radical feminist, who argues that women's oppression is rooted in the objectification of women in sexuality, and that law is essentially concerned with maintaining this victimization of women. Pornography and violence against women are the main two substantial topics covered.

O'Donovan, Katherine. *Sexual Divisions in Law*. London: Weidenfeld and Nicholson, 1985

Women's oppression is organized primarily through the division between the public (regulated) sphere and the private (unregulated) sphere. An influential text which suffers from some conceptual problems noted by Fran Olsen (see next entry).

Olsen, Frances E. 'The Family and the Market: A Study of Ideology and Legal Reform.' *Harvard Law Review* 96 (7, May 1983): 1497–1578

An extremely important contribution to political theory that questions many assumptions about the private/public split used by feminist (and non-feminist) legal scholars. Published not as political theory but rather in a journal read almost exclusively by legal scholars, it has not been as influential as it might have been.

Rifkin, Janet. 'Toward a Theory of Law and Patriarchy.' *Harvard Women's Law Review* 3 (1, Spring,1980): 83–95

A brief article stating that the law is a 'symbol' of patriarchy. It is said to be the most often quoted piece in feminist legal circles, despite the vagueness of its central terms.

Sheehy, Elizabeth A. *Personal Autonomy and the Criminal Law: Emerging Issues for Women*. Ottawa: Canadian Advisory Council on the Status of Women, 1987. (Background paper). (PO Box 1541, Station B, Ottawa, Ontario K1P 5R5)

Suggestions for reforming criminal law in a feminist direction are made in this paper, focusing particularly on wife assault, sexual assault and abortion.

Smart, Carol. 'Feminism and Law: Some Problems of Analysis and Strategy.' *International Journal of the Sociology of Law* 14 (2, May, 1986): 109–23
A useful recent overview, this article questions the liberal feminist strategy of using existing legal structures to demand more 'rights' from the state. Recent issues of this journal have carried many articles written from a feminist perspective.

Tong, Rosemarie. *Women, Sex and the Law.* Totowa, NJ: Rowman and Allanheld, 1984
Containing chapters on prostitution, sexual harassment, pornography and wife abuse, this book denounces the law as part of the patriarchal system, but at the same time claims that women can use the law to their advantage.

SEXUAL AND REPRODUCTIVE POLITICS

Bell, Laurie, ed. *Good Girls/Bad Girls: Sex Trade Workers and Feminists Face to Face.* Toronto: Women's Press, 1987
Proceedings of a conference held in Toronto with participation from grassroots feminists, sex trade workers and academic feminists. Although focused mainly on prostitution, there are some materials on pornography.

Burstyn, Varda, ed. *Women Against Censorship.* Vancouver: Douglas and McIntyre, 1985
A collection of articles from feminist activists, lawyers, artists and journalists all opposing censorship of pornography and suggesting some alternative ways to minimize male violence and to empower women.

Corea, Gena. *The Mother Machine: Reproductive Technologies From Artificial Insemination to Artificial Wombs.* New York: Harper and Row, 1985
The use of new reproductive technologies to further disempower women is analyzed and denounced.

Delacoste, Frederique and Alexander, Priscilla, eds. *Sex Work: Writings by Women in the Sex Industry.* Pittsburgh, PA: Cleis Press, 1987
A collection of autobiographies and semi-fictional accounts by women sex workers, together with an important selection of documents from prostitutes' organizations in various countries.

Feminist Review, ed. *Sexuality: A Reader.* London: Virago, 1987
Leading American and English feminist thinkers are represented in an anthology of writings from the 'pro-sex' camp of the feminist sexuality debates, including reprints of influential articles. Issues covered include

sexual violence, feminist sexual politics, psychoanalysis and pornography.

Gavigan, Shelley. 'On 'Bringing On the Menses': The Criminal Liability of Women and the Therapeutic Exception in Canadian Abortion Law' *Canadian Journal of Women and the Law* 1 (1986): 279–312
An historical study of the criminalization of abortion in Canada, and its partial legalization in 1969; published prior to the Supreme Court's striking down of the abortion law in January, 1988. Gavigan published a similar article, but addressed to a feminist-activist audience, rather than a legal audience, in *Feminism and Political Economy*, edited by Meg Luxton and Heather Jon Maroney. Toronto: Methuen, 1987.

Lowman, John, et al, eds. *Regulating Sex: An Anthology of Commentaries on the Findings and Recommendations of the Badgley and Fraser Reports*. Burnaby, B.C.: Simon Fraser University, School of Criminology, 1986. (Simon Fraser University, Burnaby, B.C. V5A 1S6)
Contains several critiques of the regulations proposed by the royal commissions on child sexual abuse (Badgley) and pornography and prostitution (Fraser).

Petchesky, Rosalind P. *Abortion and Woman's Choice: The State, Sexuality and Reproductive Freedom*. Boston, Mass: Northeastern University Press, ©1984
This massive and thorough study is acknowledged as the key feminist text on both the regulation of abortion and feminist perspectives on reproductive politics. It emphasizes class and race factors in their interaction with gender.

Stanworth, Michelle, ed. *Reproductive Technologies: Gender, Motherhood and Medicine*. Minneapolis: University of Minnesota, 1987.
An important collection of articles (mostly British). Leading thinkers in the field, such as Rosalind Petchesky, Ann Oakley and Carol Smart are represented.

Vance, Carole S., ed. *Pleasure and Danger: Exploring Female Sexuality*. Boston and London: Routledge and Kegan Paul, 1984
Proceedings of the controversial and high profile feminist conference held at Barnard College in 1982.

Walkowitz, Judith R. *Prostitution and Victorian Society: Women, Class and the State*. Cambridge; New York: Cambridge University Press, 1980
A classic study of the regulation of prostitutes in Victorian England, and of the feminist struggle against this regulation.

FEMINIST ANALYSES OF VIOLENCE

Breines, Wini and Gordon, Linda. 'The New Scholarship on Family Violence.' *Signs: Journal of Women in Culture and Society.* 8 (3, Spring, 1983): 490–531
A review of scholarship in all areas of family violence, which highlights feminist research, and provides some interesting comments on feminists' lack of theorizing on the issue of child abuse.

Dobash, R. Emerson and Dobash, Russell. *Violence Against Wives: A Case Against the Patriarchy.* New York: Free Press, 1979
An historical analysis of wife battering, concentrating on how western capitalism and the state lessened the power of women and made them more susceptible to violence.

'Family Secrets: Child Sexual Abuse.' *Feminist Review* 28 (Spring 1988): special issue
A special issue on the occasion of the Cleveland child sexual abuse scandal in Britain, including articles by noted feminist scholars, Mary McIntosh and Linda Gordon.

Gordon, Linda. *Heroes of Their Own Lives: The Politics and History of Family Violence.* New York: Viking, 1988
An historical study of child welfare work in the United States, emphasizing that although mothers were often harassed and stigmatized by agencies, they could also manipulate social workers, and mobilize them against violent husbands. Gordon uses her evidence to question the usefulness of social control theory to understand women's experience.

Guberman, Connie and Wolfe, Margie, eds. *No Safe Place: Violence Against Women and Children.* Toronto: Women's Press, 1985
A collection of articles on issues ranging from rape to pornography.

Loseke, Donileen R. and Cahill, Spencer E. 'The Social Construction of Deviance: Experts on Battered Women.' *Social Problems* 31 (3, February, 1984): 296–310
An analysis of the rise of 'experts' on wife battering. The authors argue that the experts redefine a battered woman's experience of the relationship and battering to 'fit' a feminist explanation of battering.

MacLeod, Linda. *Wife Battering in Canada: The Vicious Circle.* Hull, Que: Canadian Government Publishing Centre, Supply and Services Canada, 1980
Based on data collected from transition houses located across Canada, this book describes and analyses the wife battering phenomenon in this country.

Pagelow, Mildred Daley. *Woman-Battering: Victims and Their Experiences.* Beverly Hills, CA: Sage Publications, 1981. (Sage Library of Social Research; Vol. 129)

The perspective of battered women about the abusive relationship and the response of various social agencies is examined. Pagelow uses social learning theory and Lemert's ideas of primary and secondary deviance to construct an explanation.

Rubesaat, Gisela. 'Sexual Assault Legislation in Canada, an Evaluation: The New Sexual Assault Offences: Emerging Legal Issues, Report No.2.' Ottawa: Department of Justice, 1985

The legal ramifications of recent changes in legislation are discussed primarily for lawyers and law students.

Schechter, Susan. *Women and Male Violence: The Visions and Struggles of the Battered Women.* Boston: South End Press, 1982

Discussion focuses on how feminists 'discovered' violence against women by men and struggled for social change.

Stanley, Marilyn. 'Sexual Assault Legislation in Canada, An Evaluation: The Experience of the Rape Victim with the Criminal Justice System Prior to Bill C-127, Report No.1.' Ottawa: Department of Justice, 1985

This report discusses the experience of the rape victim as affected and shaped by the legal framework of the criminal justice system. Past and present laws on sexual assault are evaluated.

WOMEN, SOCIAL CONTROL AND THE STATE

Andrew, Caroline. 'Women and the Welfare State.' *Canadian Journal of Political Science* 17 (4, December, 1984): 667–83

An understanding of the welfare state is incomplete, even inadequate, without an examination of gender, the role played by women's organizations, women as workers and as clients of the welfare state. The importance of gender in political struggles is also discussed.

Bennett, Fran. 'The State, Welfare and Women's Dependence' In *What Is To Be Done About the Family*? pp. 190–214. Edited by Lynne Segal. Harmondsworth, Middx: Penguin, 1983

An overview of the ways in which the welfare apparatus reinforces patriarchal structures both within the family and between the state and women. Based on the British situation (like most of the literature available on this topic) but applicable to Canada as well.

Burstyn, Varda 'Masculine Dominance and the State.' In *Women, Class, Family and the State*, pp. 45–89 by Varda Burstyn and Dorothy E. Smith. Toronto: Garamond Press, 1985. (Reprinted from the *Socialist Register*, 1983)

A critique of Marxist perspectives on the state from a feminist viewpoint, this article argues that masculine dominance is as integral to state formation as class rule.

Dale, Jennifer and Foster, Peggy. *Feminists and State Welfare*. London: Routledge and Kegan Paul, 1986.
The book begins with an historical overview of the relation of women to the British state, both as recipients of government programs and as active participants in the development of welfare programs, and goes on to critically examine current programs.

McIntosh, Mary. 'The State and the Oppression of Women.' In *Feminism and Materialism: Women and Modes of Production*, pp. 254–89. Edited by Annette Kuhn and Anne Marie Wolpe. London, Boston: Routledge and Kegan Paul, 1978
An early and influential socialist-feminist argument claiming that the state reinforces traditional family forms, and thus contributes to women's oppression.

Ungerson, Clare, ed. *Women and Social Policy: A Reader*. Basingstoke: Macmillan Education, 1985
A comprehensive anthology providing gender analyses of social security, housing, health care and education policies in Britain, as well as a look at women's inferior status in personal services and the voluntary sector.

Ursel, Jane. 'The State and the Maintenance of Patriarchy' In *Family, Economy and State: Essays on the Social Reproduction Process Under Capitalism*, pp. 150–91. Edited by James Dickinson and Bob Russell. Toronto: Garamond Press, 1986
The development of Canadian protective legislation, singling out women and the reform of family law to give mothers more rights, is analyzed here as the replacement of 'familial' patriarchy by 'social' (state) patriarchy.

10

Juvenile Delinquency and Juvenile Justice in Canada

W. Gordon West

Introduction

Over the last two decades, research on juvenile delinquency and juvenile justice in Canada has expanded dramatically, partly in response to vigorous popular discussions about our errant young. Potentially reformable 'youth in conflict' have reemerged on the public stage with the debate over the recent passage and continuing difficulties in implementation of the Canadian *Young Offenders Act*. Drugs, precocious sexuality, racism, and gang violence fill the national press, appear on research agendas, and persistently concern parents (for an historical perspective, see earlier studies, such as Rogers, 1945; Seeley, Sim and Loosley, 1956).

This short review initially raises some issues regarding the relationship between some popular notions based on our collective or individual experiences of delinquent acts and our attempts at legal resolution. For instance, the images of delinquency portrayed in the mass media of film, television, and newspapers overemphasize violence compared with its actual occurrence; in our adult condemnation of youthful pranks we often conveniently forget our own younger participation in such activities. Some of the specific legal issues embodied in legislation are outlined, followed by a discussion of our social scientific knowledge of delinquency. A review of the most important contributions toward an understanding of delinquency in Canada includes comprehending Canadian juvenile justice, the officially sanctified, governmentally organized response to those we deem our errant young.

Popular Culture, Morality and Delinquency

Popular culture consists of the shared meanings manifest in art, artifact, and behaviour, understood and used by people in going about their ordinary everyday business (Hall, et al, 1980). It includes, for instance, notions of what kinds of property are private under what circumstances (for example, when can a rake, a car, or foodstuffs be appropriated from a neighbour?); it includes notions of propriety (for example, regarding eating behaviour and clothing); it includes notions of collective symbols (such as the hometown team, or the national flag). It is distinguished from 'high culture' (for example, fine art, drama, classical music) in that it is composed of understandings widely shared in the population; it is culture as anthropologists have used the term.

Clearly included in popular culture are notions of morality, of the distinction between good and evil. Specifically, within contemporary industrial societies, popular culture includes notions of 'a good home,' 'the well-behaved child,' – and conversely, 'the delinquent.'

Our everyday perceptions continually shape our understanding of juvenile delinquency, not only influencing political definitions of the phenomenon, but also research funding priorities. Errant youth continue to fill our streets (Fleming and Visano, 1983), resorting to the traditional mainstay of petty property crime (West, 1979), instead of working hard at legitimate enterprises, such as selling newspapers they also sell 'speed,' 'crack,' and their very bodies and souls. (Ng, 1982; Visano, 1987). Direct experience of such behaviour is drawn upon in our reading of more abstract reports, whether in the popular press or research journals.

Many of the violations resulting in criminal justice processing of young people include not just crimes by young people (such as theft), but also quite petty acts, considered to be juvenile delinquency only if committed by the young. Truancy, sexual activeness, and smoking tobacco are examples of many acts which have been legal infractions only for the young in this century.

In the nineteenth century, the Industrial Revolution initially increasingly drew children as well as their parents into waged labour. The horrendous factory conditions brought humanitarian efforts, concern for the biological 'stock' of the nation, and adult unionized pressure to preserve jobs for men and eventually resulted in the progressive exclusion of children from the labour force. In general, participation in activities increasingly reserved for their elders finally resulted in many of these activities being defined as delinquent (Musgrove, 1964). By the end of the nineteenth century, the larger Canadian cities were experiencing many of the same problems with street urchins as Europe, exacerbated by the arrival of tens of thousands of

British waifs (Sutherland, 1976). The federal and provincial governments resorted to strategies similar to those used in Europe. Exclusion from employment, requirements regarding compulsory school attendance, prohibition from participation in any 'vices' (such as alcohol consumption, vagrancy, and sexual activity) – all were proscribed for children in an attempt to build a new Jerusalem for the younger generation through legislation such as the *Juvenile Delinquents Act*.

The Legal Frameworks: The 1908 *Juvenile Delinquents Act* and the 1984 *Young Offenders Act*

In addition to the passage of compulsory school attendance legislation (in 1870 in Ontario), other legislation favoured sending young offenders to juvenile reformatories and offered probation (Leon, 1978). Against this background, the 1908 Canadian *Juvenile Delinquents Act* formally established the legal category of juvenile delinquency, and allowed organized systems of probation and juvenile courts. Thus, for most of this century, the Act has defined as a 'delinquent':

> any child who violates any provision of the *Criminal Code* or of any Dominion or provincial statute, or of any by-law or ordinance of any municipality, or who is guilty of sexual immorality or any similar form of vice, or who is liable by reason of any other act to be committed to an industrial school or juvenile reformatory under the provisions of any Dominion or provincial statute.

In English common law, age seven was the minimum age for knowing right from wrong. In Canada, the upper age limit has varied from sixteen to eighteen years, and sometimes by sex, from province to province. Key terms such as 'sexual immorality' or 'any other vice' are nowhere explicitly defined in the *Juvenile Delinquents Act*, 1908. With such undefined, sweeping powers, juvenile court trials were conducted by special judges (usually lacking legal training), in separate courts, in private and with minimal attention to procedural rules. Judges and probation officers had special investigatory powers such as access to hearsay evidence and no necessity to reveal confidential information to defendants. Automatic right to appeal was not present. Dispositions ranged from warning and release to indeterminate sentences, with the guilty remaining under the courts' jurisdiction until age twenty-one, and sentences were quite unlinked to gravity of offence. Instead, sentences were to be tailored to the child's court-defined 'needs.' Definitional vagueness, lack of due process (i.e., traditionally legally ensconced rights to self-defence, exclusion of hearsay evidence, or a trial by peers), inclusion of juvenile status offences (such as truancy), and wide dispositional powers left the treatment of juveniles open to judicial and administrative arbitrariness.

This legally sanctioned arbitrariness in the definition and processing of delinquency must be recognized as fundamental in understanding our response to juvenile misbehaviour. Whereas (at least ideally) the adult-applicable *Criminal Code* attempts to be as explicit as possible regarding offences, the *Juvenile Delinquents Act* was intentionally vague, to allow judges to act in the roles of concerned and caring parents. In practice, this has allowed them to symbolically and ritually play out popular social concerns regarding not only clearly offending youngsters (for example, those who kill or steal), but also those who make us uncomfortable by not fulfilling our often inexplicable, very often unexamined expectations of what a 'good child' is.

Training school placement became the ultimate sanction of the juvenile law. Youngsters who were neglected by parents, and had no community facility able to take them, were sent to training schools ('juvenile reform-atories,' or more realistically, juvenile jails), and legally classified as 'delinquent' (West, 1984). The result was that most of the girls sent to training schools in the last hundred years went 'for their protection' (that is, their supposed sexual precocity), not for any crime committed. Almost a third of the boys sent to training schools were also deemed to be inadequately cared for, because they lived in conditions of poverty, or their parents allowed them to be vagrant (that is, to exercise their own choice regarding freedom of movement in the urban environment – which adults assume as a fundamental right). Native children have also been grossly overrepre-sented in training school populations. Official figures indicate that 'juvenile justice' has been as much concerned with establishing a particular morality as preventing serious crimes, let alone minor ones, or guarding public safety.

The new Canadian *Young Offenders Act* (1984) has formally eliminated all status offences from the federal code (such as truancy and 'sexual immorality') confining delinquency to acts prohibited in the federal *Criminal Code* (such as theft and assault). The juvenile age has been raised from a minimum of seven to twelve years, and the maximum age from sixteen to eighteen across the country. The *Young Offenders Act* encourages screening or diversion procedures by which youngsters avoid formal court and legal processing. It also provides for the addition of some safeguards in the trial stage, such as the right to legal counsel, stricter rules of evidence and proof, press access, and appeals (Leon, 1978, p. 167). Three-year maximum sentences have replaced the former indefinite terms. Administra-tive review of any special treatment is required, as well as voluntary consent to 'treatment.'

Of course, any and all legal revisions are still implemented through our judicial system: the kids still face the arbitrariness of victims reporting or not, police using discretion or not, overworked social workers and probation officers making pre-sentence reports based upon one-hour interviews, harried judges' efforts to clear court dockets while making sensitive, psychological assessments with universally acknowledged inadequate tests, and perhaps worst of all for children, the traumatic possibility of removal from their homes and loved ones for residential placement – even if their home environments are indisputably horrendous. The 'system' is clearly disjointed, a 'non-system' in many respects.

With the *Young Offenders Act* itself, many problems remain: the age of legal accountability is fiercely disputed in the media (especially by the Toronto police, who want a much younger age limit – in part, to give them more control over management of disreputable, difficult populations, for example in the seven to eleven age group), the exercise of police discretion, and the requirement that juveniles give voluntary consent for 'treatment' (Leschied, 1991). Furthermore, the police have been hampered by restrictions on public disclosure of names. They feel that the three-year maximum penalty is inadequate for capital offences, and they are inconvenienced by Ontario's maintenance of a two-tier system which still effectively segregates twelve to fifteen-year-olds from those aged sixteen and seventeen. And where the framers of the *Young Offenders Act* sought more use of community alternatives and less use of removal from home, early research reports indicate greater use of coercive sanctions. Some revisions of the legislation can be expected in the next few years. But enough discussion of some of the legal issues which have vexed us for the last century. What have we learned of the real misbehaviour of children?

Social Knowledge and Theories of Delinquency

In the years before 1960, research reports often consisted of anecdotes and judges' reminiscences mixed with reports from official government commissions (which were largely composed of such judges), with little objective evidence other than that questionably proffered by police or judicial reports (but see Rogers, 1945, for a lively antidote). Empirical social scientific criminological research was very weakly supported in Canada until the founding of four or five academic centres in the 1960s. Ever since, these centres have relied heavily upon government funding, and therefore address politically defined issues. The enormous expansion of social science faculties in the universities during the 1960s and 1970s brought to research on delinquency in Canada many younger researchers who do not subscribe to traditional and conservative assumptions about controlling the young.

They have used their own experiences and understanding of popular culture in defining what it means to be a worthwhile young person in this society – and, conversely, what type of youthful behaviour is not permissable. The result has been a veritable multiplication of research materials on errant Canadian youth: where we had perhaps two books on Canadian delinquency in 1975, we now have some two dozen.

I) METHODS OF RESEARCH

The methods employed in such research have varied in popularity over time. Before 1960, almost all research reports relied upon official statistics from courts or police regarding those youngsters processed, which obviously excluded the hordes of the unapprehended. We now know that very few self-reported delinquencies (admitted by youngsters themselves in anonymous questionnaires) actually result in official processing. In addition, researchers relied upon formal academic analyses of legal issues, often quite unrelated to actual administrative processing, and upon informal wisdom passed on by the resident sages of juvenile justice: the judges, not the kids.

By the 1950s and 1960s the analyses of official statistics became more mathematically sophisticated, but perhaps has not led to a deeper understanding of fundamental issues. Computer analyses of self-report survey questionnaire data revealed enormous amounts of unofficially recorded delinquency, especially by middle and upper class youths, and also by females. These self-report studies were complemented by some participant observation studies, in which researchers attempted to understand delinquent youths by actually living with and among them. Even today, such participant observation research causes moral consternation and fears of their older and more conservative colleagues (for instance, that a researcher could be accused of being an accomplice to a crime before, during, or after the fact by not fully complying with the citizen's duty to report law-breaking). Furthermore, all the research sophistication of controlled experimental design has been imported into criminology wherever possible, such as in the evaluation of social experiments (Morton and West, et al, 1980). But no research methods are infallible, and each one needs a major effort to interpret and comprehend the results produced.

In the 1980s, as in previous decades, young people continue to appear disproportionately, not only in popular images of deviance, but also in official police statistics, and in self-report surveys of misbehaviour. Half of serious property crime incidents (which constitute two-thirds of the total crimes recorded) are committed by those under age eighteen. Although most serious violent crimes are by those within the first decade of legal adulthood, the young nonetheless remain threatening. Self-report surveys indicate that the young are probably more likely to commit an offence than those over age twenty. They also show that almost all young males (and only slightly fewer young females) violate the law every year at least once, if not a number of times (Bennett and West, 1983; West, 1984).

Such data and events are not infrequently taken up by various groups and bureaucracies to generate 'moral panics' among the general public (Cohen, 1980; Hall, et al, 1978). 'Moral panics' are those regularly recurring occasions generated in liberal-democracies when popularly irritating concerns achieve front-page status as political issues regarding the definition of the boundary line between right and wrong. Clearly, abortion, corporate environmental pollution, and child abuse have become such issues, but errant juvenile misbehaviour continues as a mainstay: 'gangs' (too many rough-looking kids at the bus stop); 'drugs' (instead of just getting drunk as we did, they are using this stuff from Colombia); 'sex' ('you can no longer tell the girls from the boys, and they're all doing it, and what about AIDS?'); random vandalism ('parking my car on the street gets the hundred dollar aerial broken off!'). Such moral issues use juvenile misbehaviour to justify campaigns of legal repression (often not so subtly directed against ethnic minority groups, the lower classes, women, and others).

Yet we must also recognize that some children really have been more obstreperous, revolting, or downright nasty and threatening to others' property and lives. How can we understand and explain their undesirable behaviour?

II) THEORETICAL EXPLANATIONS

Empirical criminological research offers a number of theories for understanding these behaviours, some more intriguing and scientifically supported than others (Silverman and Teevan, 1986; West, 1979).

Anomie theory, for instance, basically postulates that the disadvantaged (in a system proclaiming common goals such as economic success, but with differential access to adequate means) are more likely to become delinquent (Leyton, 1979). Unfortunately, the self-report survey statistics suggest that middle class youngsters are almost as likely to deviate as working class ones (Gomme, 1982).

Control theory postulates that 'bonds' to social order restrain delinquency. Bonds can be emotional attachments to significant others, conventional commitments (e.g., to success in school), belief in the legitimacy of the social order, and time-committing involvement (e.g., in sports and recreation) (Frechette and Leblanc, 1987). Control theory succeeds in identifying those youngsters most likely to deviate, but does not well explain why there are more male delinquents, nor how those bonds are more loosely constructed for adolescents (Langelier-Biron, 1983; Reitsma-Street, 1985; West, 1984).

Interactionist ('labelling') theory offers more 'humanistic' approaches (largely through participant observation studies) in arguing that 'delinquency' must be seen as a social construction, emerging from the interaction between youngsters and social controllers (parents, teachers, police). Labelling theory emphasizes the importance of youth subcultures which define the world views of our young (Dorn and South, 1983).

Some research tries to combine these theories (Greenberg, 1977), for instance in investigating the finding that school failure affects delinquency (Gomme, 1982). Critical (neo-Marxist/feminist) theories argue that delinquency results from not only many of the above factors, but that it is orchestrated by the needs of production and reproduction through the state: our orchestration of controlling youthful delinquency is not only morally, but politically, economically – and familially organized. (Morton, 1988; Schwendinger and Schwendinger, 1985; West, 1984).

None of these theories are perfect, either in terms of the available facts, or in terms of offering practical solutions to delinquency problems. Young people have been deemed to be of a fundamentally different nature than adults (such as, immature, dependent, ignorant, frivolous, happy, and unable to work, socialize independently, or act maturely and responsibly). In Canada, ironically it has become illegal for a person under eighteen to act as an adult!

Self-report studies have conclusively indicated that there is far too much delinquency for the legal apparatus to deal with, as almost every adolescent commits some delinquencies (West 1984). Reformist policies, such as diversion from formal judicial processing, must be seen as an attempt by the state to 'save' the liberal notion that each violation not only must, but also can, be punished.

Conclusion

In the past decade, some of the worst inequities in juvenile justice have been formally addressed: abuses against people because of sex, race, class, or age. Increased police discretion (regarding the laying of charges), court diversion and decarceration from training schools to community-based group homes has led to administrative attempts to improve the system (Langelier-Biron, 1983). We can claim to have made some humane improvements in the system.

Yet historical evidence makes it difficult to deny that the *Juvenile Delinquents Act* – and the *Young Offenders Act* – have exemplified through legislation the domination by some groups over others. Upper and middle-

class old white Protestant and Catholic males dominated their opposites –
lower and working class, non-religious or other religious, female – and
especially young people. Many argue that this legalistically enshrined
domination continues today, bluntly evident in any statistical analysis of
delinquency, which reveals the Canadian state's attempts to manage our
young through coercive legislation.

None of our theories are entirely adequate, nor our methods of trying to
understand what we elders deem to be the misbehaviour of our young people. Perhaps humbly and humanely recognizing our ignorance is the most
important message which a century of delinquency research should give us.

Reading List

Ariés, Philippe. *Centuries of Childhood.* New York: Knopf, 1962
    Provocative historical review of (especially French) pre-industrial
    childhood.
Bala, Nicholas C. and Clarke, Kenneth L. *The Child and the Law.* Toronto:
    McGraw-Hill Ryerson, 1981
    A good legal overview of the *Juvenile Delinquents Act.*
Barrett, Michele, and McIntosh, Mary. *The Anti-Social Family.* London:
    Verso/New Left, 1982
    Major feminist argument that the contemporary heterosexist patriarchal
    family form is contrary to the social good.
Bennett, Eldon J., and West, W. Gordon. 'Criminal and Deviant Acts.' In
    Introduction to Sociology: An Alternate Approach, pp. 456–82. Edited
    by John Paul Grayson. Toronto: Gage, 1983
    Review of crime and delinquency materials and theories in Canada.
Brake, Mike. *Comparative Youth Cultures.* London: Routledge and Kegan
    Paul, 1985
    A good review of delinquency and subcultural theories, with compara-
    tive data from the United States, Britain and Canada.
Brickey, Stephen, and Comack, Elizabeth, eds. *The Social Basis of Law:
    Critical Readings in the Sociology of Law.* Toronto: Garamond, 1986
    A good critical collection, with a number of papers on delinquency and
    juvenile justice.
Central Toronto Youth Services. *Youth Opportunity Action: Towards
    Ontario's New System for Young Offenders.* Toronto: Central Toronto
    Youth Services (27 Carlton St, M5B 1L2), 1982
    Practical assessment of issues, especially regarding urban street youth.
Cohen, Stan. *Folk Devils and Moral Panics: The Creation of the Mods and
    Rockers.* 2nd ed. New York: St. Martins Press, 1980
    The original reconceptualization of the topical use of juvenile mis-
    behaviour as a political issue.

Chunn, Dorothy. 'From Punishment to Doing Good: The Origins and Impact of Family Courts in Ontario, 1888–1942.' Unpublished PHD thesis, University of Toronto, 1986
Socio-legal analysis of how family court legislation and procedures administer family relations.
Cusson, Maurice. *Why Delinquency?* Toronto: University of Toronto Press, 1983
Well translated and intriguing theoretical essay from Montreal on delinquency as adolescent rebellion.
Donzelot, Jacques. *The Policing of Families*. New York: Pantheon Books, 1979
A controversial structuralist analysis of mainly French materials, arguing that women united with the state and professionals to control errant men (and children).
Dorn, Nick, and South, Nigel. *Males and Markets: A Critical Review of Youth Culture Theory*. London: Middlesex Polytechnic, 1983. (Research paper no.l); reprinted (in Spanish) in *Modernizacion: Un Desafio para la Educacion*. Edited by Marianella Cerri, Luis-Eduardo Gonzalez, and W. Gordon West. Santiago: CIDE/PIIE/UNESCO, 1988
Perhaps the best recent overview of youth subculture theory, with an excellent feminist critique of the traditional male bias in studies of adolescent subcultures.
Ellis, Desmond. *The Wrong Stuff: An Introduction to the Sociological Study of Deviance*. Don Mills, Ont: Collier Macmillan Canada, 1987
A lively general introduction, drawing on some delinquency material.
Fitz, John, 'The Child as Legal Subject.' In *Education and the State*, Vol. 2, pp. 285–302. Edited by Roger Dale, et al. Milton Keynes: Open University Press, 1981. 2 vols
A brilliant analysis of the legal construction of childhood and delinquency, using Foucault.
Fitz, John, 'Welfare, the Family and the Child'; Shaw, Jenny, 'Family, State, and Compulsory Education,' Units 12–13, Block 5, Course E-353. In *Education, Welfare and the Moral Order*. Milton Keynes: Open University Press. 1981
Thorough analyses of how schooling has been used to monitor errant families and children.
Fleming, Thomas, ed. *The New Criminologies in Canada: State, Crime and Control*. Toronto: Oxford University Press, 1985
A somewhat uneven collection of critical papers (some on delinquency).
Fleming, Thomas and Visano, Livy, eds. *Deviant Designations*. Toronto: Butterworths, 1983
A good, although sometimes uneven, collection of especially ethnographic research, many dealing with delinquency in Canada.

Frechette, Marcel and LeBlanc, Marc. *Delinquances et Delinquants.* Chicoutimi, Quebec: Gaetan Morin, 1987
A thorough and theoretically brilliant attempt (grounded in extensive longitudinal data) to integrate psychological and social control theories. The presentation of decades of extensive and painstakingly careful work on delinquency by the 'Montreal School' demands an English-language translation-which is due to appear.

Gaffield, Chad and West, W. Gordon. 'Children's Rights in the Canadian Context.' In *Children's Rights: Legal and Educational Issues*, pp. 1–14. Edited by Heather Berkeley, Chad Gaffield, and W. Gordon West. Toronto: OISE Press, 1978
A somewhat dated (1970s) cheer for children's rights, but some good articles retain their poignancy.

Gillis, John R. *Youth and History: Tradition and Change in European Age Relations, 1770–Present.* New York: Academic Press, 1974
Another excellent long-term historical overview of European youth, with a focus on England.

Gomme, Ian M. 'A Multivariate Analysis of Juvenile Delinquency Among Students.' Ontario Public and Separate School thesis, EDD, University of Toronto, 1982
A very good secondary analysis of a data set on schooling and delinquency, with an excellent critical review.

Gomme, Ian M., Morton, Mary E., and West, W. Gordon. 'Rates, Types and Patterns of Male and Female Delinquency in an Ontario County.' *Canadian Journal of Criminology* 26 (3, July 1984): 313–23
A succinct summary of some of the above.

Greenberg, David F. 'Delinquency and the Age Structure of Society.' *Contemporary Crises* 1 (1977): 189–223
One of the best theoretical integrations of anomie, control, interactionist and neo-Marxist theory – all in 30 pages!

Hackler, James C. *The Prevention of Youthful Crime: The Great Stumble Forward.* Toronto: Methuen, 1978
An occasionally rambling, but wisely sceptical overview of attempts at delinquency prevention and therapy by an expert with decades of dedicated experience.

Hall, Stuart, et al. *Policing the Crisis: Mugging, the State and Law and Order.* London: Macmillan, 1978
A somewhat disjointed, but landmark application of state theory and ideology towards understanding delinquency and moral panics.

Hall, Stuart, Hobson, Dorothy, Lowe, Andrew, and Willis, Paul, eds. *Culture, Media, Language: Working Papers in Cultural Studies, 1972–79.* London: Hutchinson, 1980

A collection of classic pieces, outlining the work of the 'Birmingham School' at the Centre for Contemporary Cultural Studies, Birmingham England.

Houston, Susan. 'The Victorian Origins of Juvenile Delinquency.' *History of Education Quarterly* 12 (1972): 254–80
Excellently detailed historical analysis of Canadian delinquency.

Ishwaran, K., ed. *Childhood and Adolescence in Canada*. Toronto: Mc-Graw-Hill Ryerson. 1979
An increasingly dated, quite uneven collection of research materials; needs to be superseded with new, more critical work, but the best available collection on Canadian adolescence.

Langelier-Biron, Louise. 'The Delinquent Young Girl: a Non-Entity?' In *Current Issues in Juvenile Justice*, pp. 61–72. Edited by Raymond Corrado, Marc LeBlanc, and Jean Trepanier. Toronto: Butterworths, 1983
A presentation of more of the landmark research from Montreal, this specifically in regard to young women.

LaPrairie, Carol Pitcher. 'Native Juveniles in Court: Some Preliminary Observations.' In *Deviant Designations*, pp. 337–50. Edited by Thomas Fleming and L.A. Visano. Toronto: Butterworths, 1983
A focus on the systematic discrimination in juvenile justice against native Canadians, about which much more research needs to be done.

Leon, Jeffrey. 'Children's Rights Revisited.' In *Children's Rights: Legal and Educational Issues*. Edited by Heather Berkeley, Chad Gaffield and W. Gordon West. Toronto: OISE Press, 1978.
An historical review of the *Juvenile Delinquents Act* and an update regarding the *Young Offenders Act* raising questions about children's competency.

Leschied, Alan, and Jaffe, Peter, eds. *The Young Offenders' Act Revolution: Changing the Face of Canadian Juvenile Justice*. Toronto: University of Toronto Press, 1991 (April)
Promising to be the definitive collection on difficulties in implementing the *Young Offenders Act*.

Leyton, Elliott. *The Myth of Delinquency: An Anatomy of Juvenile Nihilism*. Toronto: McClelland and Stewart, 1979
An engaging ethnographic presentation of some eight young delinquents, although the theoretical analysis is weak.

Linden, Rick, and Caputo, Tullio, eds. *Criminology: A Canadian Perspective*. Toronto: Holt Rinehart and Winston of Canada, 1987
A very thorough and well-integrated overview of criminological research (with much reference to delinquency) from a neo-positivist orientation.

Maclean, Brian D., ed. *The Political Economy of Crime: Readings for a Critical Criminology.* Scarborough, Ont: Prentice-Hall Canada, 1986
A first-rate collection from a Marxist perspective, again with some excellent readings on delinquency.

Matthews, Fred. *Familiar Strangers: A Study of Adolescent Prostitution.* Toronto: Central Toronto Youth Services (27 Carlton St., M5B 1L2), 1987
Revised report from an Ontario Institute for Studies in Education PHD thesis, describing the juvenile prostitution scene on Yonge Street.

Miles, Ian, and Irvine, John. 'The Critique of Official Statistics.' In *Demystifying Social Statistics,* pp. 113–29. Edited by John Irvine, Ian Miles and Jeff Evans. London: Pluto, 1979
A ground-breaking radical critique, which argues that statistics can never be assumed to be neutral, but are almost always generated with some practical interest embodied in their collection.

Morton, Mary E. 'Dividing the Wealth, Sharing the Poverty: The (Re)Formation of 'Family' in Law in Ontario.' *Canadian Review of Sociology and Anthropology* 25 (2, May 1988): 254–75
An excellent feminist-informed analysis of the effects of family law reform.

Morton, Mary E., West, W. Gordon, et al. 'A Research Evaluation of the Frontenac Juvenile Diversion Project.' Ottawa: Solicitor General Canada, 1980
An evaluation of the 'flagship' Canadian Diversion Project which was successfully implemented, but not noticeably effective in regard to delinquency prevention.

Musgrove, Frank. *Youth and the Social Order.* London: Routledge & Kegan Paul, 1964
A classic on the topic: mostly English, and now somewhat dated.

Ng, Yvonne. 'Ideology, Media and Moral Panics: An Analysis of the Jaques Murder.' Unpublished MA thesis, Centre of Criminology, University of Toronto, 1982
A brilliant analysis of state agency ideological manipulation of one of the major recent 'moral crises' in Canada: the 1977 Yonge Street 'shoeshine boy' murder. Drugs, sex, delinquency, murder and media analyzed cogently.

Platt, Anthony N. *The Child-Savers: The Invention of Delinquency.* 2nd ed. enl. Chicago, IL: University of Chicago Press, 1977
Ground-breaking left critique, arguing that juvenile justice legislation has oppressed the young, to reinforce class interests.

Prentice, Alison L. *The School Promoters: Education and Social Class in Mid-Nineteenth-Century Upper Canada.* Toronto: McClelland and Stewart, 1977

Excellent, well-documented historical research on the social control role of schooling.

Ratner, Robert S. 'Inside the Liberal Boot : The Criminological Enterprise in Canada.' In *The New Criminologies in Canada: Crime, State and Control*, pp. 13–26. Edited by Thomas Fleming. Toronto: Oxford University Press, 1985
An overview of Canadian criminal justice policy as it has been affected by ideologies.

Ratner, Robert S. and McMullan, John L., eds. *State Control: Criminal Justice Politics in Canada*. Vancouver: University of British Colombia Press, 1987
A heavy, theoretical collection mainly from a critical viewpoint.

Reitsma-Street, Marge. 'Delinquency and Conformity in Adolescent Sisters.' Unpublished DWS thesis, University of Toronto, 1988
Intriguing feminist re-analysis of secondary data from the massive data bank collected by Dan Offord in the McMaster University study comparing officially delinquent with officially non-delinquent siblings. Demonstrates how officially labelled female delinquents differ from their siblings by challenging sex-role stereotypes.

Reitsma-Street, Marge. 'More Control Than Care.' University of Toronto, School of Social Work, 1985
Forceful critique of the sexism of juvenile justice by a former social worker.

Rogers, Kenneth H. *Street Gangs in Toronto: A Study of the Forgotten Boy*. Toronto: Ryerson, 1945
Out of print, but precious in documentarily reminding us that people were worrying about incipient gangs and loose girls on our streets almost half a century ago, much as we still are.

Schur, Edwin M. *Radical Nonintervention: Rethinking the Delinquency Problem*. Englewood Cliffs, NJ: Prentice-Hall, 1973
The classic labelling theory critique of intervention into juvenile lives: leave the kids alone.

Schwendinger, Herman and Schwendinger, Julia. *Adolescent Subcultures and Delinquency*. New York: Praeger, 1985
One of the best recent 'blockbuster' theoretically-synthesizing delinquency books, some two decades in the making, but hardly recognized in 'mainstream' U.S. delinquency research because of its critical viewpoint.

Seeley, John R., Sim, Alexander, and Loosley, Elizabeth W. *Crestwood Heights: A North American Suburb*. Toronto: University of Toronto Press, 1956
Perhaps the classic on problems of growing up in a middle class suburb (Forest Hill, Toronto) in postwar Canada.

Silverman, Robert A. and Teevan, James J.,eds. *Crime in Canadian Society.* Toronto: Butterworths, 1975; 2nd ed., 1980; 3rd ed., 1986
Good general collections on Canadian crime and delinquency.

Sutherland, Neil. *Children in English-Canadian Society: Framing the Twentieth Century Consensus.* Toronto and Buffalo: University of Toronto Press, 1976
An exceptionally well-documented historical work, dealing with child care, schooling, public health and delinquency.

Visano, Livy. *This Idle Trade: The Occupational Patterns of Male Prostitution.* Concord, Ont: Vita-Sana, 1987
A very graphic depiction and analysis of adolescent male prostitution on Yonge Street, Toronto.

Walker, Horacio. 'Marginal Youth in Chile: Deviance Within a Context of Social Reproduction.' *Canadian Criminology Forum* 6 (1, Fall 1983): 19–33
Good description of how traditional cultural patterns combine with imperialism to produce ordinary delinquency in a Third World context.

West, W. Gordon. 'La Marginalidad, La Inmoralidad, La Desviacion, y La Juventud del Tercer Mundo,' In *Modernizacion: Un Desafio Para La Educacion.* Edited by Marianella Cerri, Luis-Eduardo Gonzalez, and W. Gordon West. Santiago, Chile: CIDE/PIIE/UNESCO, 1988
An analysis of Third World exploitation of children and the development of delinquency as a consequence of imperialism.

West, W. Gordon. 'Serious Thieves: Lower Class Adolescent Males in Short-Term Occupation.' In *Crime and Delinquency in Canada,* pp. 247–68. Edited by Edmund W. Vaz and Abdul Q. Lodhi. Scarborough, Ont: Prentice-Hall of Canada, 1979
An early ethnographic study of the most ordinary delinquency; the overall collection is very good.

West, W. Gordon. *Young Offenders and the State: A Canadian Perspective on Delinquency.* Toronto: Butterworths, 1984
Reviews and synthesizes Canadian delinquency and juvenile justice research, from a critical, neo-Marxist-feminist perspective. Shortly will need a revision or successor.

Notes on Contributors

John M. Beattie (PHD Cantab., FRSC) is Director of the Centre of Criminology and University Professor of History and Criminology. His book, *Crime and the Courts in England, 1660–1800*, Princeton University Press and Oxford University Press, was published in 1986.

Richard V. Ericson (PHD Cantab., FRSC) is Professor of Criminology and Sociology at the University of Toronto. His major research interest in recent years has been mass media coverage of crime, law and justice. His research has resulted in three books published by University of Toronto Press and Open University Press: *Visualizing Deviance, Negotiating Control* and *Representing Order*. Dr Ericson has also written books on detective work, police patrol work, accused persons in the criminal justice system, penal institutions and sociological theories of crime.

Jane Gladstone (BA Manitoba, MLS Toronto) is a reference librarian and book selector at the Centre of Criminology Library, University of Toronto. She has worked in special libraries in the fields of science, engineering, and education in universities and colleges in England and in Canada.

Mary Jackson was a Junior Fellow at the Centre of Criminology and taught at Ryerson and at Humber College. She is now a law student at the University of Toronto. She compiled the reading list in this volume with Mariana Valverde for the chapter 'Feminist Perspectives on Criminology.'

Chester N. Mitchell (LLM Harvard) is Associate Professor, Department of Law, Carleton University and was a Visiting Fellow at the Centre of Criminology, University of Toronto during the 1988–89 academic year. As well as his interest in drug regulation, drug decriminalization and demedicalization, he has written on subjects such as criminal law, insanity, intoxication, responsibility and punishment, taxation and the economic analysis of law and the professions.

Jim Phillips (PHD Dalhousie, LLB Dalhousie) is Assistant Professor in the Faculty of Law, Department of History, and Centre of Criminology at the University of Toronto. He edited *Essays in the History of Canadian Law. Vol. 3: Nova Scotia*, University of Toronto Press, 1990, with Philip Girard. His research interests are in Canadian criminal justice history, Canadian legal history and trusts law.

Kent Roach (LLM Yale) is Assistant Professor, Faculty of Law and Centre of Criminology, University of Toronto. He has taught criminal law and procedure, the criminal process and a graduate course on the courts with colleagues at the Centre since he joined the faculty in 1989. He edited *Cases and Materials on Criminal Law and Procedure* with Martin L. Friedland, to be published by Emond-Montgomery in 1991. Various areas of criminal justice, such as prosecutors and the police and constitutional remedies are among his research interests.

Clifford D. Shearing (PHD Toronto) is Professor of Criminology and Sociology at the University of Toronto. He has written extensively on sociological and criminological theory and social ordering within both the public and private spheres. He has contributed to the development of policy on policing and regulation through a variety of forums in Canada and elsewhere. His current research interests include resistance and policing in South Africa and the ordering of financial markets.

Peter H. Solomon Jr. (PHD Columbia) is Professor of Political Science and Criminology at the University of Toronto. His book *Criminal Justice Policy: From Research to Reform* was published by Butterworths in 1983. He has written on proposals to reform police powers and acted as a consultant to the Supreme Court of Canada. Soviet criminal justice under Stalin, Soviet penal policy, discretion, parole, and the sociology of law in the USSR are among his research interests.

Philip C. Stenning (LLM Osgoode, SJD Toronto) is Associate Professor at the Centre of Criminology, University of Toronto. His research and writing is mainly on policing subjects, such as police mortality in Canada, the legal status of the police, police accountability, community policing, and private policing. His book on criminal prosecutorial authority in Canada, *Appearing for the Crown*, was published by Brown Legal Publications in 1986.

Mariana Valverde (PHD, York) is Associate Professor of Sociology at York University and Special Lecturer at the Centre of Criminology, University of Toronto. Her areas of specialization include feminist theory, and state regulation of sexuality. *Sex, Power and Pleasure* was published by Women's Press in 1985. A book on the social purity movement in English Canada, 1885–1925, will be published in 1991.

Christopher D. Webster (PHD, Dalhousie) is Head of the Department of Psychology and Research Scientist at the Clarke Institute of Psychiatry in Toronto, and Professor of Psychiatry, Psychology and Criminology at the University of Toronto. Dangerousness, particularly the clinical prediction of violent behaviour, has been a research focus for over a decade. Forensic psychiatry and psychology, narcotics treatment, and expert witness testimony in courts are subjects he has written on, and he co-edited one book entitled *Clinical Criminology* in 1985 and another with the same main title in 1990. The subject of crime in literature is of considerable interest to Dr Webster.

W. Gordon West (PHD, Northwestern) is Associate Professor of Sociology in Education and Criminology. His most recent book *Just Revolution: Popular Insurrection, Sandinista Justice and American State Terrorism in Nicaragua* is forthcoming. Young delinquents have been a central research interest to Dr West for over twenty years. *Young Offenders and the State: A Canadian Perspective on Delinquency* was published by Butterworths in 1984. At present, his work includes the subject of marginal Latin American youth.